Oh My Goddess!

ああっ女神さまっ **7**

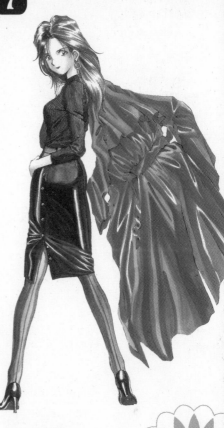

STORY AND ART BY
Kosuke Fujishima

TRANSLATION BY
Dana Lewis AND Toren Smith

LETTERING AND TOUCH-UP BY
Susie Lee AND Betty Dong
WITH Tom2K

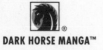

DARK HORSE MANGA™

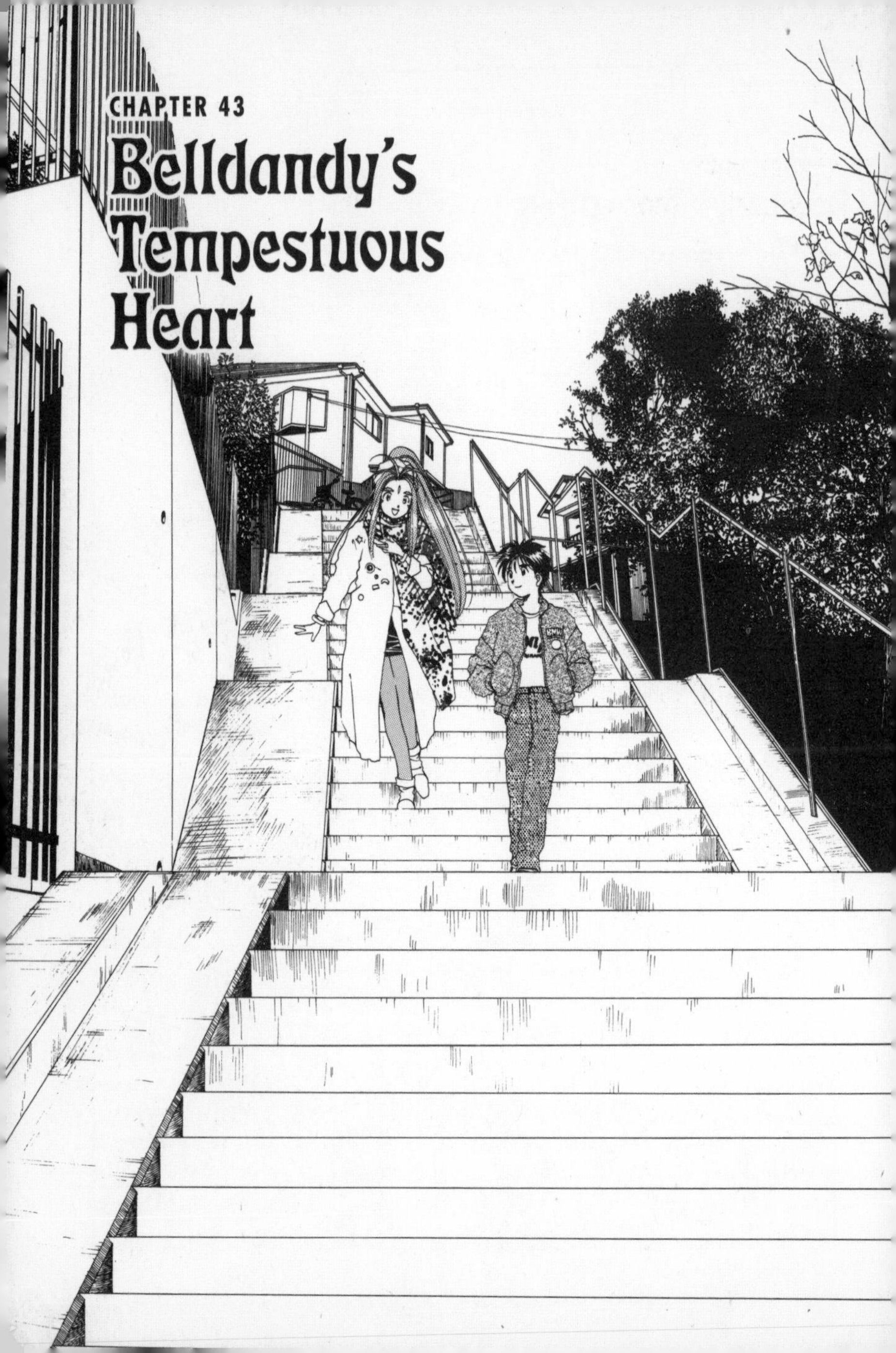
CHAPTER 43
Belldandy's Tempestuous Heart

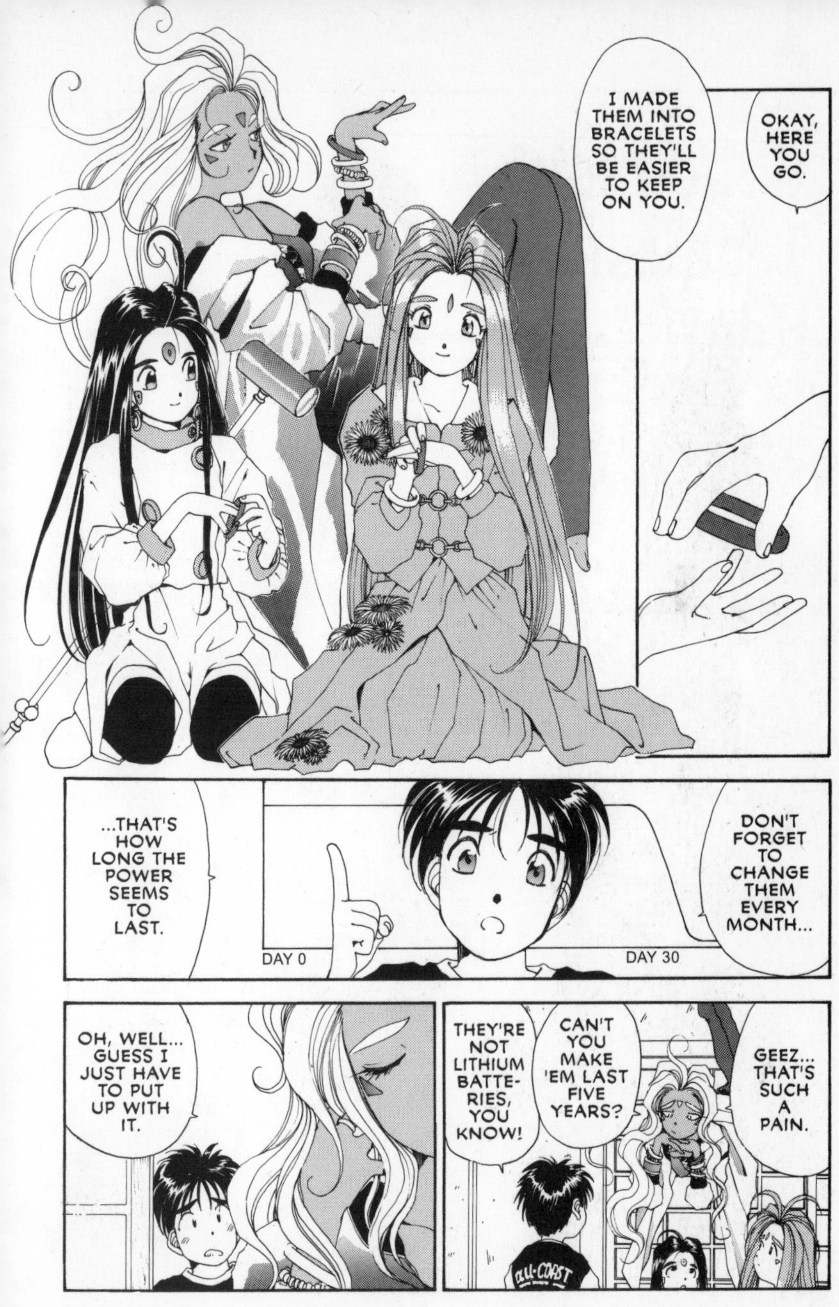
OKAY, HERE YOU GO.
I MADE THEM INTO BRACELETS SO THEY'LL BE EASIER TO KEEP ON YOU.
DON'T FORGET TO CHANGE THEM EVERY MONTH...
DAY 30
DAY 0
...THAT'S HOW LONG THE POWER SEEMS TO LAST.
GEEZ... THAT'S SUCH A PAIN.
CAN'T YOU MAKE 'EM LAST FIVE YEARS?
THEY'RE NOT LITHIUM BATTE-RIES, YOU KNOW!
OH, WELL... GUESS I JUST HAVE TO PUT UP WITH IT.

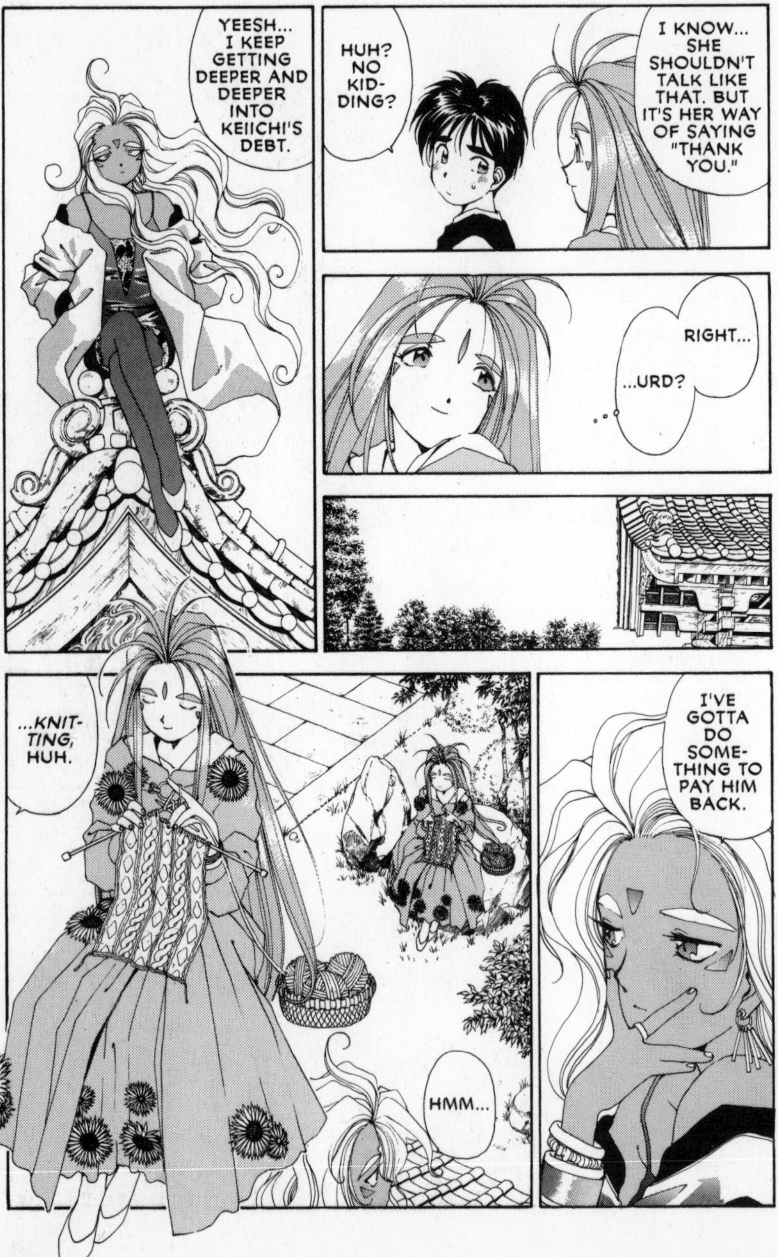
I KNOW... SHE SHOULDN'T TALK LIKE THAT. BUT IT'S HER WAY OF SAYING "THANK YOU."
HUH? NO KID-DING?
RIGHT...
...URD?
YEESH... I KEEP GETTING DEEPER AND DEEPER INTO KEIICHI'S DEBT.
I'VE GOTTA DO SOME-THING TO PAY HIM BACK.
...KNIT-TING, HUH.
HMM...

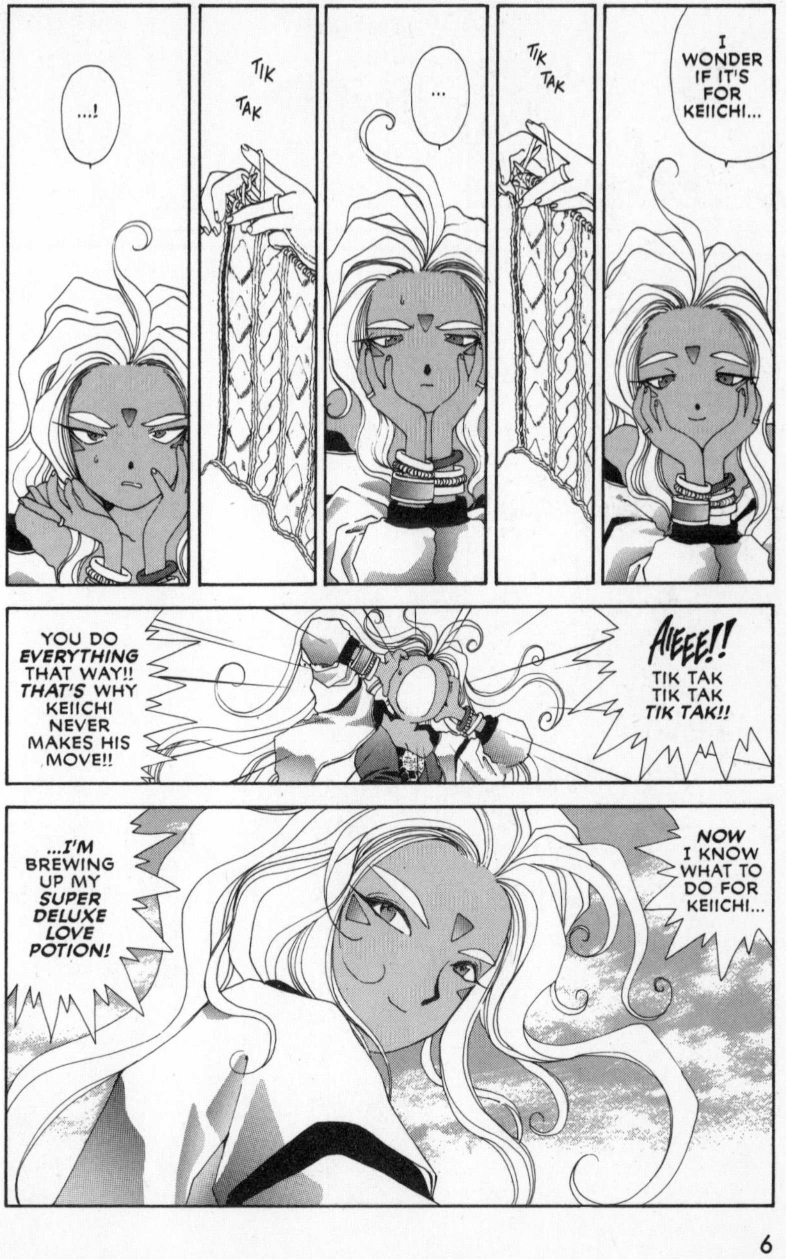
I WONDER IF IT'S FOR KEIICHI...
TIK TAK
...
TIK TAK
...!
AIEEE!!
TIK TAK TIK TAK TIK TAK!!
YOU DO EVERYTHING THAT WAY!! THAT'S WHY KEIICHI NEVER MAKES HIS MOVE!!
NOW I KNOW WHAT TO DO FOR KEIICHI...
...I'M BREWING UP MY SUPER DELUXE LOVE POTION!

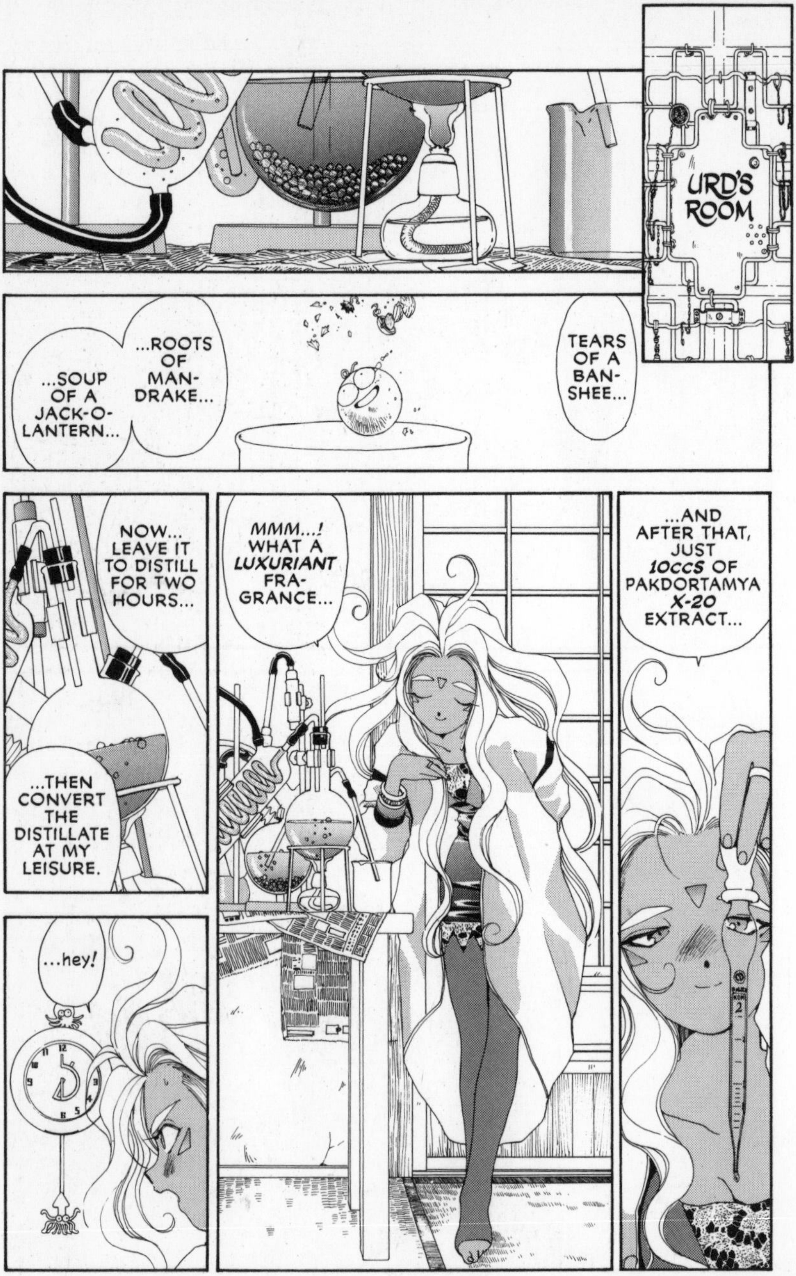
URD'S ROOM
TEARS OF A BANSHEE...
...ROOTS OF MANDRAKE...
...SOUP OF A JACK-O-LANTERN...
...AND AFTER THAT, JUST 10CCS OF PAKDORTAMYA X-20 EXTRACT...
MMM...! WHAT A LUXURIANT FRAGRANCE...
NOW... LEAVE IT TO DISTILL FOR TWO HOURS...
...THEN CONVERT THE DISTILLATE AT MY LEISURE.
...hey!

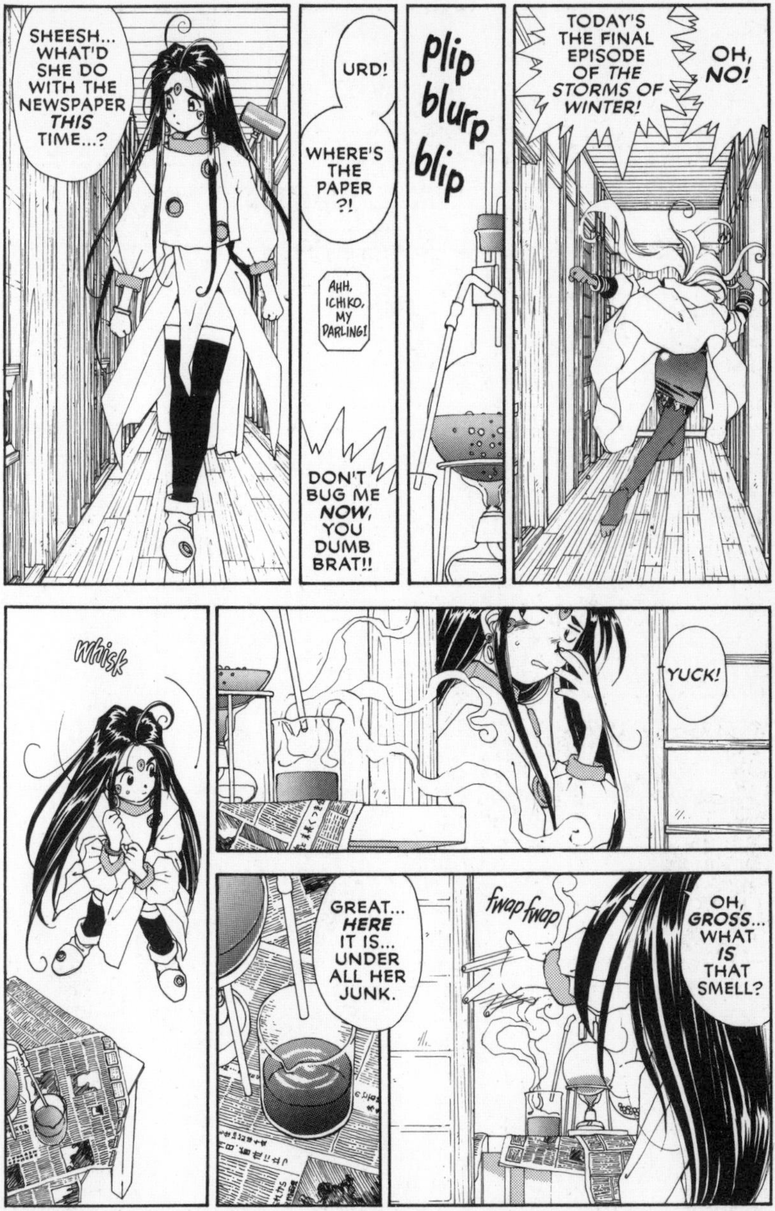
OH, NO!
TODAY'S THE FINAL EPISODE OF THE STORMS OF WINTER!
plip blurp blip
URD!
WHERE'S THE PAPER?!
AHH, ICHIKO, MY DARLING!
DON'T BUG ME NOW, YOU DUMB BRAT!!
SHEESH... WHAT'D SHE DO WITH THE NEWSPAPER THIS TIME...?
YUCK!
OH, GROSS... WHAT IS THAT SMELL?
fwap fwap
GREAT... HERE IT IS... UNDER ALL HER JUNK.
whisk

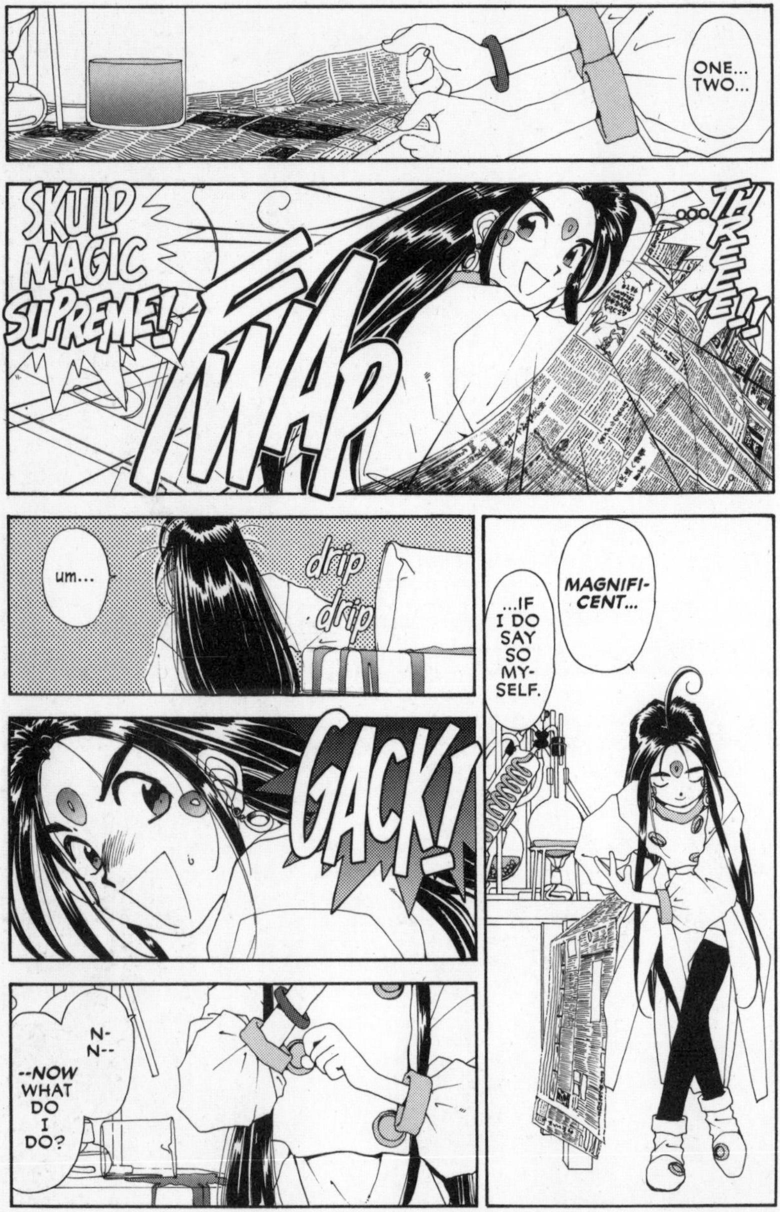
ONE... TWO...
...THREE!!
SKULD MAGIC SUPREME!
FWAP
MAGNIFI-CENT...
...IF I DO SAY SO MY-SELF.
um...
drip drip
GACK!
N-N--
--NOW WHAT DO I DO?

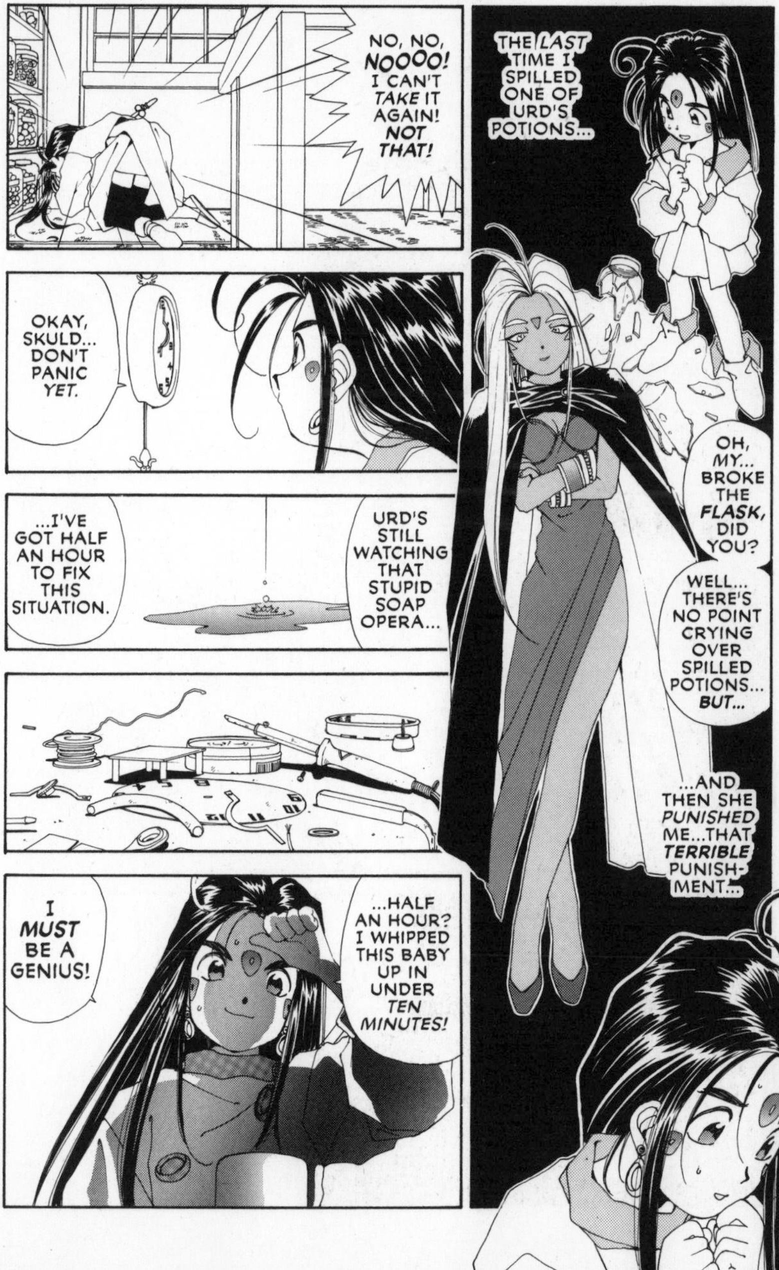
THE *LAST* TIME I SPILLED ONE OF URD'S POTIONS...
OH, *MY*... BROKE THE ***FLASK***, DID YOU?
WELL... THERE'S NO POINT CRYING OVER SPILLED POTIONS... ***BUT...***
...AND THEN SHE *PUNISHED* ME...THAT ***TERRIBLE*** PUNISH-MENT...
NO, NO, ***NOOOO!*** I CAN'T *TAKE* IT AGAIN! ***NOT THAT!***
OKAY, SKULD... DON'T PANIC *YET.*
URD'S STILL WATCHING THAT STUPID SOAP OPERA...
...I'VE GOT HALF AN HOUR TO FIX THIS SITUATION.
...HALF AN HOUR? I WHIPPED THIS BABY UP IN UNDER *TEN MINUTES!*
I ***MUST*** BE A GENIUS!

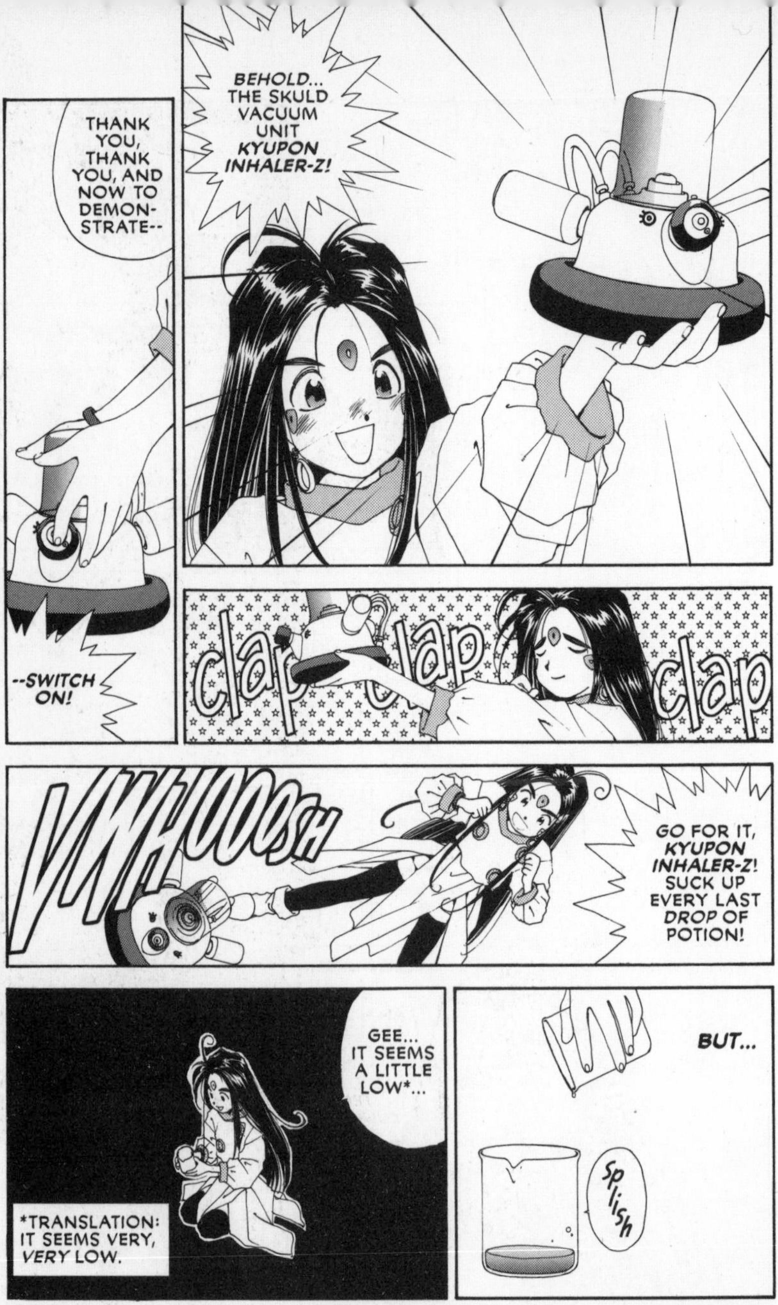
BEHOLD... THE SKULD VACUUM UNIT KYUPON INHALER-Z!
clap clap clap
THANK YOU, THANK YOU, AND NOW TO DEMON-STRATE--
--SWITCH ON!
VWHOOOSH
GO FOR IT, KYUPON INHALER-Z! SUCK UP EVERY LAST DROP OF POTION!
BUT...
splish
GEE... IT SEEMS A LITTLE LOW*...
*TRANSLATION: IT SEEMS VERY, VERY LOW.

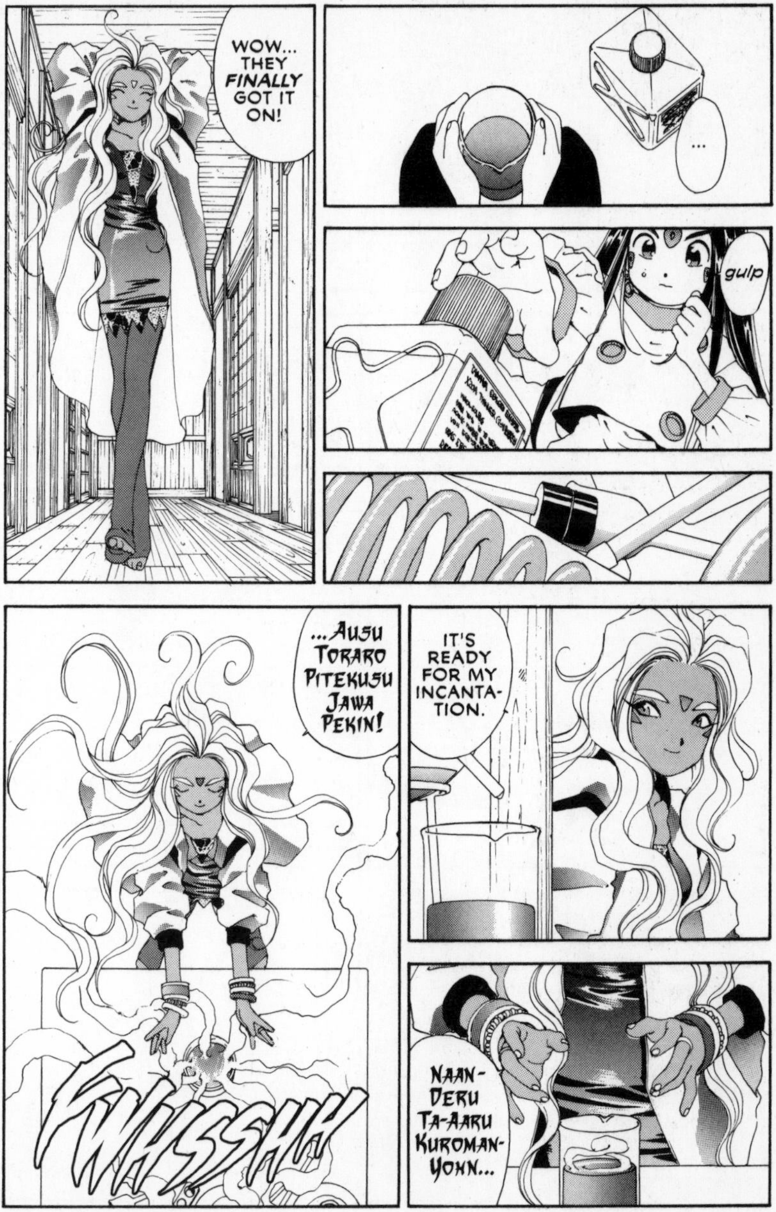
...
gulp
WOW... THEY FINALLY GOT IT ON!
IT'S READY FOR MY INCANTATION.
NAAN-DERU TA-AARU KUROMAN-YOHN...
...AUSU TORARO PITEKUSU JAWA PEKIN!
KWHSSHH

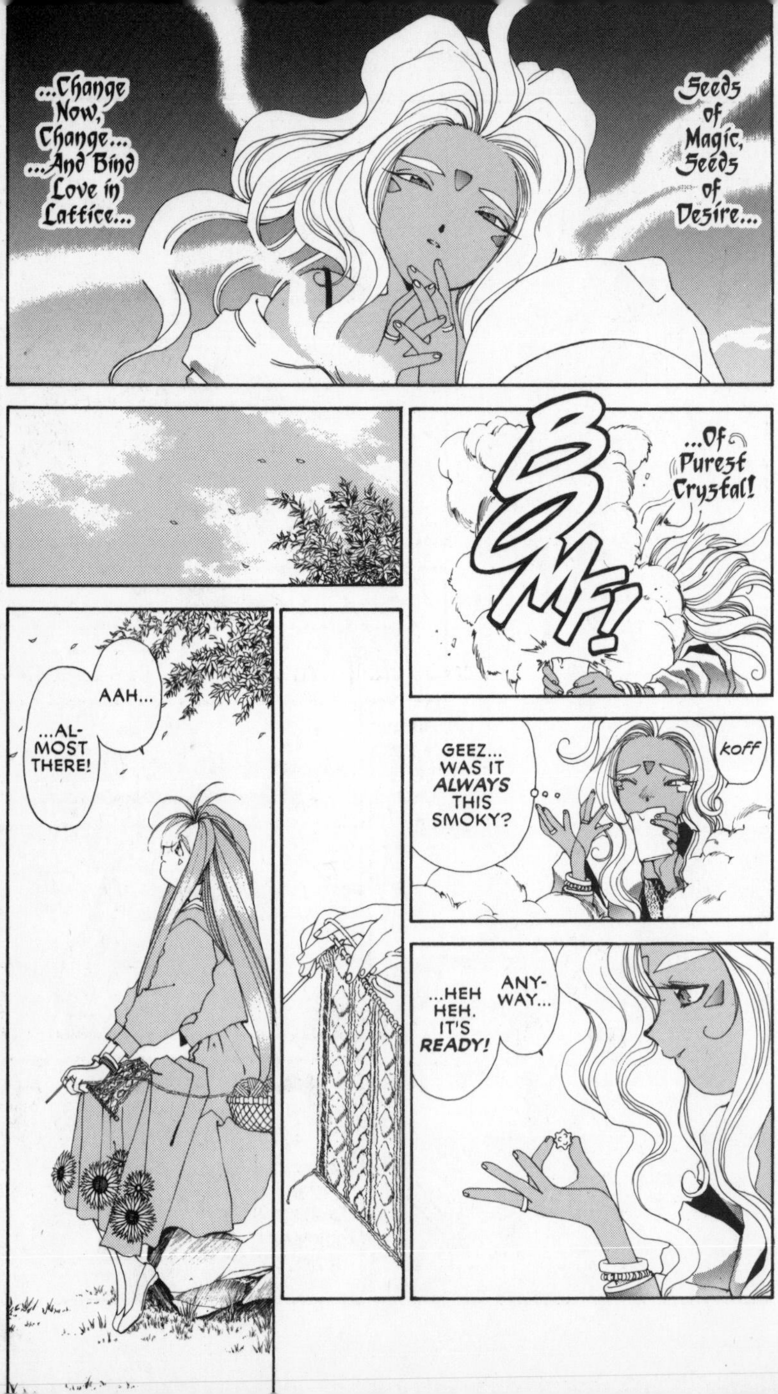
Seeds of Magic, Seeds of Desire...
...Change Now, Change... ...And Bind Love in Lattice...
BOMF!
...Of Purest Crystal!
koff
GEEZ... WAS IT ALWAYS THIS SMOKY?
ANY-WAY...
...HEH HEH. IT'S READY!
AAH...
...AL-MOST THERE!

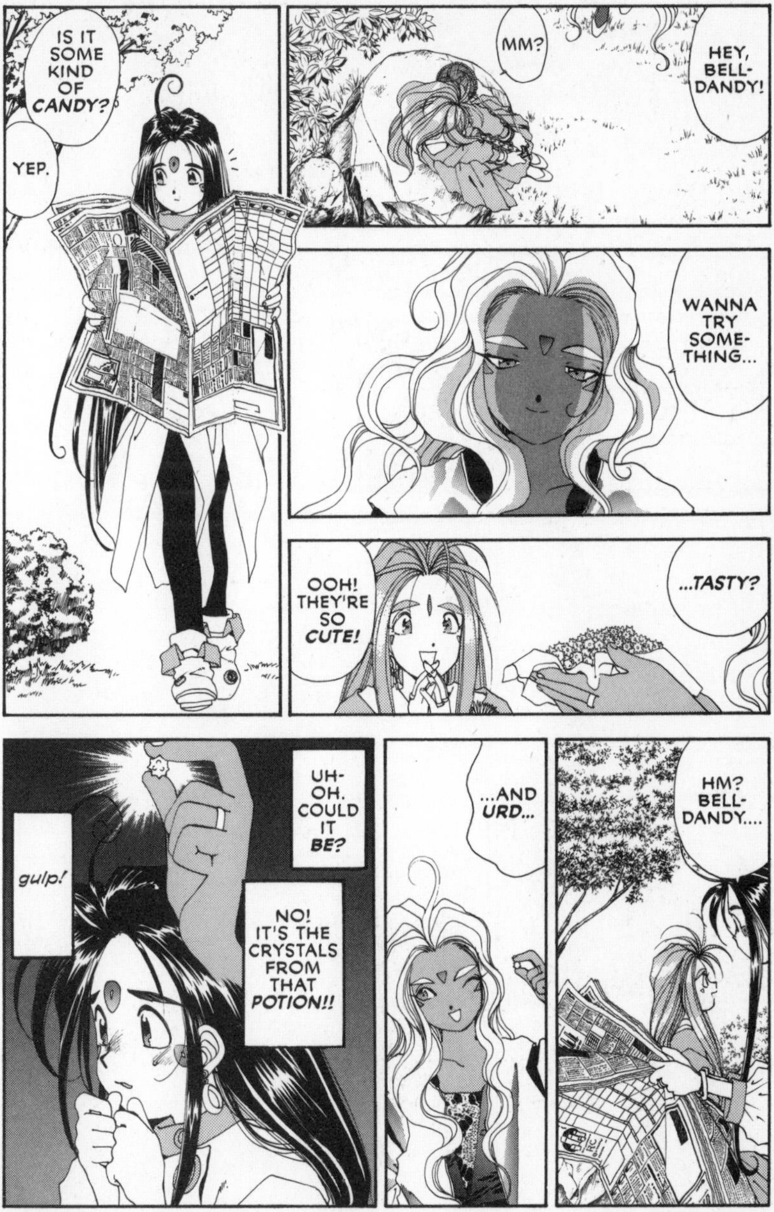
HEY, BELL-DANDY!
MM?
WANNA TRY SOME-THING...
...TASTY?
OOH! THEY'RE SO CUTE!
IS IT SOME KIND OF CANDY?
YEP.
HM? BELL-DANDY....
...AND URD...
UH-OH. COULD IT BE?
NO! IT'S THE CRYSTALS FROM THAT POTION!!
gulp!

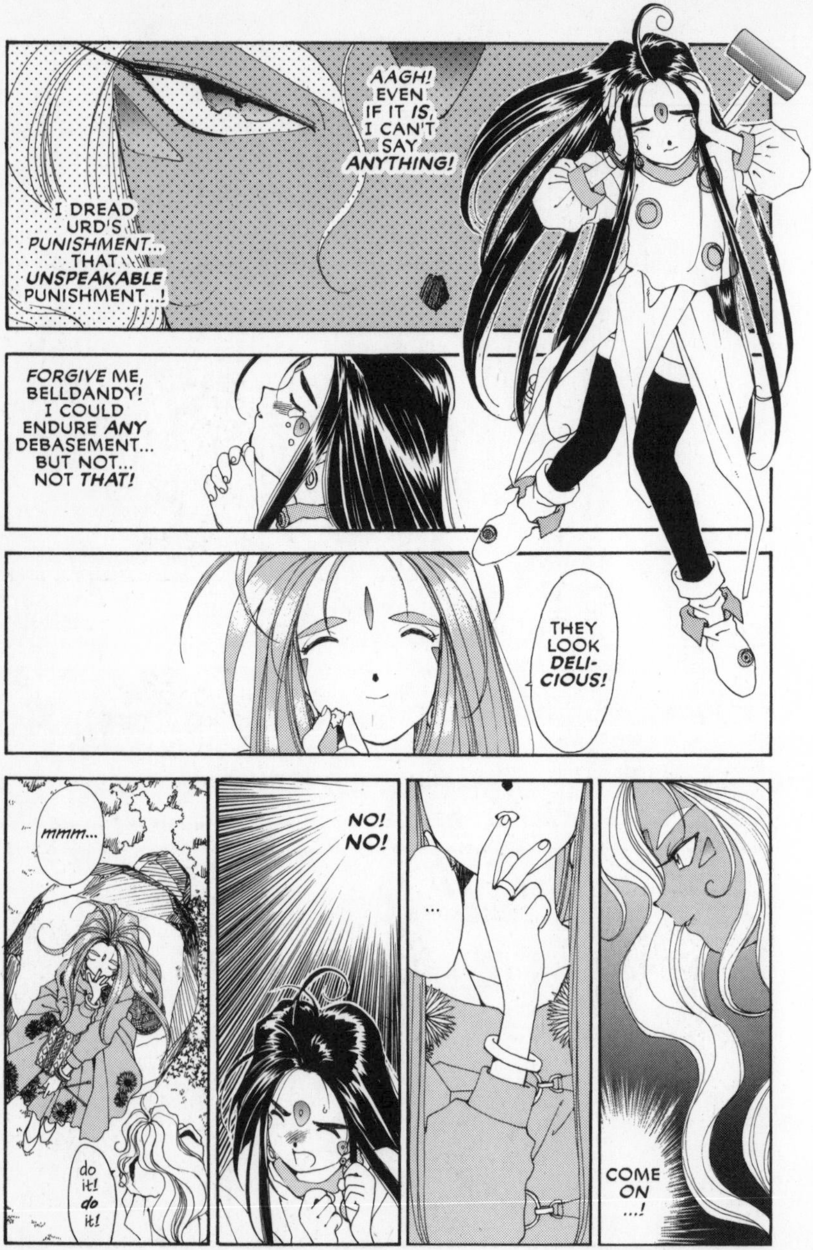

AAGH! EVEN IF IT *IS*, I CAN'T SAY *ANYTHING!*
I DREAD URD'S *PUNISHMENT*... THAT *UNSPEAKABLE* PUNISHMENT...!
FORGIVE ME, BELLDANDY! I COULD ENDURE *ANY* DEBASEMENT... BUT NOT... NOT *THAT!*
THEY LOOK *DELI-CIOUS!*
COME ON ...!
...
NO! NO!
mmm...
do it! *do* it!

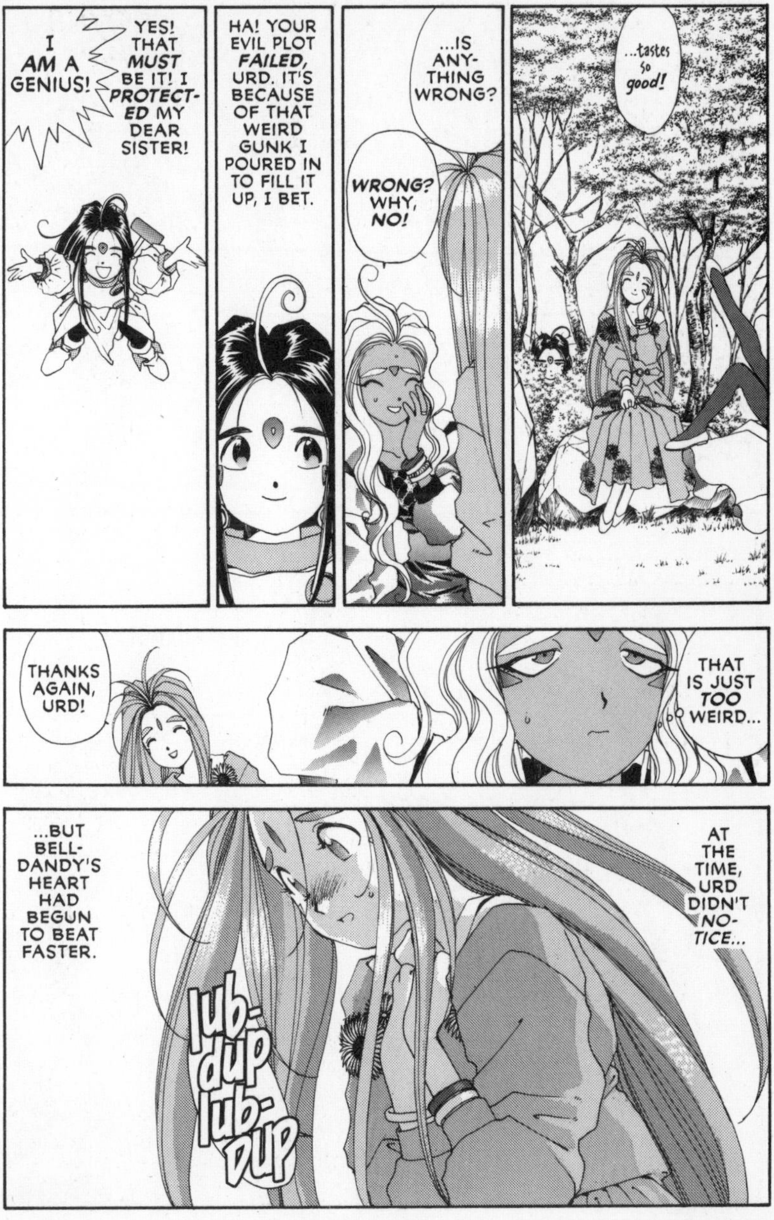
...tastes so good!
...IS ANYTHING WRONG?
WRONG? WHY, NO!
HA! YOUR EVIL PLOT FAILED, URD. IT'S BECAUSE OF THAT WEIRD GUNK I POURED IN TO FILL IT UP, I BET.
YES! THAT MUST BE IT! I PROTECTED MY DEAR SISTER!
I AM A GENIUS!
THAT IS JUST TOO WEIRD...
THANKS AGAIN, URD!
AT THE TIME, URD DIDN'T NOTICE...
...BUT BELLDANDY'S HEART HAD BEGUN TO BEAT FASTER.
lub-dup lub-Dup

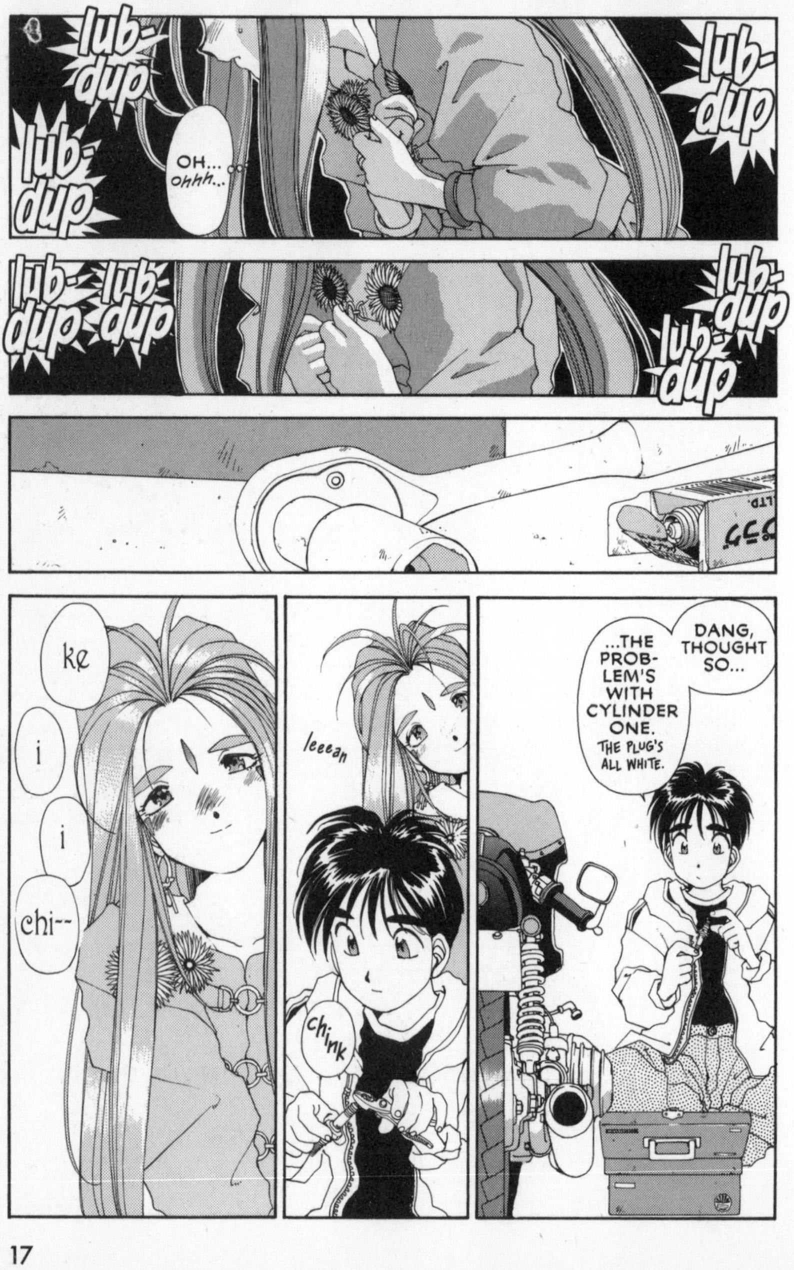
lub-dup
lub-dup
OH... ohhh...
lub-dup
lub-dup
lub-dup
lub-dup
lub-dup
DANG, THOUGHT SO...
...THE PROB-LEM'S WITH CYLINDER ONE. THE PLUG'S ALL WHITE.
leeean
chink
ke
i
i
chi--

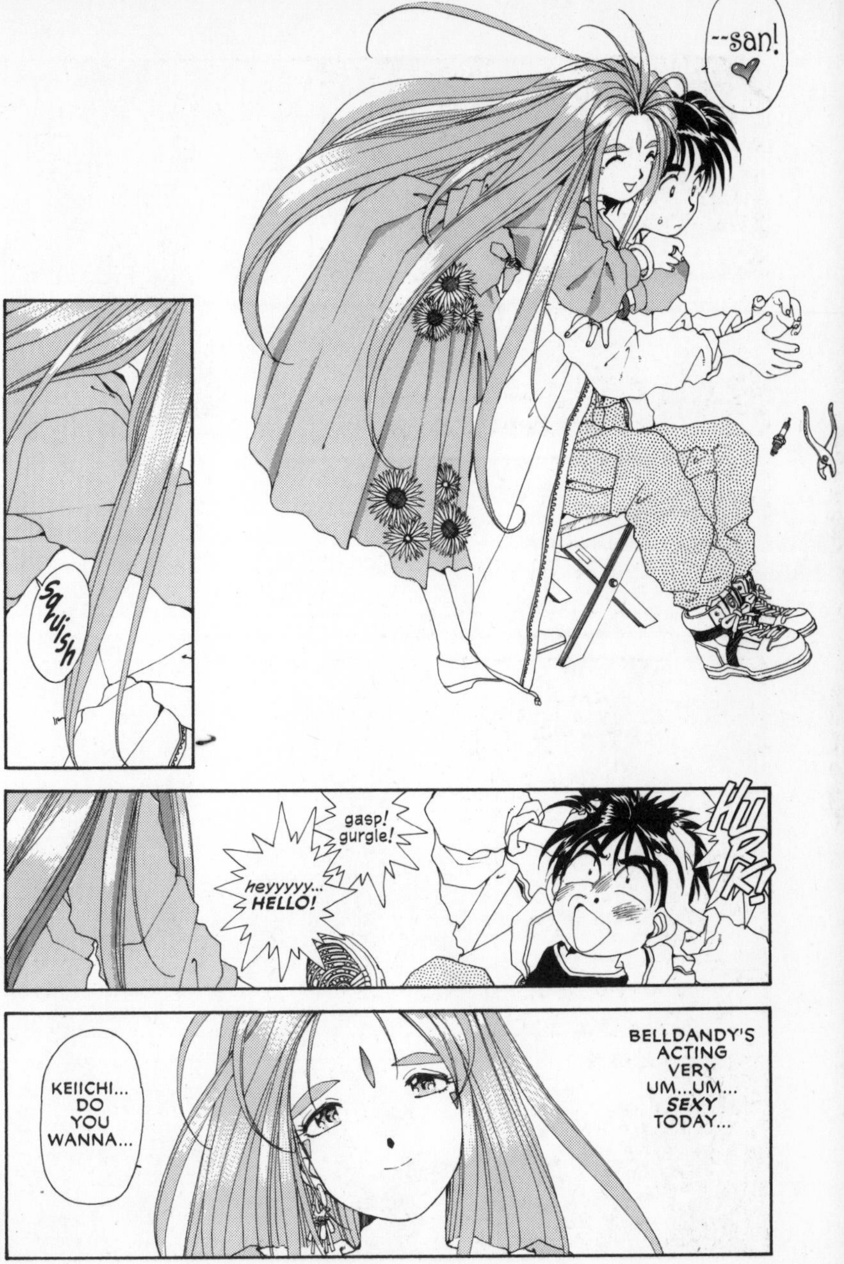
--san! ♥
squish
HURK!
gasp! gurgle!
heyyyyy... HELLO!
BELLDANDY'S ACTING VERY UM...UM... SEXY TODAY...
KEIICHI... DO YOU WANNA...

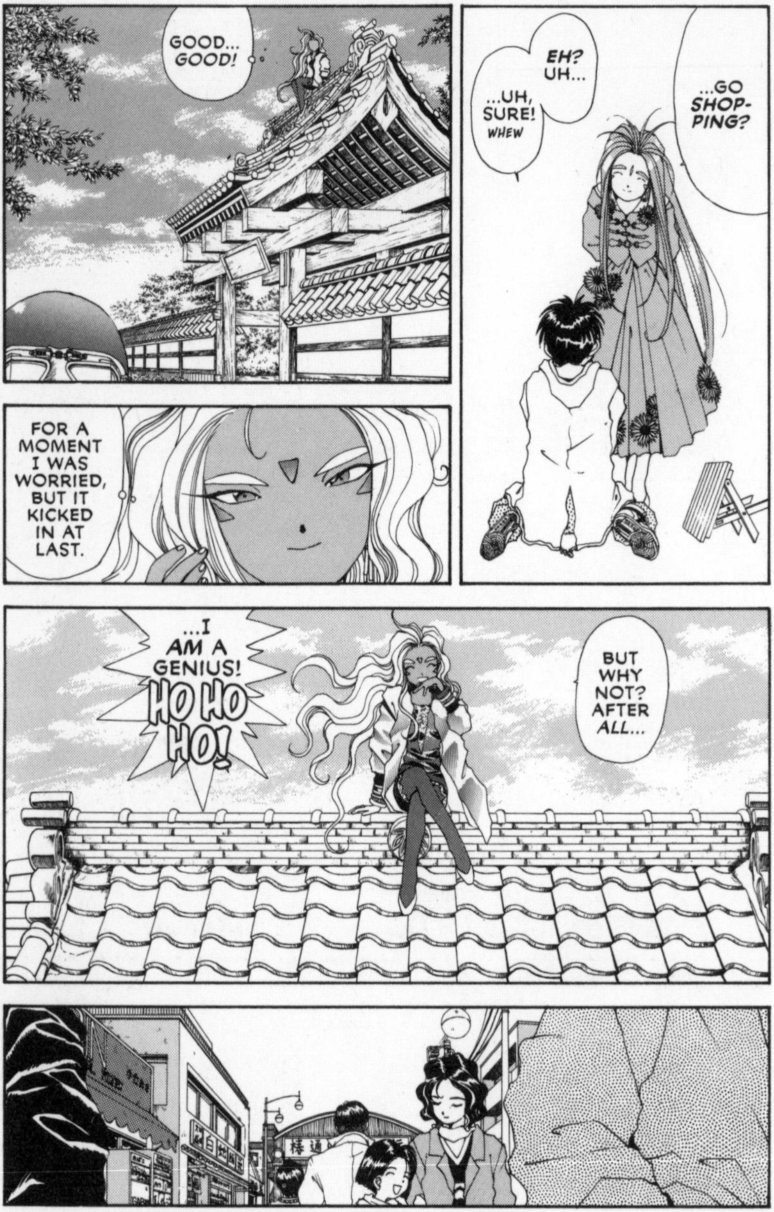
...GO SHOPPING?
EH? UH...
...UH, SURE!
WHEW
GOOD... GOOD!
FOR A MOMENT I WAS WORRIED, BUT IT KICKED IN AT LAST.
BUT WHY NOT? AFTER ALL...
...I AM A GENIUS!
HO HO HO!

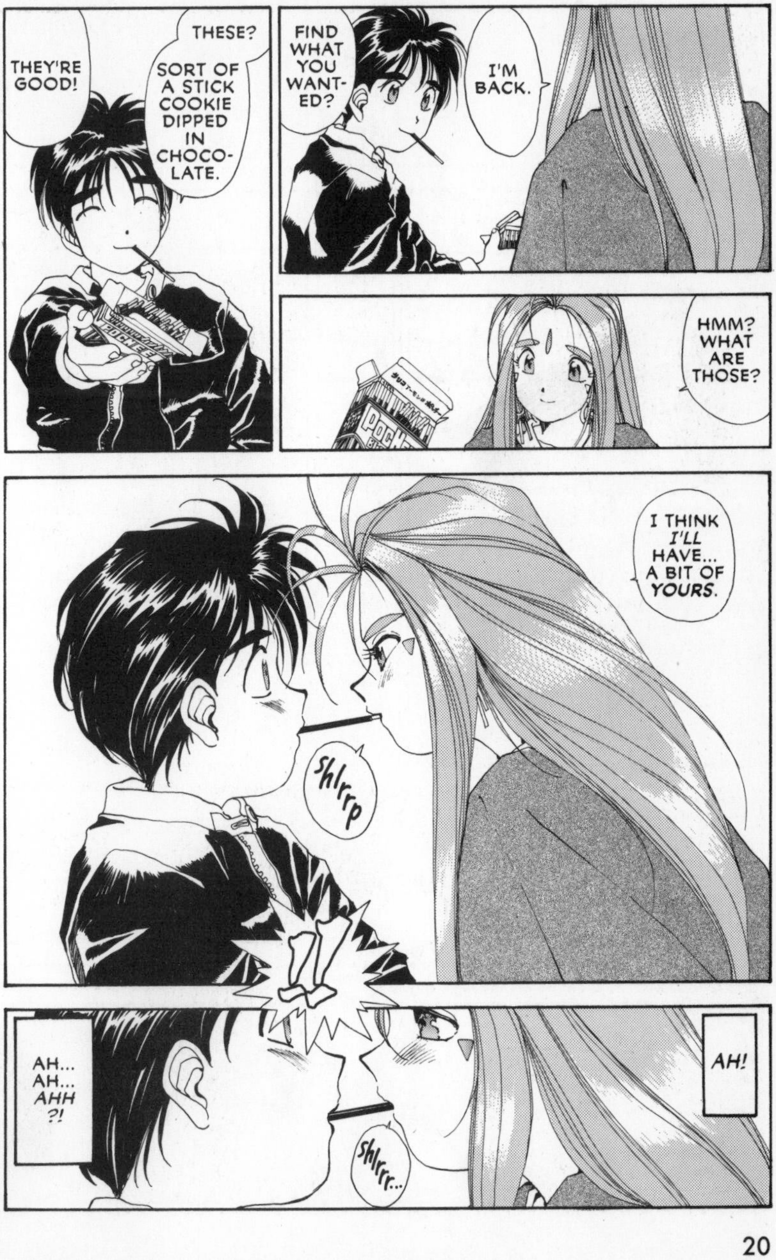
I'M BACK.
FIND WHAT YOU WANT-ED?
HMM? WHAT ARE THOSE?
THESE? SORT OF A STICK COOKIE DIPPED IN CHOCO-LATE.
THEY'RE GOOD!
POCKEE
I THINK *I'LL* HAVE... A BIT OF ***YOURS***.
Shlrrp
AH!
AH... AH... *AHH ?!*
shlrrr...

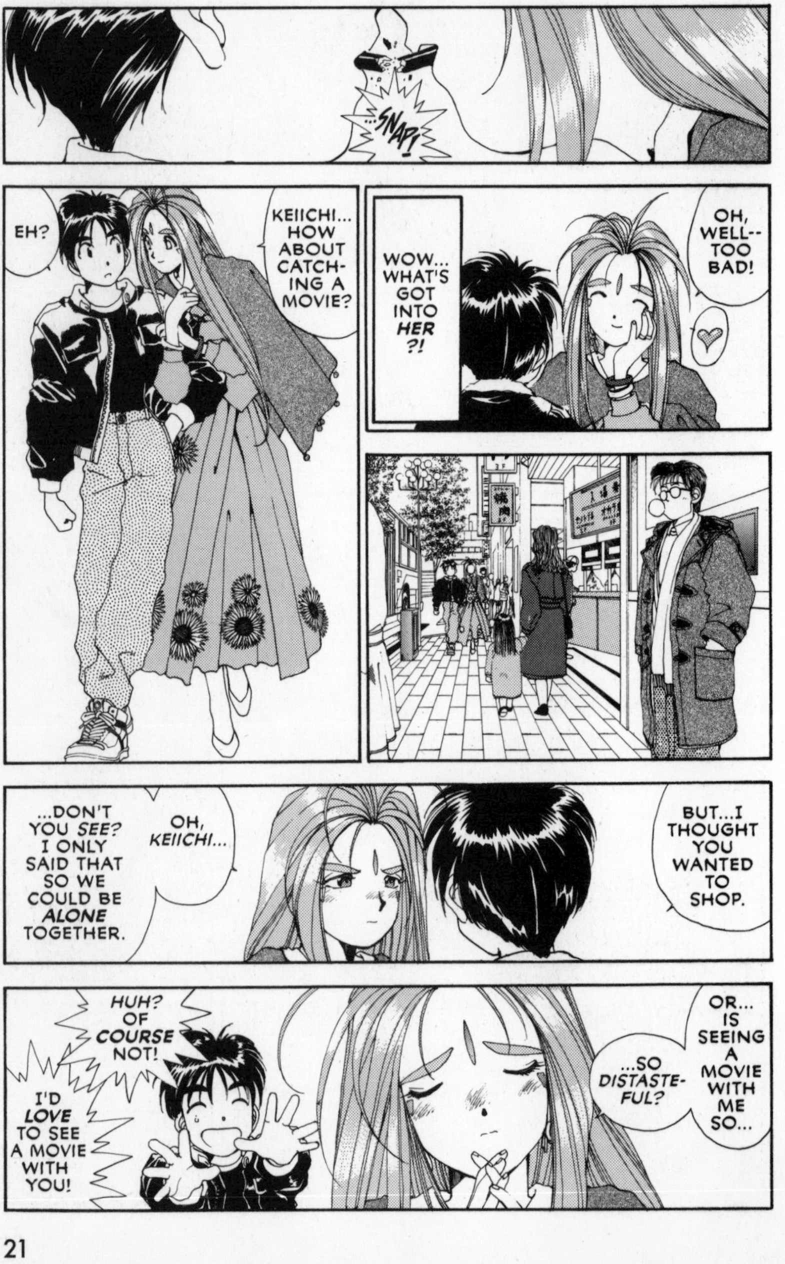
...SNAP!
OH, WELL--TOO BAD!
WOW... WHAT'S GOT INTO *HER* ?!
KEIICHI... HOW ABOUT CATCHING A MOVIE?
EH?
BUT...I THOUGHT YOU WANTED TO SHOP.
OH, *KEIICHI*...
...DON'T YOU *SEE?* I ONLY SAID THAT SO WE COULD BE *ALONE* TOGETHER.
OR... IS SEEING A MOVIE WITH ME SO...
...SO *DISTASTEFUL?*
HUH? OF *COURSE* NOT!
I'D *LOVE* TO SEE A MOVIE WITH YOU!

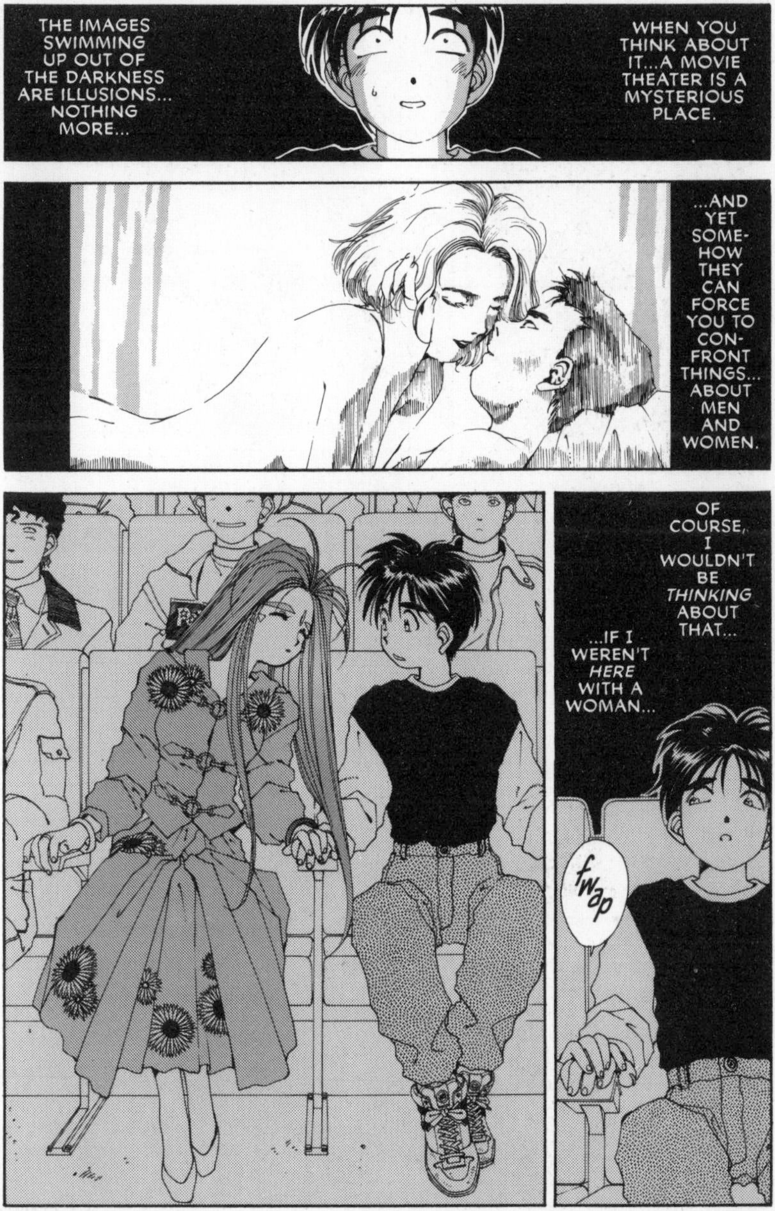
WHEN YOU THINK ABOUT IT...A MOVIE THEATER IS A MYSTERIOUS PLACE.
THE IMAGES SWIMMING UP OUT OF THE DARKNESS ARE ILLUSIONS... NOTHING MORE...
...AND YET SOMEHOW THEY CAN FORCE YOU TO CONFRONT THINGS... ABOUT MEN AND WOMEN.
OF COURSE, I WOULDN'T BE *THINKING* ABOUT THAT...
...IF I WEREN'T *HERE* WITH A WOMAN...
fwap

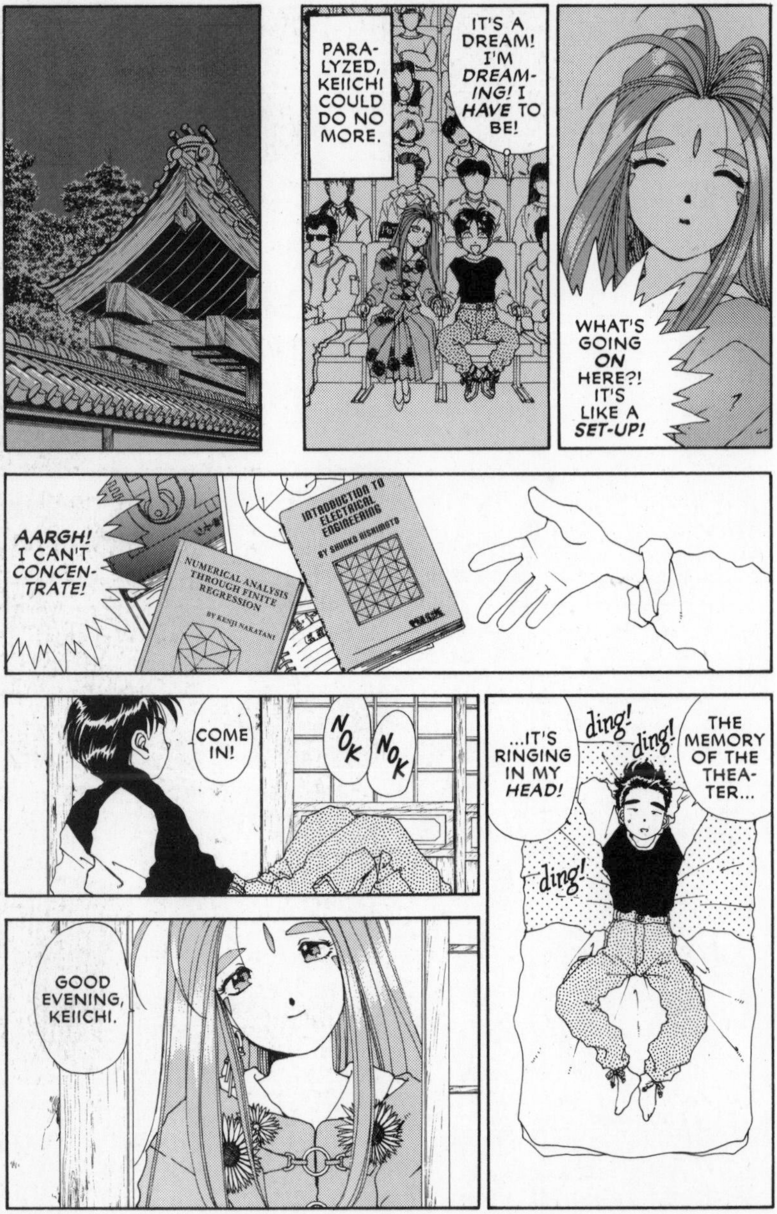
WHAT'S GOING ON HERE?! IT'S LIKE A SET-UP!
IT'S A DREAM! I'M DREAMING! I HAVE TO BE!
PARALYZED, KEIICHI COULD DO NO MORE.
AARGH! I CAN'T CONCENTRATE!
INTRODUCTION TO ELECTRICAL ENGINEERING
BY SHUNKO NISHIMOTO
NUMERICAL ANALYSIS THROUGH FINITE REGRESSION
BY KENJI NAKATANI
THE MEMORY OF THE THEATER...
ding!
ding!
...IT'S RINGING IN MY HEAD!
ding!
NOK
NOK
COME IN!
GOOD EVENING, KEIICHI.

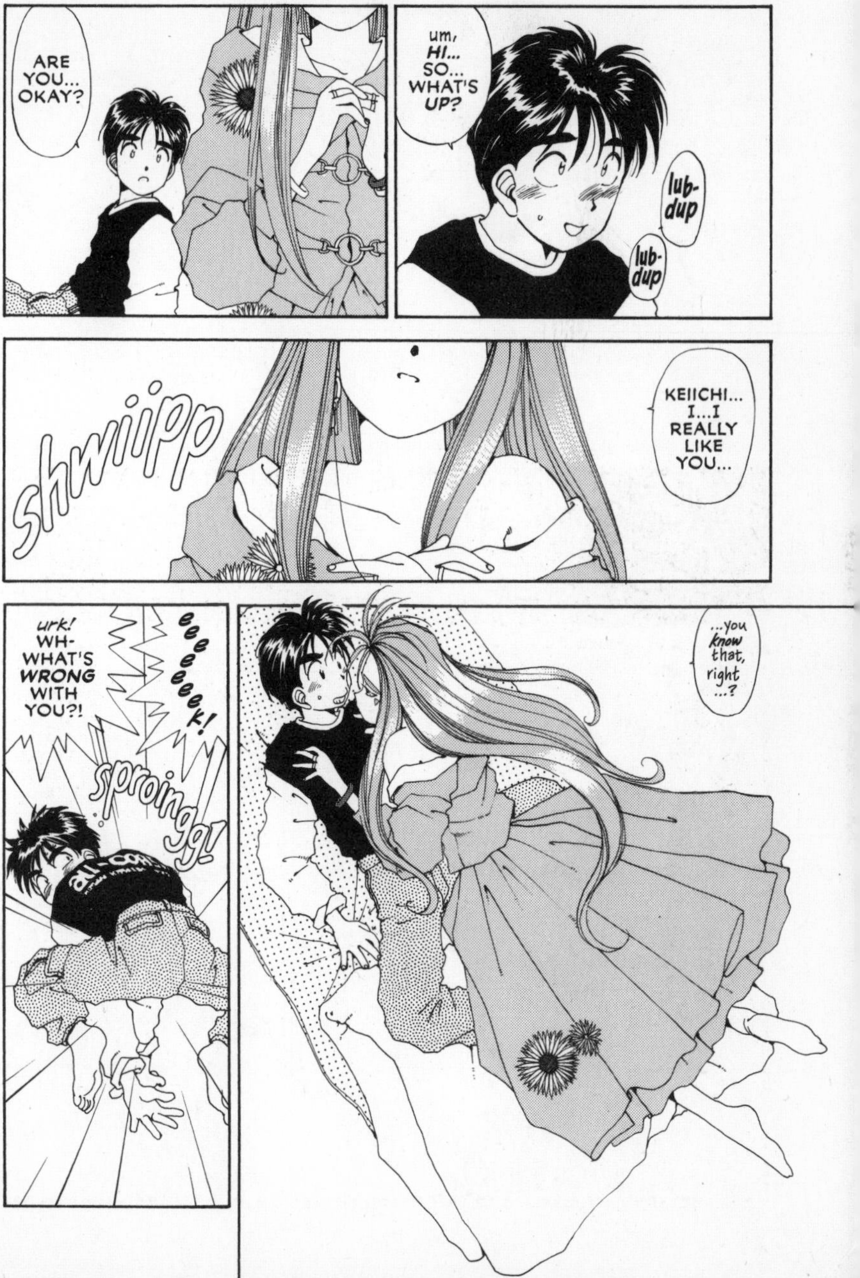

um, HI... SO... WHAT'S UP?
lub-dup
lub-dup
ARE YOU... OKAY?
KEIICHI... I...I REALLY LIKE YOU...
shwiipp
...you know that, right...?
urk! WH- WHAT'S WRONG WITH YOU?!
eeeeeeek!
sproingg!

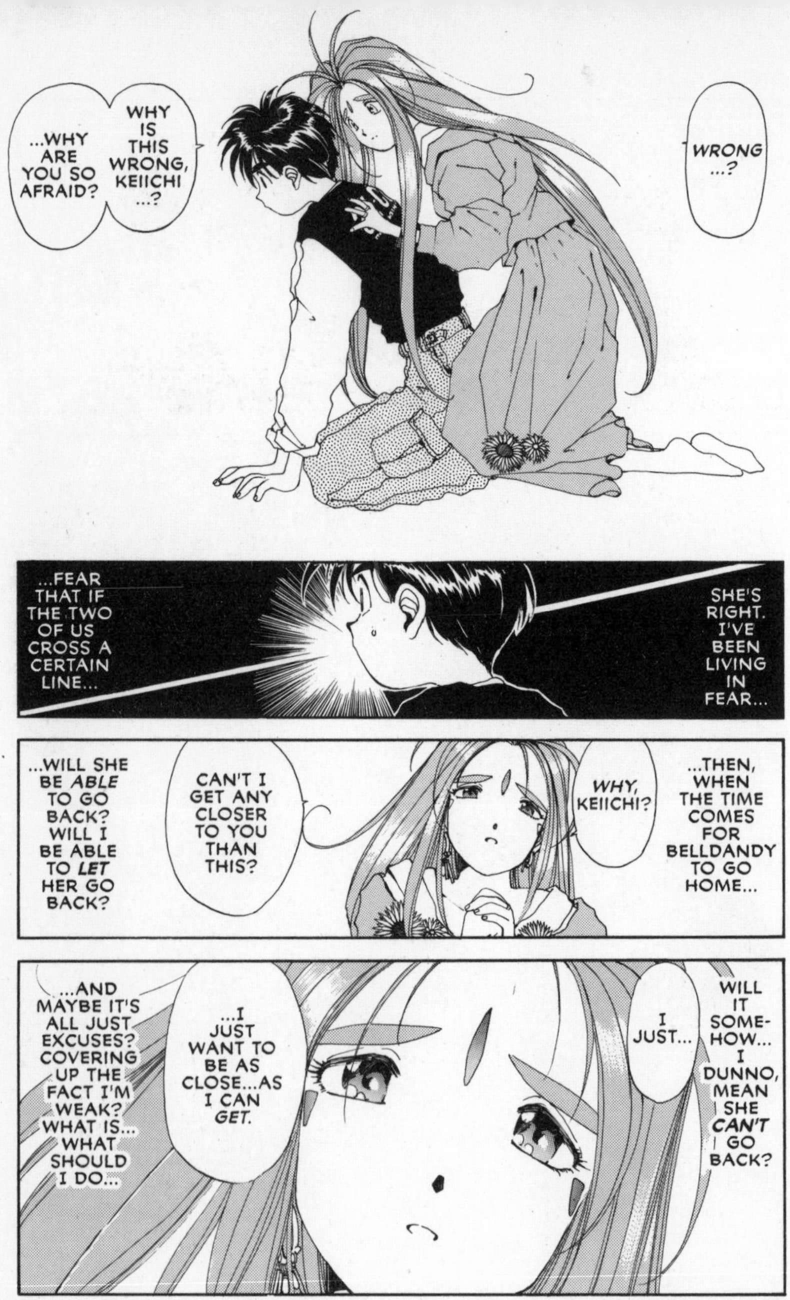
WRONG...?
WHY IS THIS WRONG, KEIICHI...?
...WHY ARE YOU SO AFRAID?
SHE'S RIGHT. I'VE BEEN LIVING IN FEAR...
...FEAR THAT IF THE TWO OF US CROSS A CERTAIN LINE...
...THEN, WHEN THE TIME COMES FOR BELLDANDY TO GO HOME...
WHY, KEIICHI?
CAN'T I GET ANY CLOSER TO YOU THAN THIS?
...WILL SHE BE ABLE TO GO BACK? WILL I BE ABLE TO LET HER GO BACK?
WILL IT SOMEHOW... I DUNNO, MEAN SHE CAN'T GO BACK?
I JUST...
...I JUST WANT TO BE AS CLOSE...AS I CAN GET.
...AND MAYBE IT'S ALL JUST EXCUSES? COVERING UP THE FACT I'M WEAK? WHAT IS... WHAT SHOULD I DO...

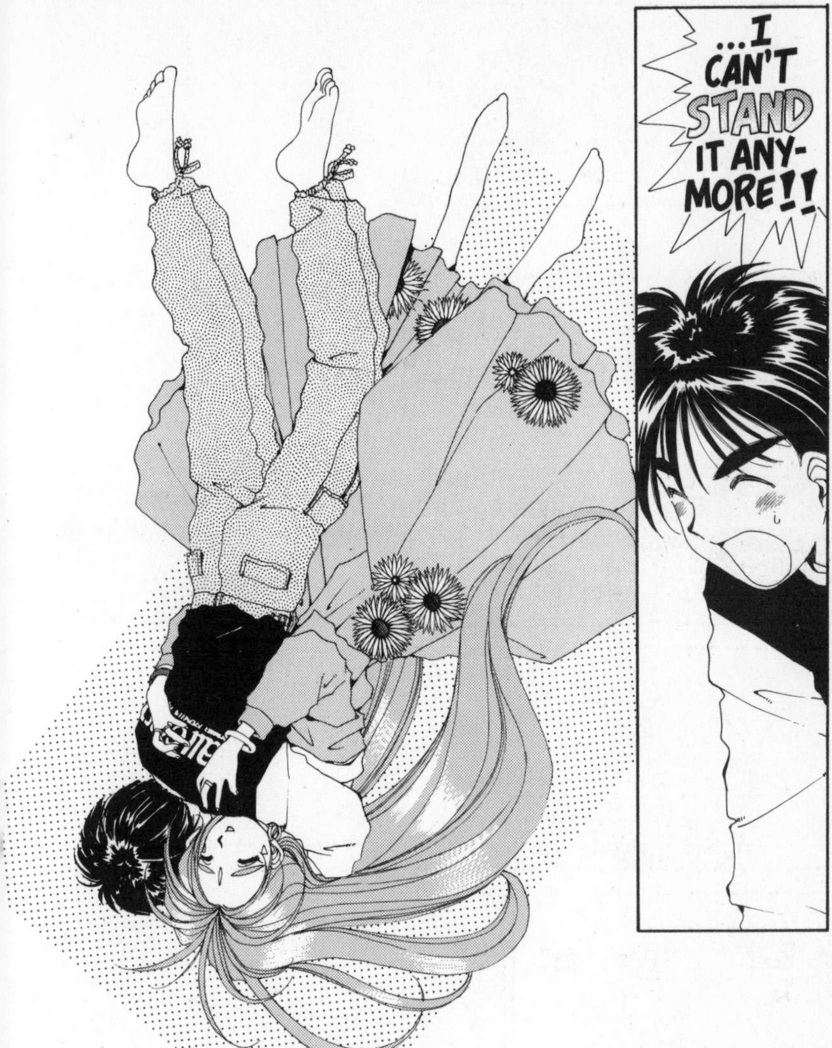
...I CAN'T STAND IT ANY-MORE!!

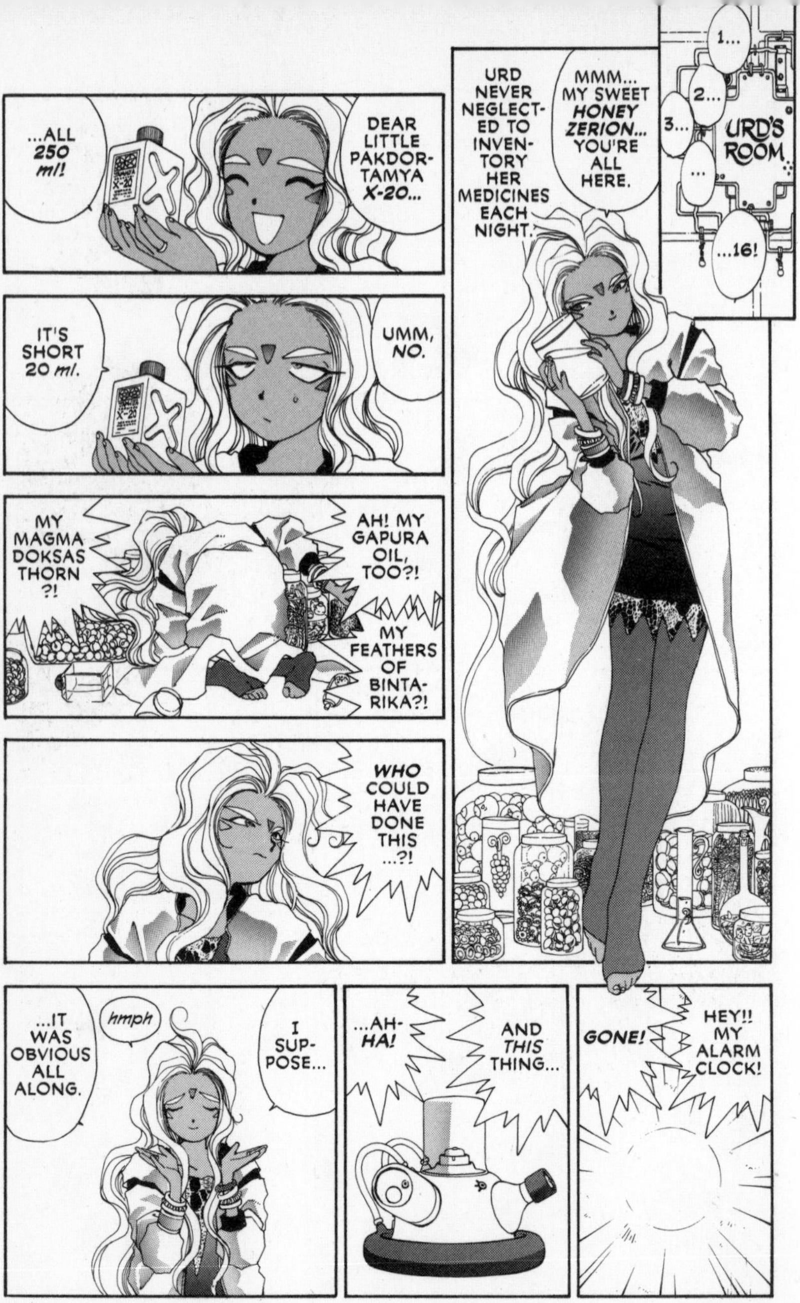
URD'S ROOM
1...
2...
3...
...
...16!
MMM... MY SWEET HONEY ZERION... YOU'RE ALL HERE.
URD NEVER NEGLECTED TO INVENTORY HER MEDICINES EACH NIGHT.
DEAR LITTLE PAKDOR-TAMYA X-20...
...ALL 250 ml!
UMM, NO.
IT'S SHORT 20 ml.
AH! MY GAPURA OIL, TOO?!
MY MAGMA DOKSAS THORN?!
MY FEATHERS OF BINTA-RIKA?!
WHO COULD HAVE DONE THIS ...?!
HEY!! MY ALARM CLOCK!
GONE!
AND THIS THING...
...AH-HA!
I SUPPOSE...
hmph
...IT WAS OBVIOUS ALL ALONG.

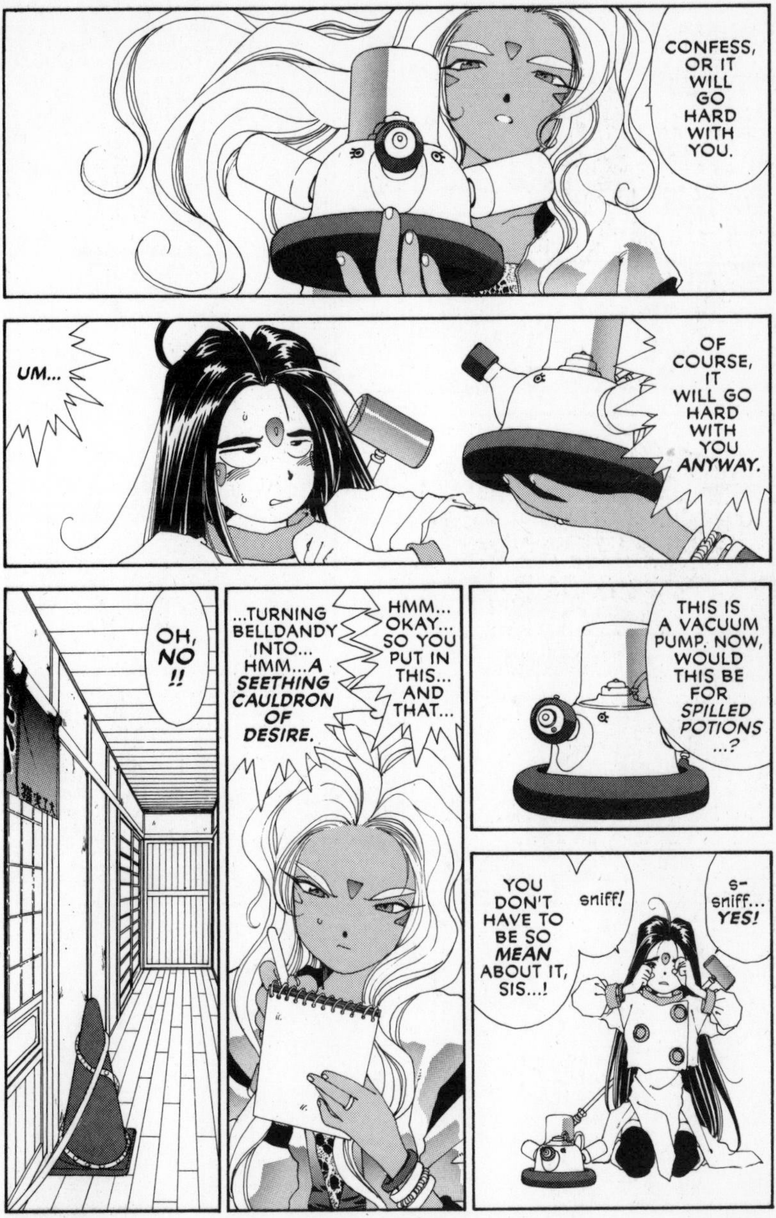

CONFESS, OR IT WILL GO HARD WITH YOU.
OF COURSE, IT WILL GO HARD WITH YOU ANYWAY.
UM...
THIS IS A VACUUM PUMP. NOW, WOULD THIS BE FOR SPILLED POTIONS ...?
S-SNIFF... YES!
SNIFF!
YOU DON'T HAVE TO BE SO MEAN ABOUT IT, SIS...!
HMM... OKAY... SO YOU PUT IN THIS... AND THAT...
...TURNING BELLDANDY INTO... HMM...A SEETHING CAULDRON OF DESIRE.
OH, NO !!

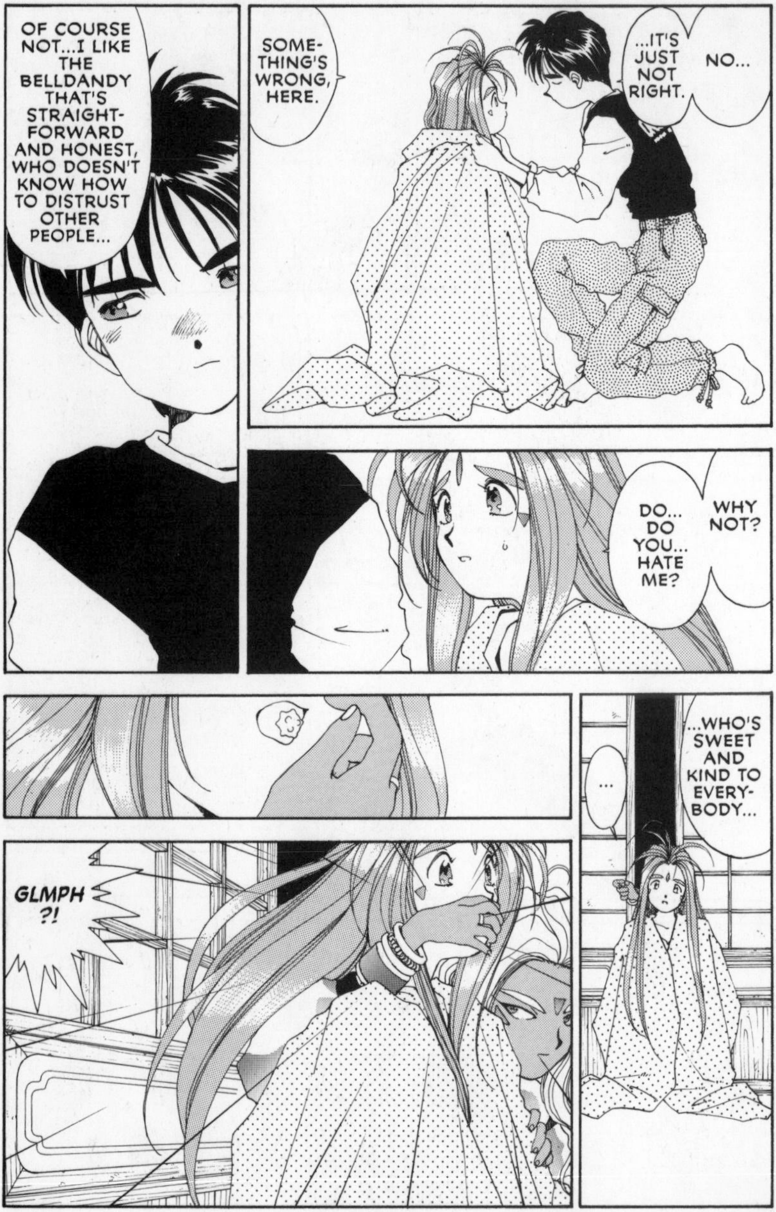
NO...
...IT'S JUST NOT RIGHT.
SOME-THING'S WRONG, HERE.
WHY NOT?
DO... DO YOU... HATE ME?
OF COURSE NOT...I LIKE THE BELLDANDY THAT'S STRAIGHT-FORWARD AND HONEST, WHO DOESN'T KNOW HOW TO DISTRUST OTHER PEOPLE...
...WHO'S SWEET AND KIND TO EVERY-BODY...
...
GLMPH ?!

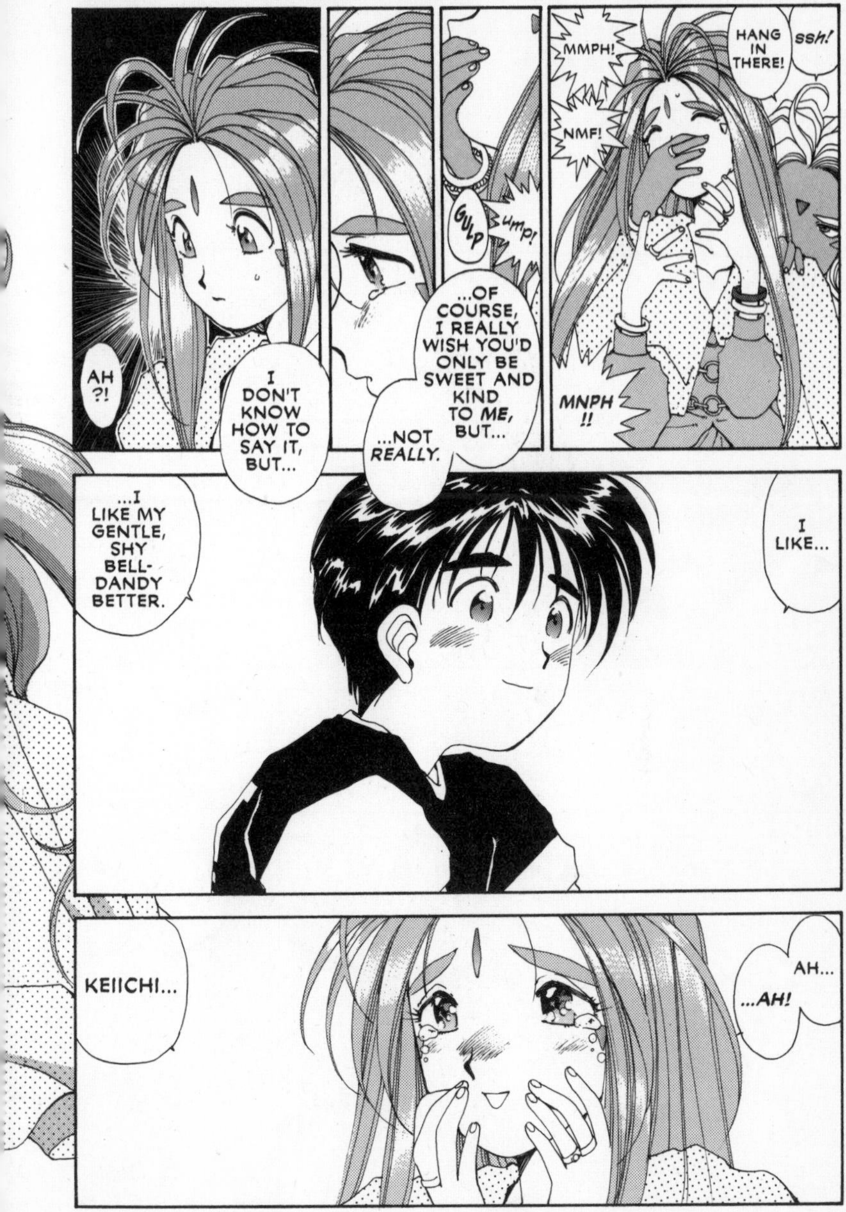

ssh!
HANG IN THERE!
MMPH!
NMF!
MNPH !!
GULP
ump!
...OF COURSE, I REALLY WISH YOU'D ONLY BE SWEET AND KIND TO *ME*, BUT...
...NOT *REALLY*.
AH ?!
I DON'T KNOW HOW TO SAY IT, BUT...
I LIKE...
...I LIKE MY GENTLE, SHY BELL-DANDY BETTER.
AH...
...*AH!*
KEIICHI...

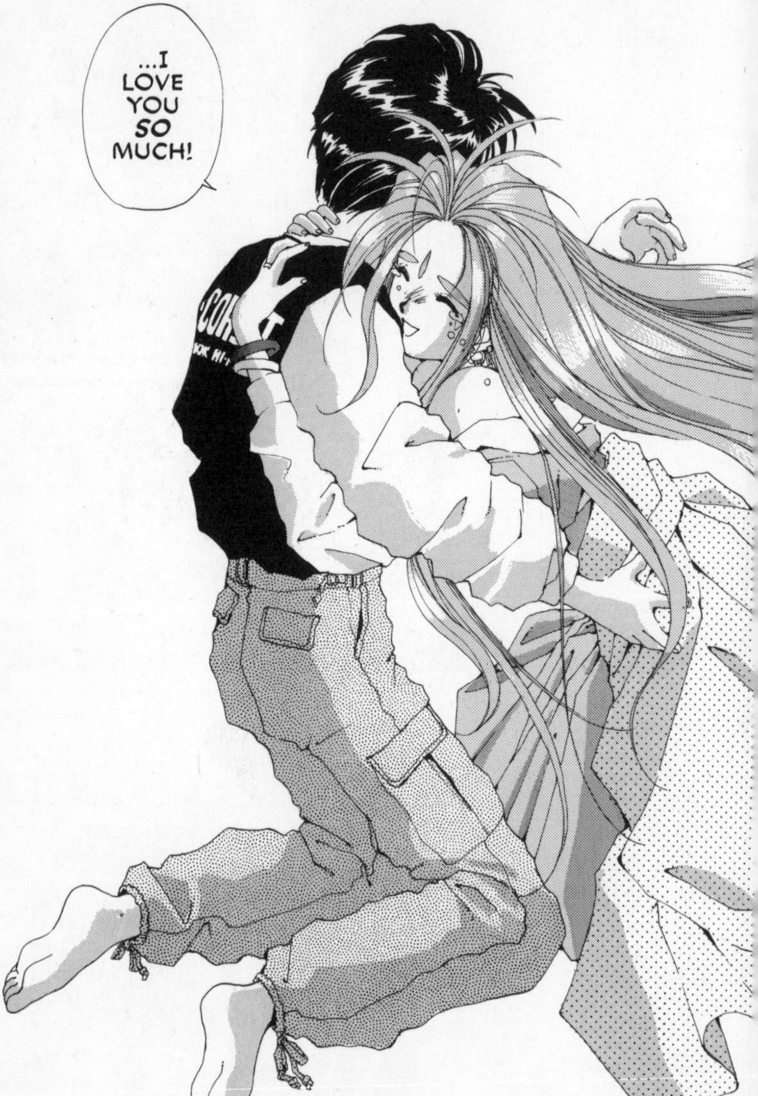
...I LOVE YOU SO MUCH!

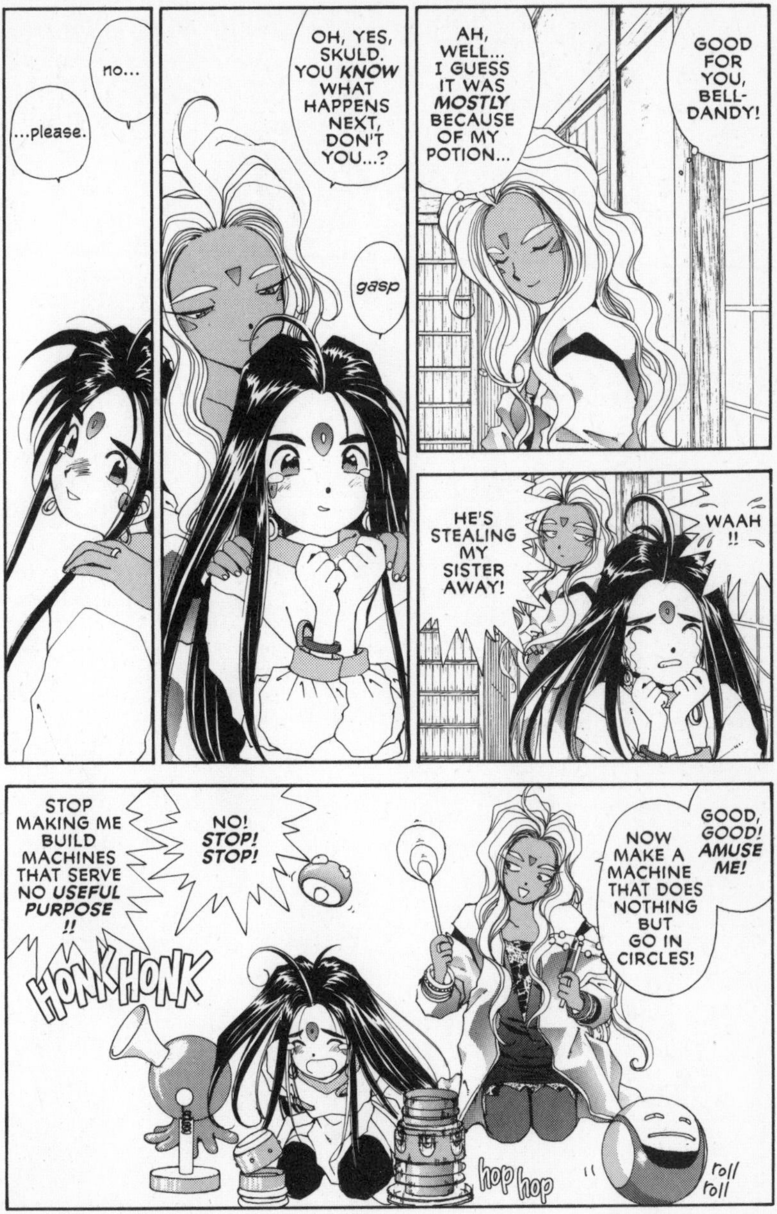
GOOD FOR YOU, BELL-DANDY!
AH, WELL... I GUESS IT WAS *MOSTLY* BECAUSE OF MY POTION...
WAAH !!
HE'S STEALING MY SISTER AWAY!
OH, YES, SKULD. YOU *KNOW* WHAT HAPPENS NEXT, DON'T YOU...?
gasp
no...
...please.
GOOD, *GOOD! AMUSE ME!*
NOW MAKE A MACHINE THAT DOES NOTHING BUT GO IN CIRCLES!
NO! *STOP! STOP!*
STOP MAKING ME BUILD MACHINES THAT SERVE NO *USEFUL PURPOSE !!*
HONK HONK
roll roll
hop hop

THE ADVENTURES OF MINI-URD

In the handy PETITE SIZE!

◆ CATCHING RAYS ◆

SSshhhsssshhh
WHEW... AM I HOT!
fwap
I'M HOT ENOUGH TO MELT...
OOOGH... IT FEELS LIKE I REALLY AM MELTING...
GLRSSHH
AH?! AAA!!
URD! DON'T YOU KNOW IT'S NOT NICE TO MELT PEOPLE?!
SSshhhss
I THOUGHT YOU WANTED TO MELT...

◆ A COOL BREEZE IN SUMMER ◆

OH, ALL RIGHT.
I'LL TAKE YOU SOME PLACE NICE AND COOL.
REAL-LY?! YOU MEAN IT?!
OOOH... IT'S TRUE!
IT'S SO COOL IN HERE!
TOLD YA SO!
PARTY ICE
THIRTY MIN-UTES LATER...
Big
NOW I'M FROZEN!!
THERE'S NO PLEAS-ING SOME PEOPLE.

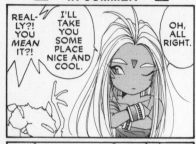

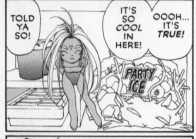

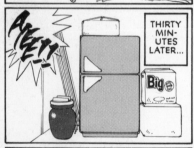

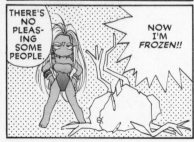

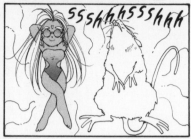

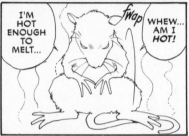

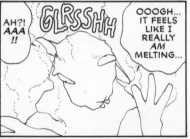

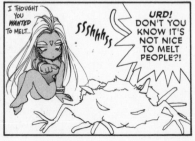

GOLDEN GOURMAND

WELCOME TO THE FIRST ANNUAL WEIRD FOOD EATING CONTEST!
SO LET'S GO!
CONTESTANT ONE-- WORM SPAGHETTI!
YEECH! GROSS!! YOU THINK YOU'RE A MOLE?!
CONTESTANT TWO-- DOUBLE-A BATTERY RECHARGE!
DAMN! IF THAT'S HOW IT'S GONNA BE...
...THEN I'VE ONLY GOT ONE CHANCE...
CONTESTANT THREE-- BBQ RAT ON A STICK!
W-WHAT DID YOU SAY ...?!

AMAZING! THE ALL-YOU-CAN-EAT CONTEST!

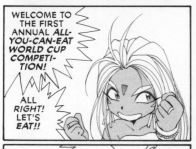

WELCOME TO THE FIRST ANNUAL ALL-YOU-CAN-EAT WORLD CUP COMPETITION!
ALL RIGHT! LET'S EAT!!
ON YOUR MARK! GET SET...
GO!
GEN THE RAT IS PACKING IT IN!
BUT WHAT'S THIS? MR. SNAKE HASN'T HAD A BITE!
WAIT! MR. SNAKE JUST ATE GEN THE RAT!!
AND IT'S MR. SNAKE BY A MILE!!
GEEZ, IT WAS JUST ANOTHER "WEIRD FOOD EATING CONTEST" AFTER ALL...

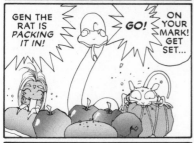

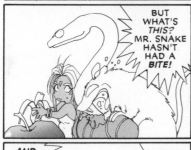

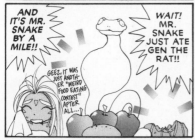

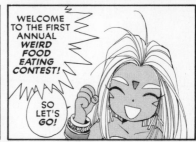

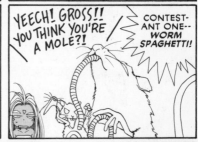

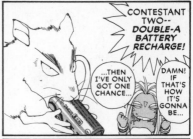

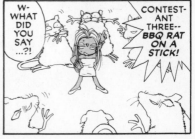

CHAPTER 44

The Queen of Vengeance

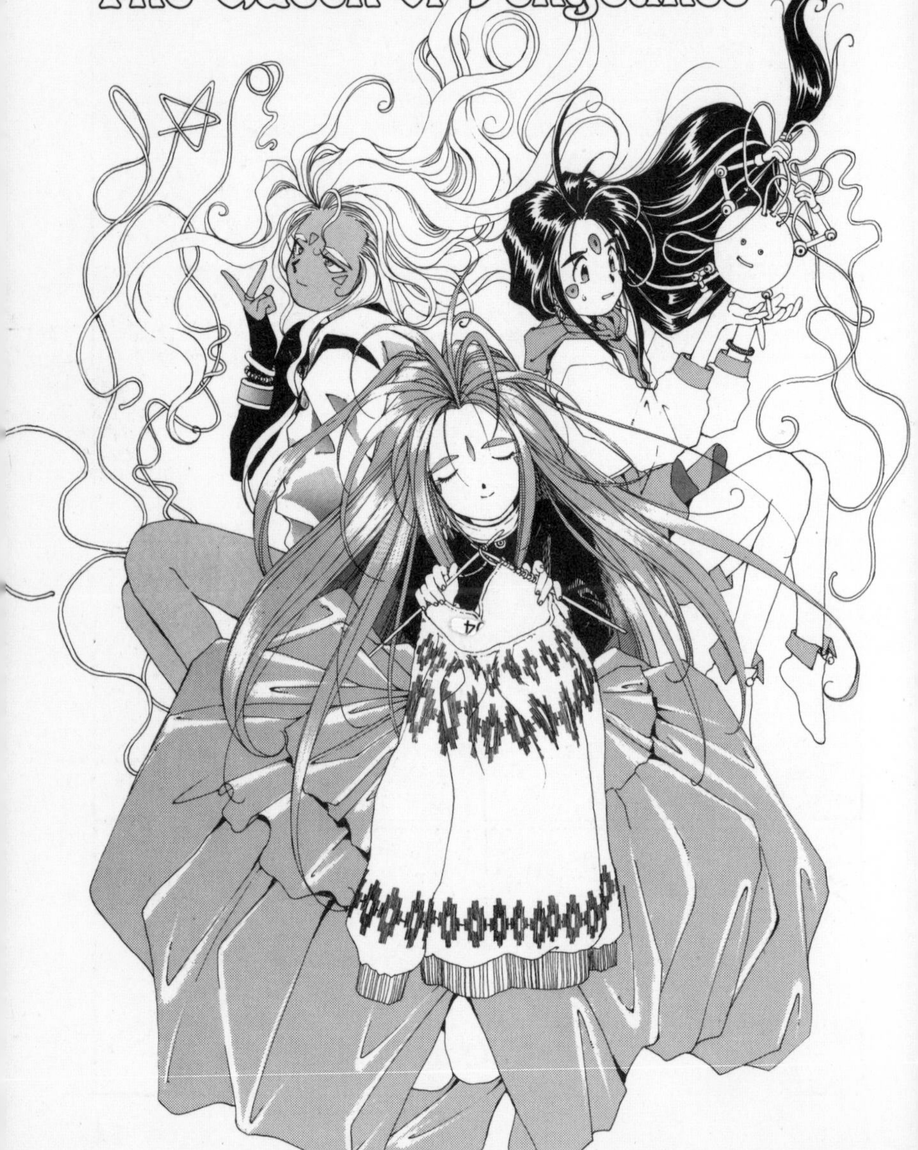

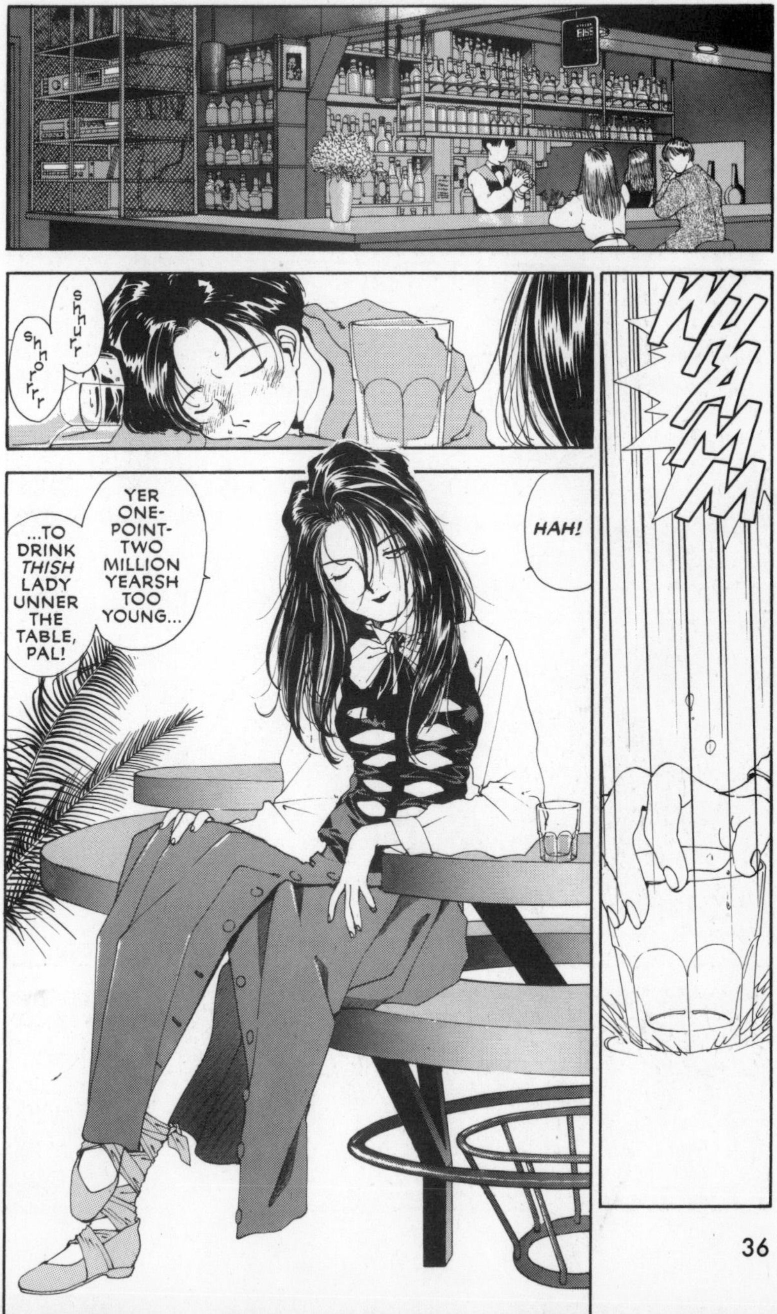
WHAMM
shnurr
shnorrrr
HAH!
YER ONE-POINT-TWO MILLION YEARSH TOO YOUNG...
...TO DRINK THISH LADY UNNER THE TABLE, PAL!

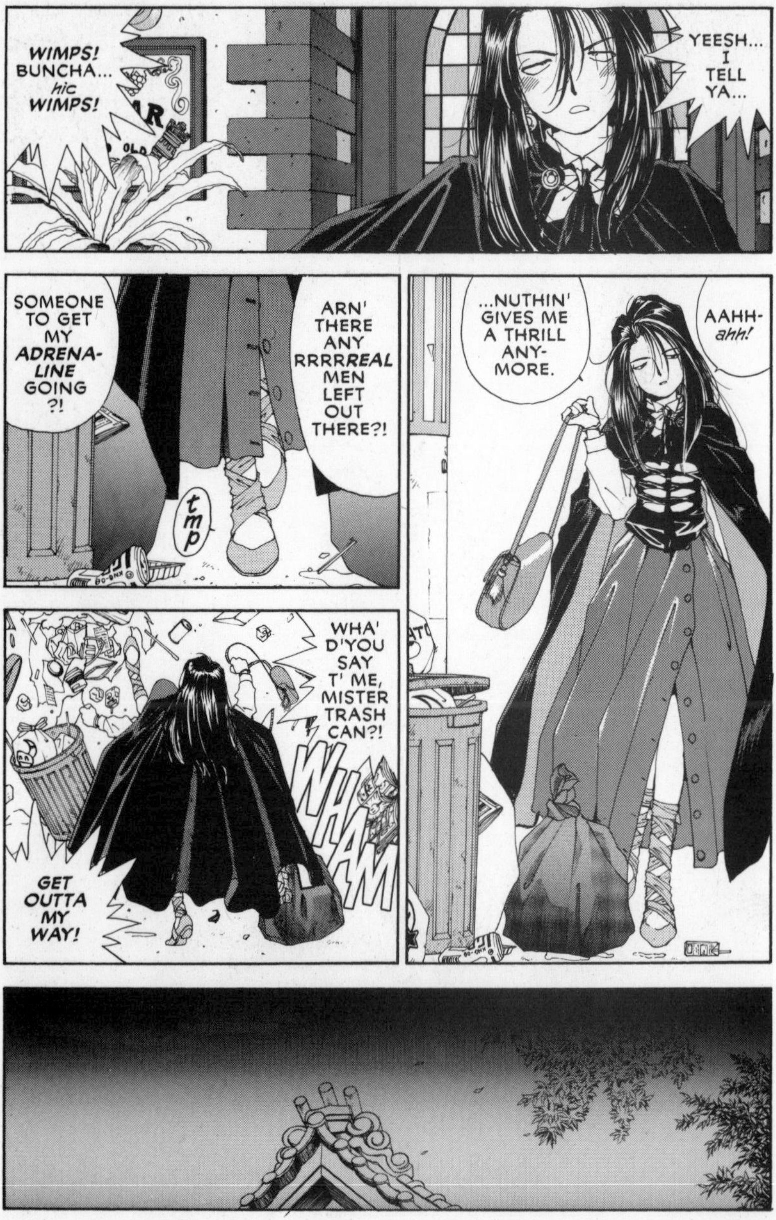
YEESH... I TELL YA...
WIMPS! BUNCHA... hic WIMPS!
AAHH-ahh!
...NUTHIN' GIVES ME A THRILL ANYMORE.
ARN' THERE ANY RRRRREAL MEN LEFT OUT THERE?!
SOMEONE TO GET MY ADRENALINE GOING?!
tmp
WHA' D'YOU SAY T' ME, MISTER TRASH CAN?!
WHAM
GET OUTTA MY WAY!

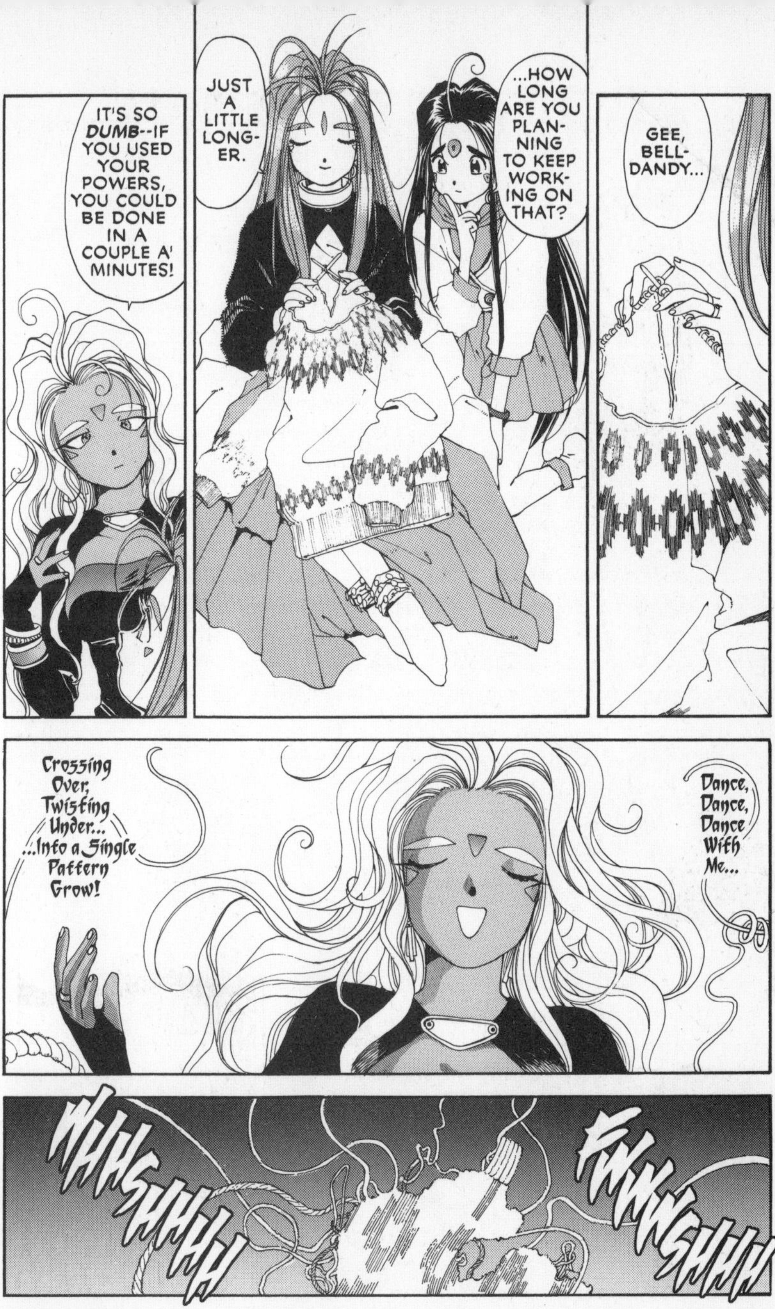
GEE, BELL-DANDY...
...HOW LONG ARE YOU PLANNING TO KEEP WORKING ON THAT?
JUST A LITTLE LONGER.
IT'S SO DUMB--IF YOU USED YOUR POWERS, YOU COULD BE DONE IN A COUPLE A' MINUTES!
Dance, Dance, Dance With Me...
Crossing Over, Twisting Under... ...Into a Single Pattern Grow!

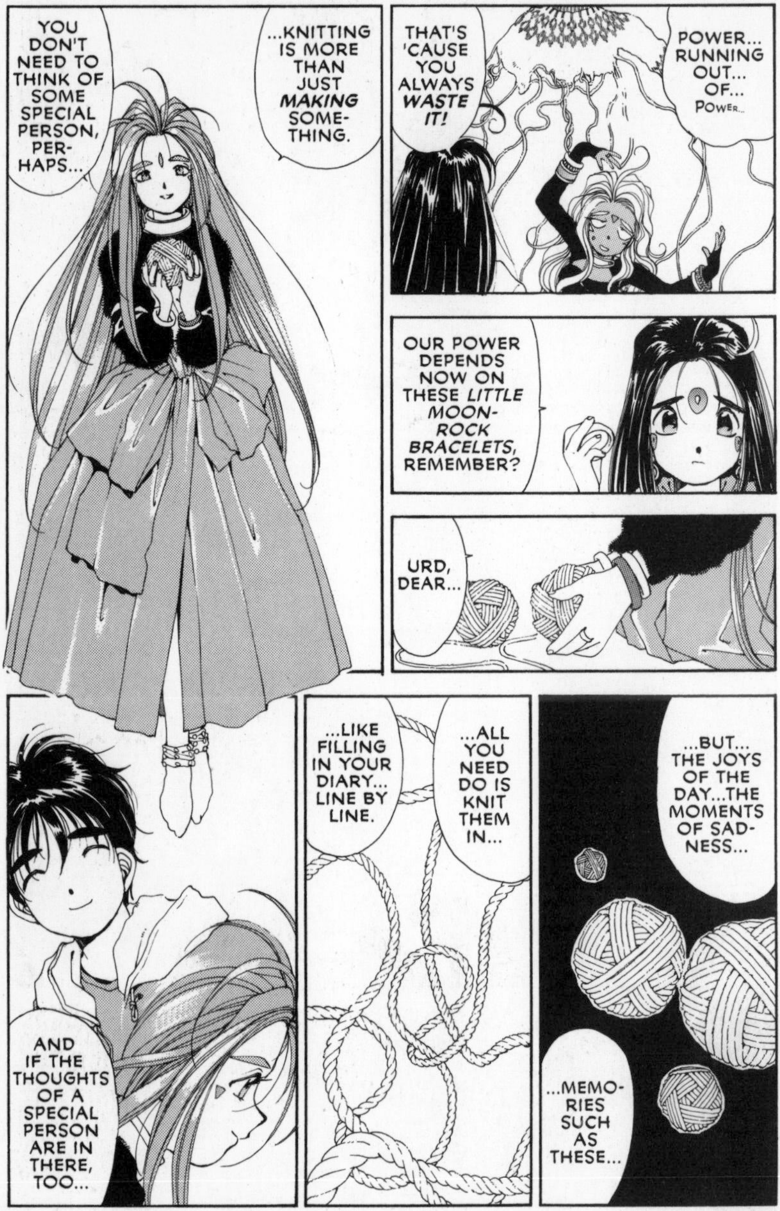
POWER... RUNNING OUT... OF... POWER...
THAT'S 'CAUSE YOU ALWAYS *WASTE IT!*
OUR POWER DEPENDS NOW ON THESE *LITTLE MOON-ROCK BRACELETS*, REMEMBER?
URD, DEAR...
...KNITTING IS MORE THAN JUST *MAKING* SOMETHING.
YOU DON'T NEED TO THINK OF SOME SPECIAL PERSON, PERHAPS...
...BUT... THE JOYS OF THE DAY...THE MOMENTS OF SADNESS...
...MEMORIES SUCH AS THESE...
...ALL YOU NEED DO IS KNIT THEM IN...
...LIKE FILLING IN YOUR DIARY... LINE BY LINE.
AND IF THE THOUGHTS OF A SPECIAL PERSON ARE IN THERE, TOO...

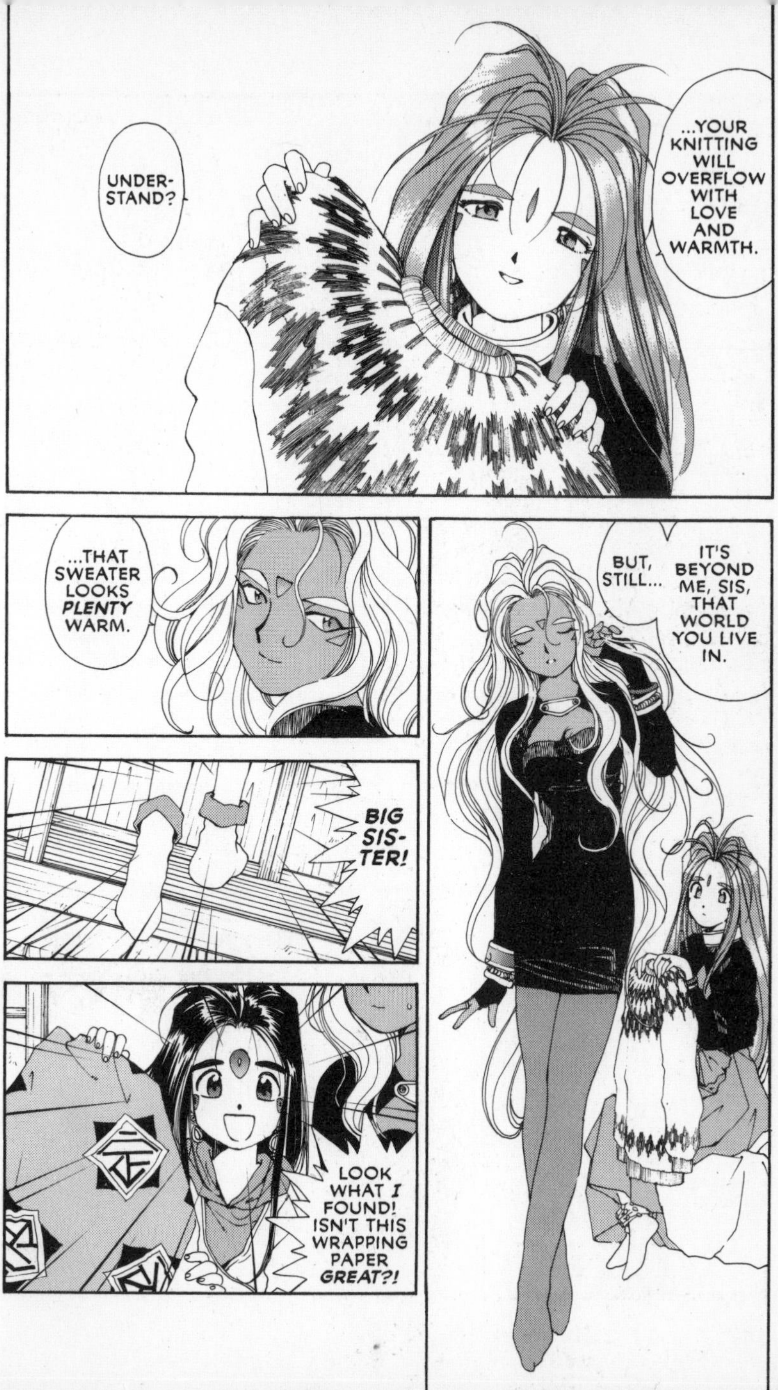
...YOUR KNITTING WILL OVERFLOW WITH LOVE AND WARMTH.
UNDER-STAND?
IT'S BEYOND ME, SIS, THAT WORLD YOU LIVE IN.
BUT, STILL...
...THAT SWEATER LOOKS *PLENTY* WARM.
BIG SIS-TER!
LOOK WHAT *I* FOUND! ISN'T THIS WRAPPING PAPER *GREAT?!*

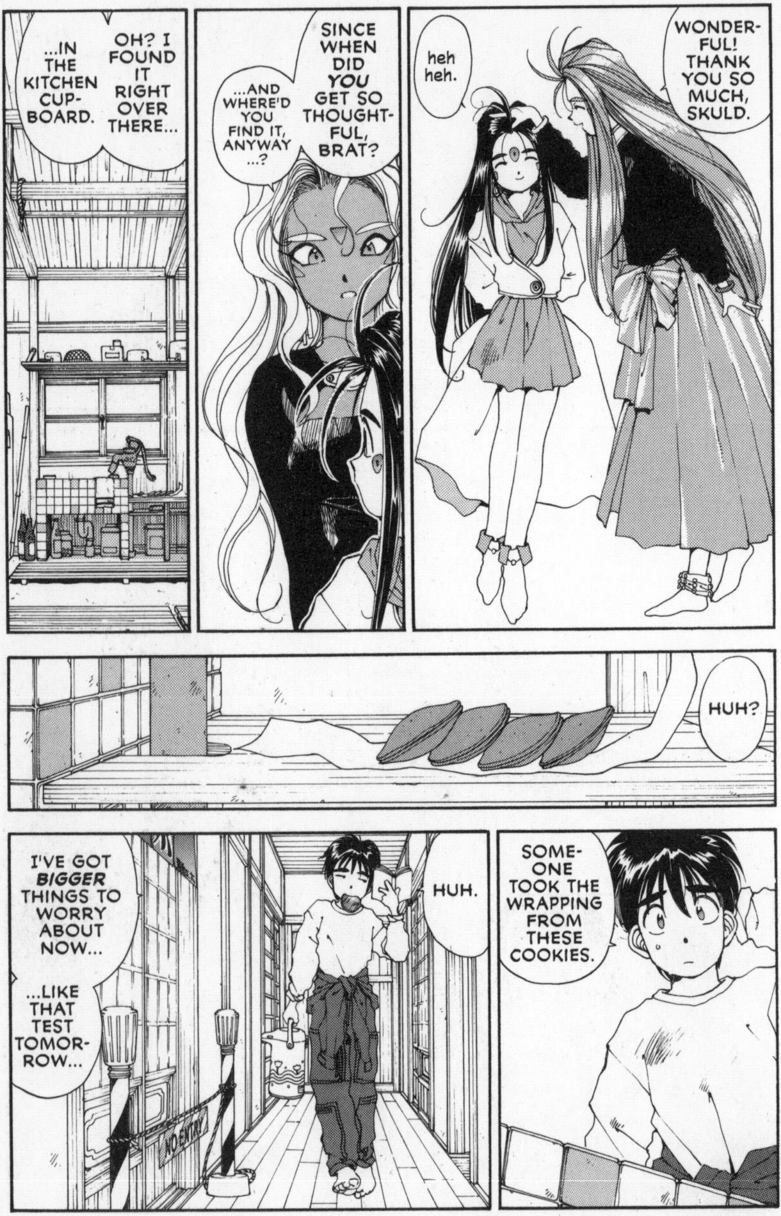
WONDER-FUL! THANK YOU SO MUCH, SKULD.
heh heh.
SINCE WHEN DID *YOU* GET SO THOUGHT-FUL, BRAT?
...AND WHERE'D YOU FIND IT, ANYWAY ...?
OH? I FOUND IT RIGHT OVER THERE...
...IN THE KITCHEN CUP-BOARD.
HUH?
SOME-ONE TOOK THE WRAPPING FROM THESE COOKIES.
HUH.
I'VE GOT ***BIGGER*** THINGS TO WORRY ABOUT NOW...
...LIKE THAT TEST TOMOR-ROW...
NO ENTRY

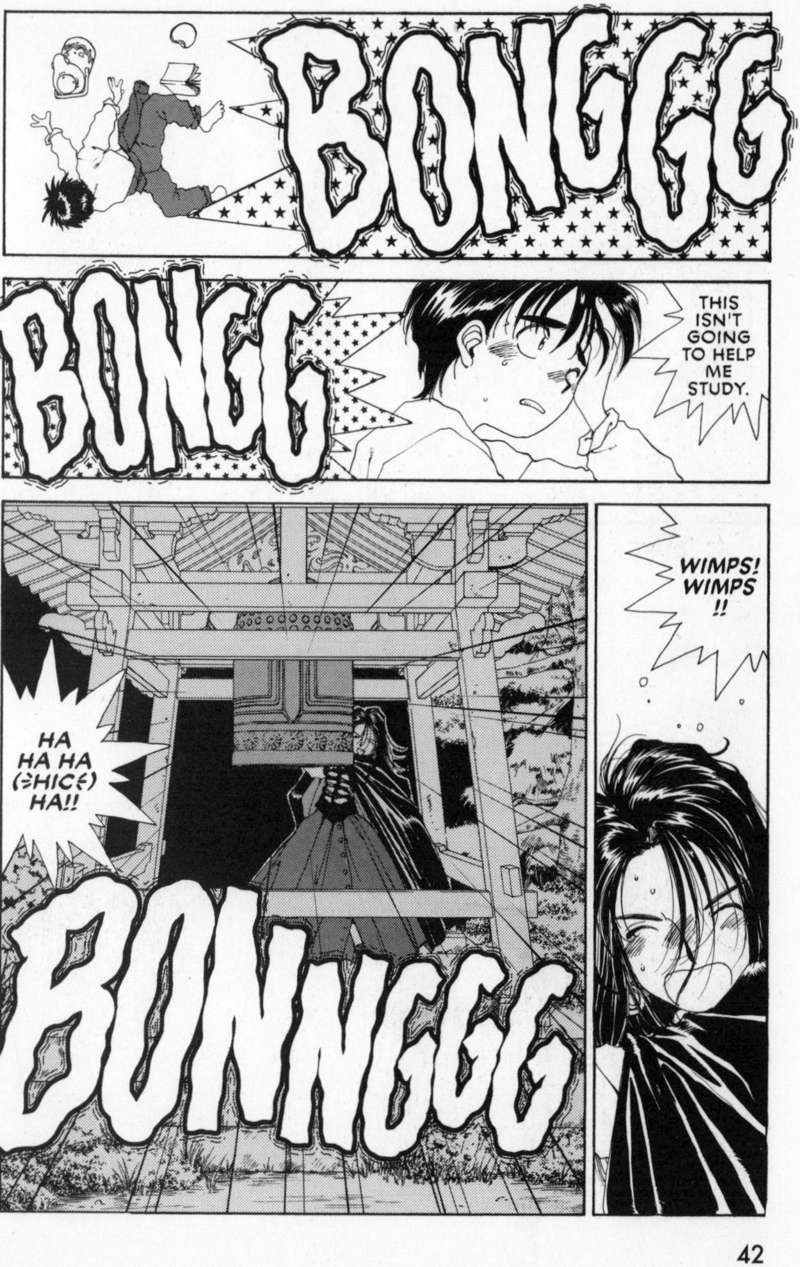
BONGGG
THIS ISN'T GOING TO HELP ME STUDY.
BONGG
WIMPS! WIMPS !!
HA HA HA (=HIC=) HA!!
BONNGGG

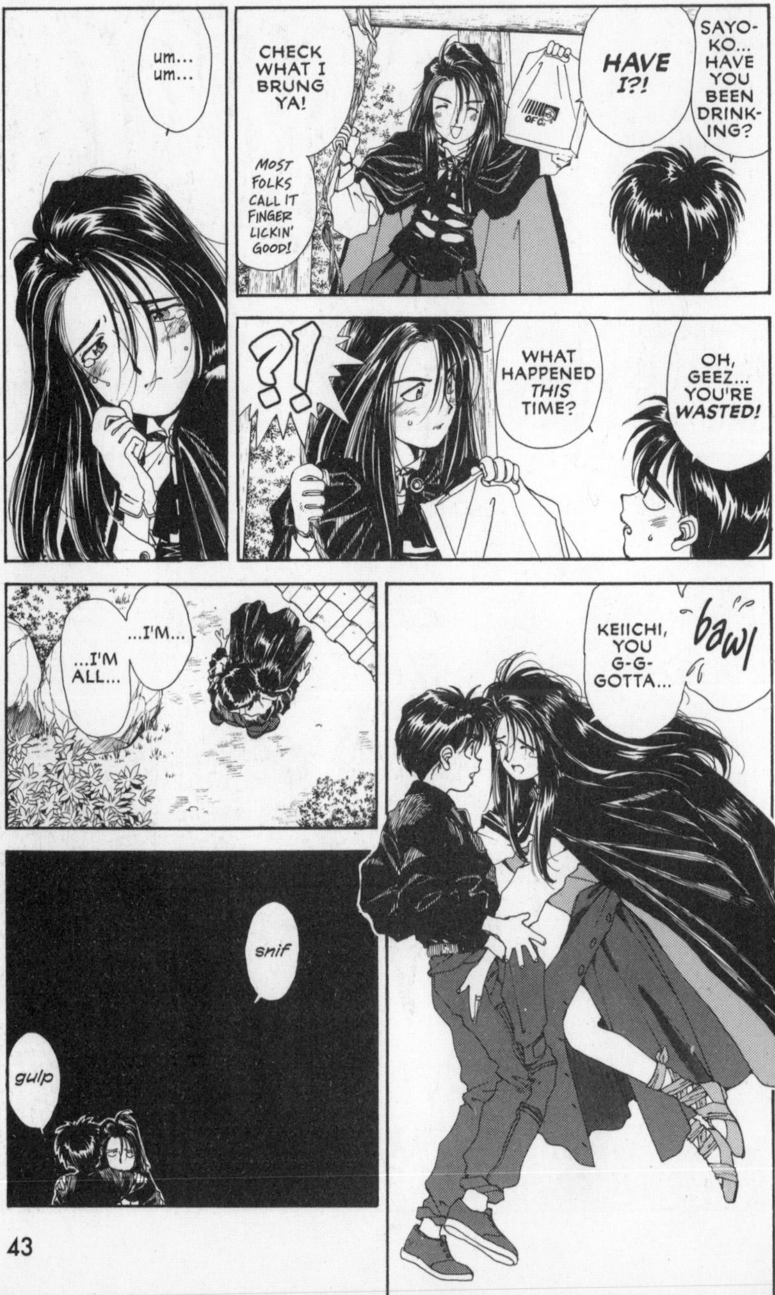
SAYO-KO... HAVE YOU BEEN DRINK-ING?
HAVE I?!
CHECK WHAT I BRUNG YA!
MOST FOLKS CALL IT FINGER LICKIN' GOOD!
OH, GEEZ... YOU'RE WASTED!
WHAT HAPPENED THIS TIME?
?!
um... um...
bawl
KEIICHI, YOU G-G-GOTTA...
...I'M...
...I'M ALL...
snif
gulp

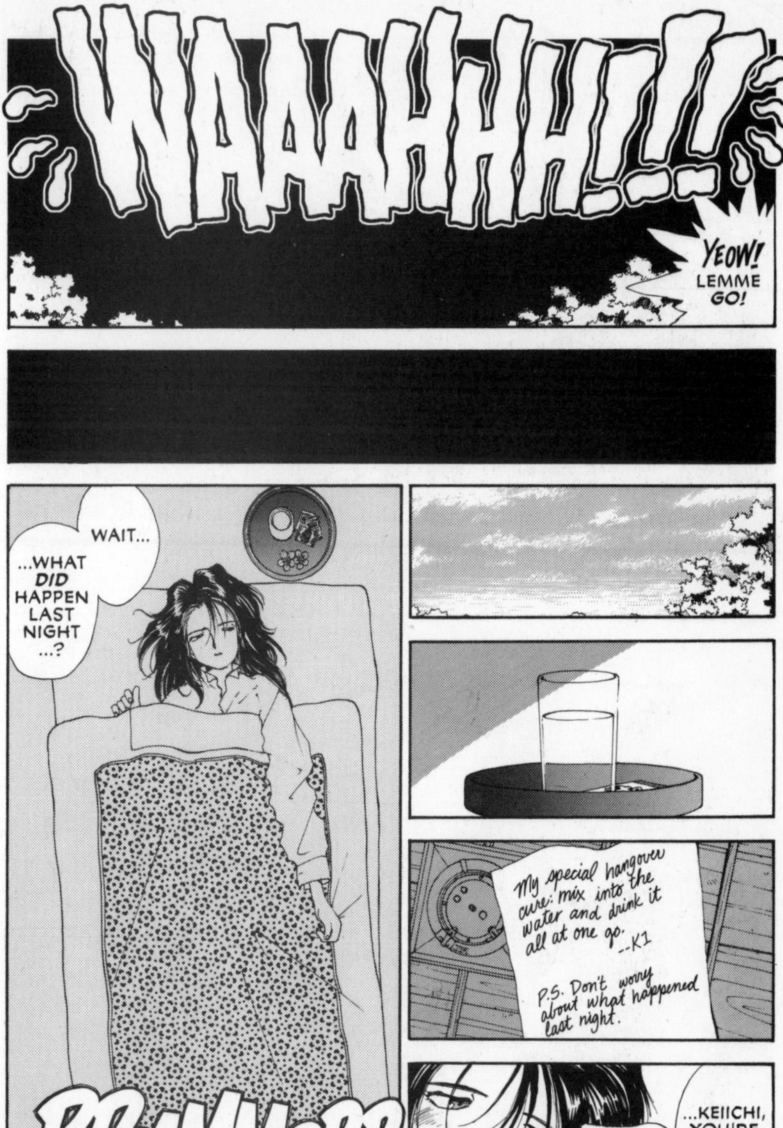
WAAHHH!!!
YEOW! LEMME GO!
My special hangover cure: mix into the water and drink it all at one go. --K1
P.S. Don't worry about what happened last night.
...KEIICHI, YOU'RE SO SWEET...
WAIT...
...WHAT DID HAPPEN LAST NIGHT ...?
BRMMMBBB

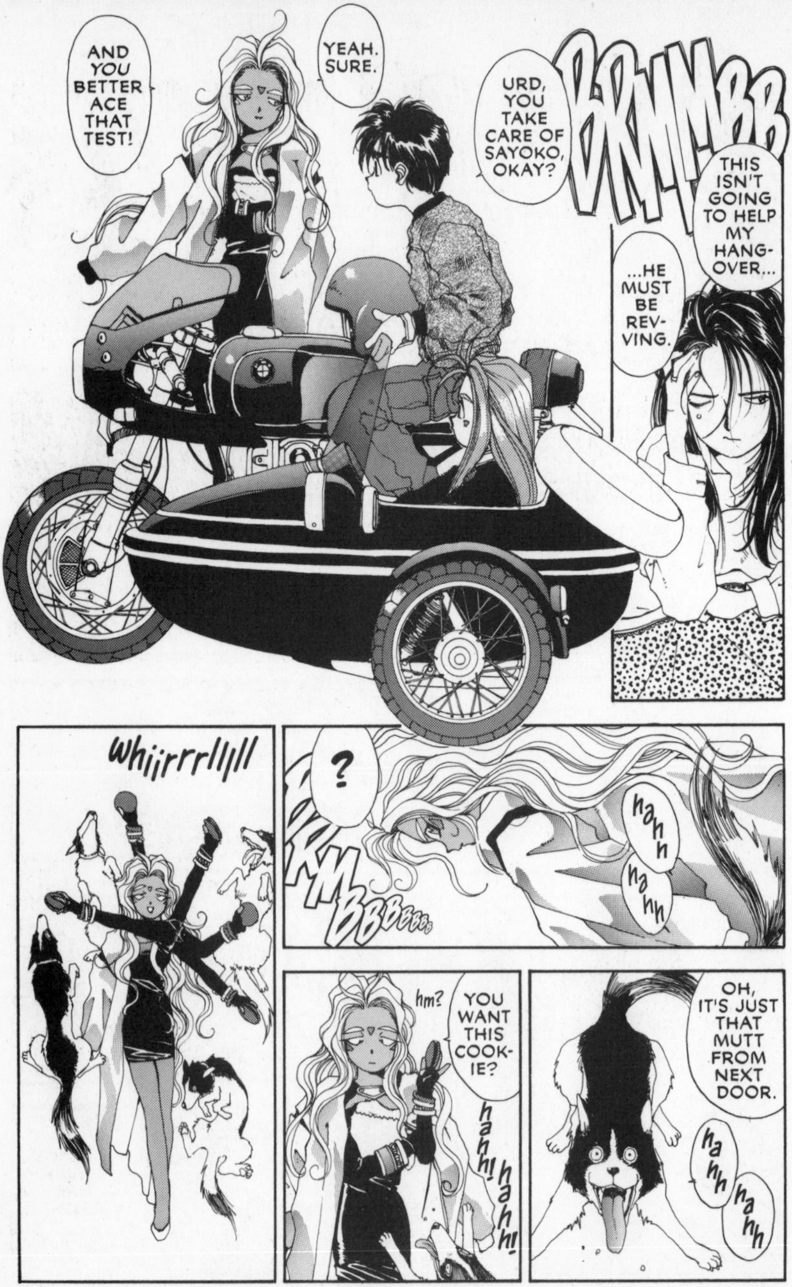

BRMMBB
THIS ISN'T GOING TO HELP MY HANG-OVER...
...HE MUST BE REV-VING.
URD, YOU TAKE CARE OF SAYOKO, OKAY?
YEAH. SURE.
AND YOU BETTER ACE THAT TEST!
?
hahh
hahh
MMBBBBbb
OH, IT'S JUST THAT MUTT FROM NEXT DOOR.
hahh
hahh
hm?
YOU WANT THIS COOK-IE?
hahh!
hahh!
hahh!
whiirrrlllll

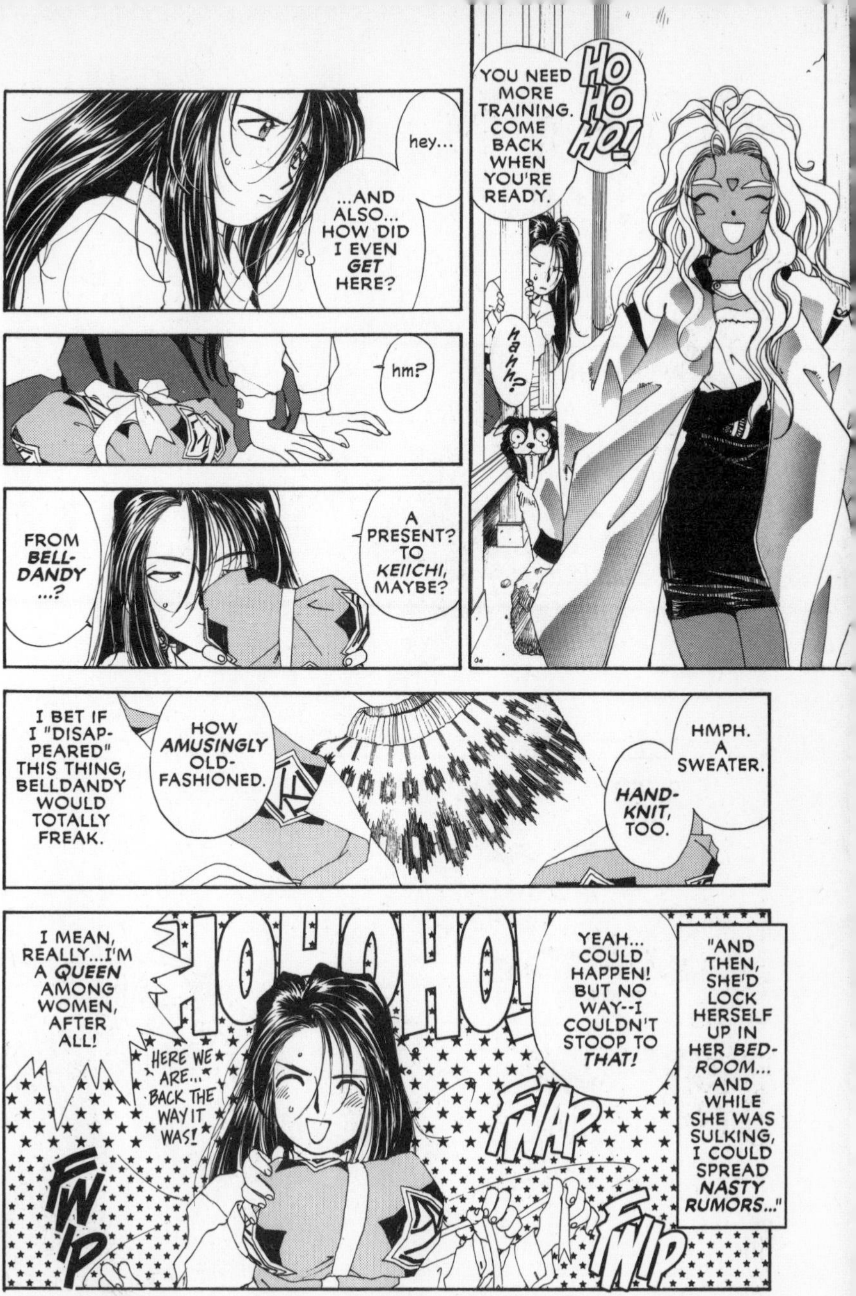
HO HO HO!
YOU NEED MORE TRAINING. COME BACK WHEN YOU'RE READY.
hahh?
hey...
...AND ALSO... HOW DID I EVEN GET HERE?
hm?
A PRESENT? TO KEIICHI, MAYBE?
FROM BELLDANDY ...?
HMPH. A SWEATER. HAND-KNIT, TOO.
HOW AMUSINGLY OLD-FASHIONED.
I BET IF I "DISAPPEARED" THIS THING, BELLDANDY WOULD TOTALLY FREAK.
"AND THEN, SHE'D LOCK HERSELF UP IN HER BEDROOM... AND WHILE SHE WAS SULKING, I COULD SPREAD NASTY RUMORS..."
YEAH... COULD HAPPEN! BUT NO WAY--I COULDN'T STOOP TO THAT!
HOHOHO
I MEAN, REALLY...I'M A QUEEN AMONG WOMEN, AFTER ALL!
HERE WE ARE... BACK THE WAY IT WAS!
FWAP
FWIP
FWIP

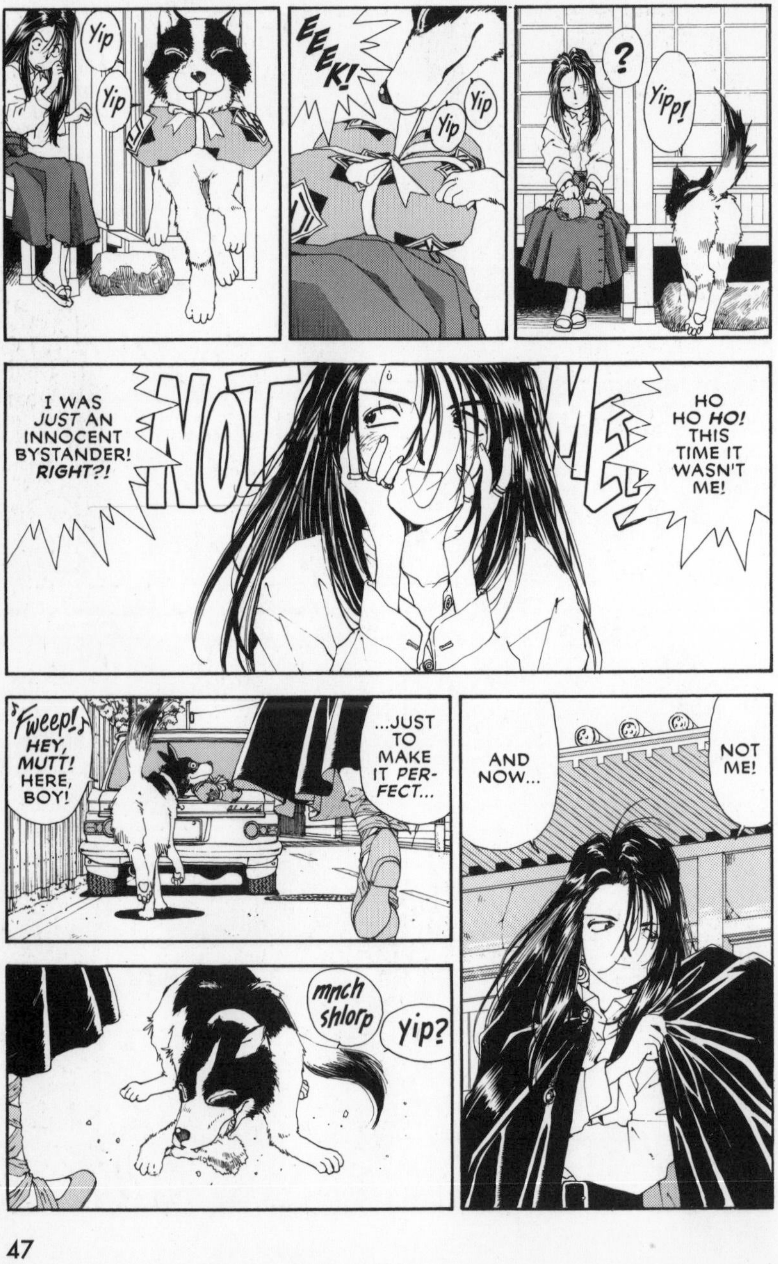
?
Yipp!
EEEK!
Yip
Yip
Yip
Yip
HO HO HO! THIS TIME IT WASN'T ME!
NOT ME!
I WAS JUST AN INNOCENT BYSTANDER! RIGHT?!
NOT ME!
AND NOW...
...JUST TO MAKE IT PERFECT...
Fweep!
HEY, MUTT! HERE, BOY!
mnch shlorp
yip?

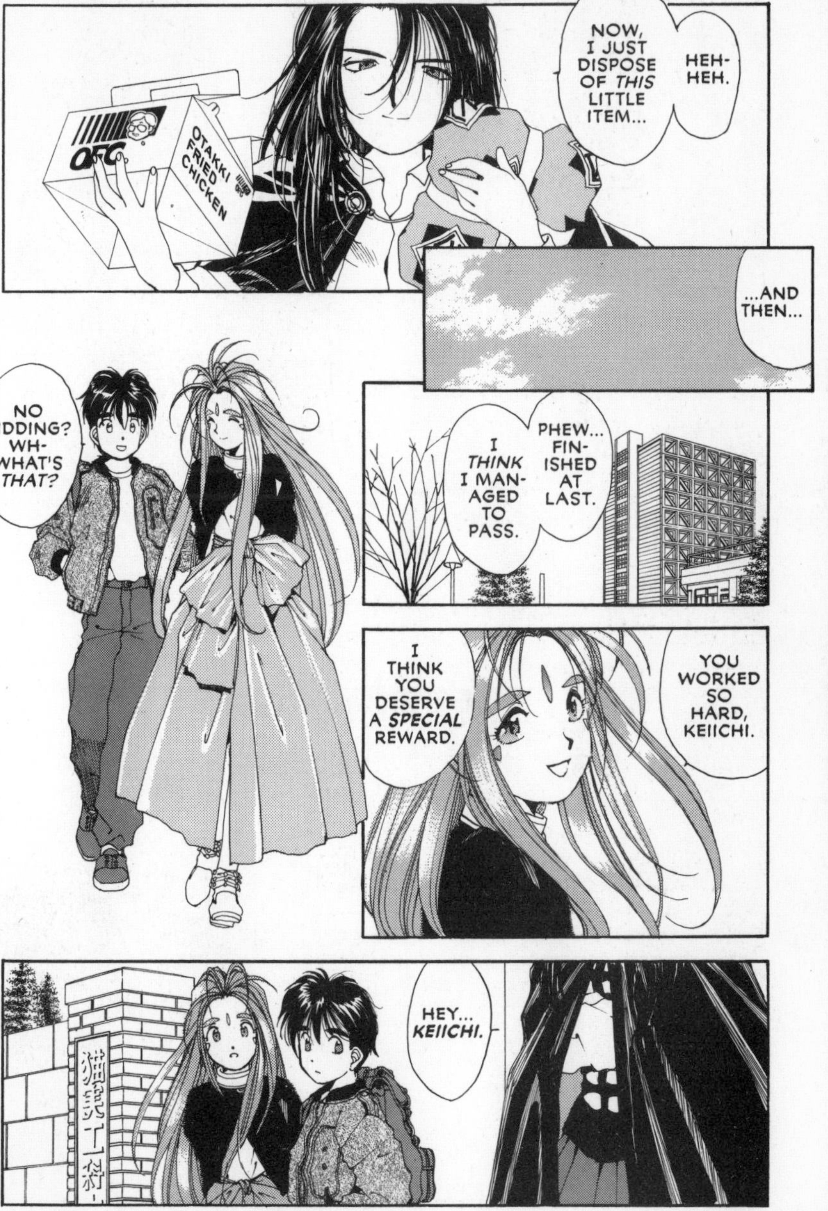
HEH-HEH.
NOW, I JUST DISPOSE OF *THIS* LITTLE ITEM...
OTAKKI FRIED CHICKEN
OFC
...AND THEN...
PHEW... FIN-ISHED AT LAST.
I *THINK* I MAN-AGED TO PASS.
YOU WORKED SO HARD, KEIICHI.
I THINK YOU DESERVE A *SPECIAL* REWARD.
NO KIDDING? WH-WHAT'S *THAT?*
HEY... ***KEIICHI.***

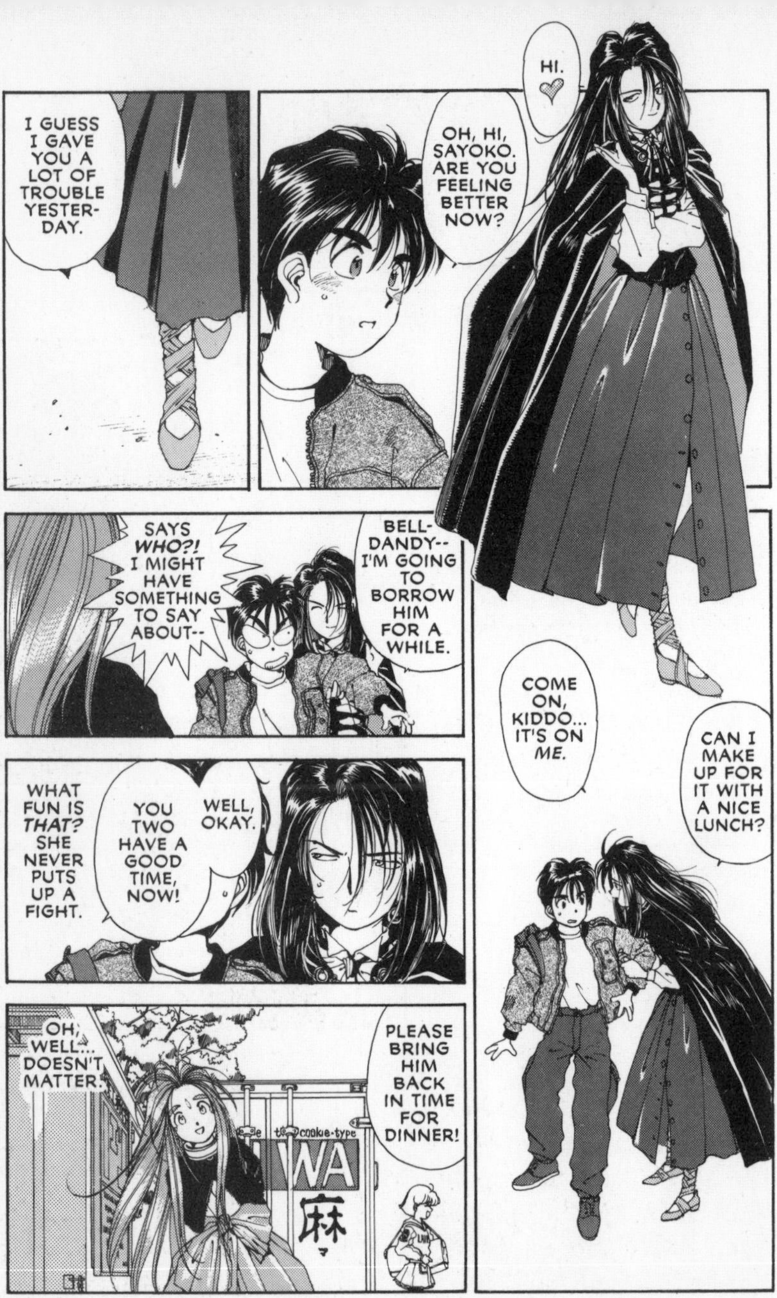
HI.
OH, HI, SAYOKO. ARE YOU FEELING BETTER NOW?
I GUESS I GAVE YOU A LOT OF TROUBLE YESTER-DAY.
CAN I MAKE UP FOR IT WITH A NICE LUNCH?
COME ON, KIDDO... IT'S ON *ME.*
BELL-DANDY-- I'M GOING TO BORROW HIM FOR A WHILE.
SAYS *WHO?!* I MIGHT HAVE SOMETHING TO SAY ABOUT--
WELL, OKAY.
YOU TWO HAVE A GOOD TIME, NOW!
WHAT FUN IS *THAT?* SHE NEVER PUTS UP A FIGHT.
PLEASE BRING HIM BACK IN TIME FOR DINNER!
OH, WELL... DOESN'T MATTER.

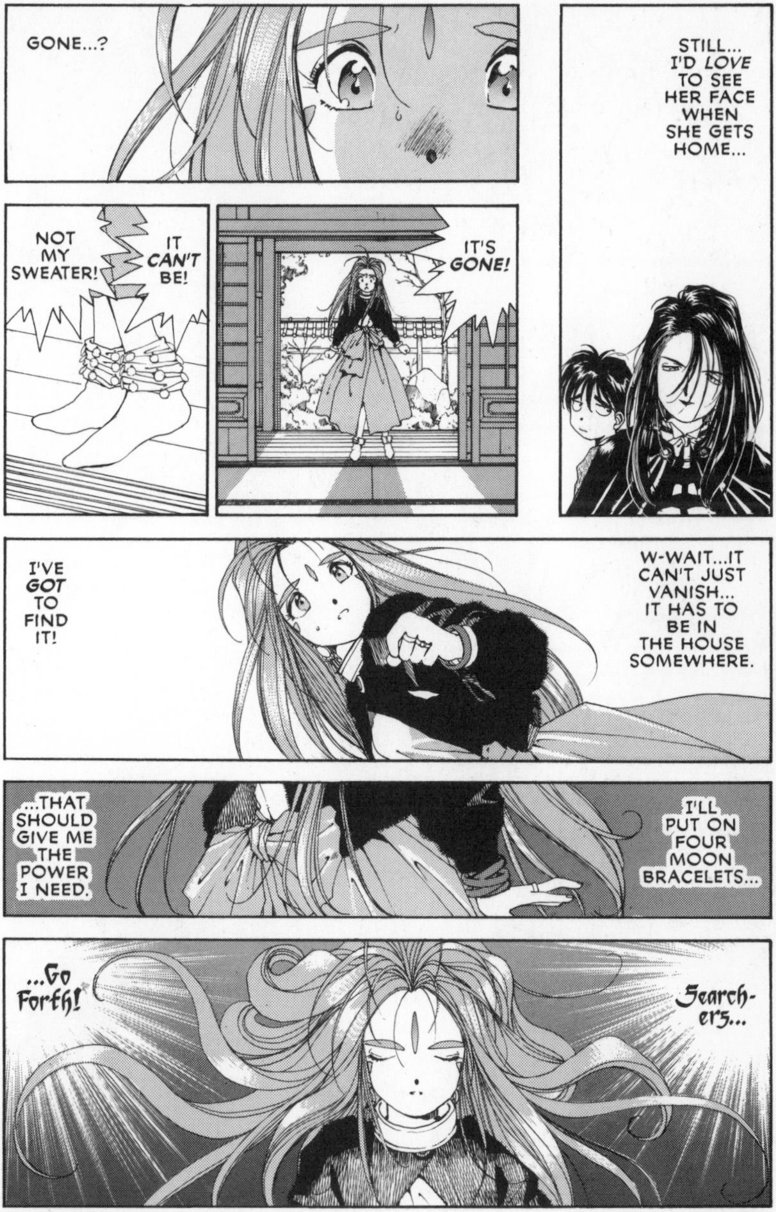
STILL... I'D *LOVE* TO SEE HER FACE WHEN SHE GETS HOME...
GONE...?
IT'S *GONE!*
IT *CAN'T* BE!
NOT MY SWEATER!
W-WAIT...IT CAN'T JUST VANISH... IT HAS TO BE IN THE HOUSE SOMEWHERE.
I'VE *GOT* TO FIND IT!
I'LL PUT ON FOUR MOON BRACELETS...
...THAT SHOULD GIVE ME THE POWER I NEED.
Searchers...
...Go Forth!

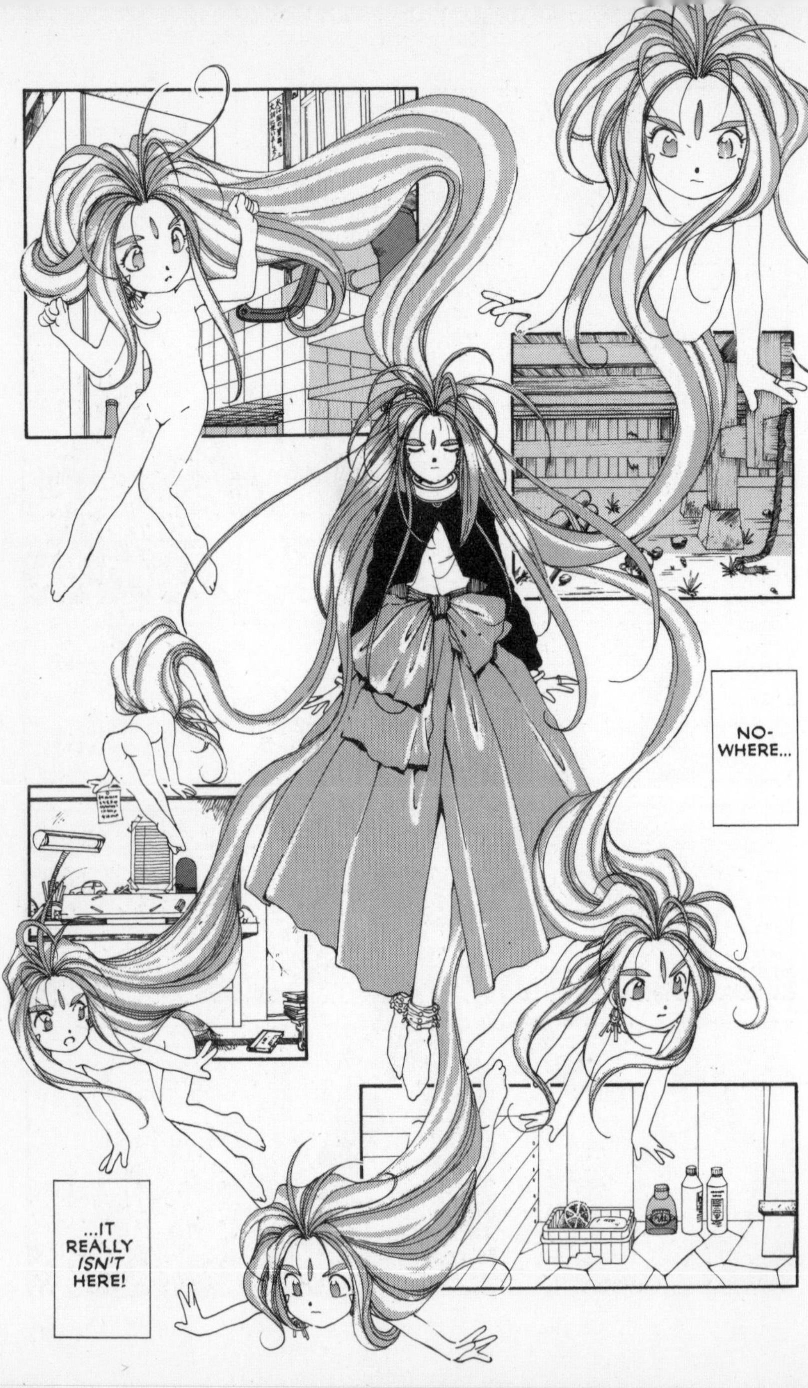
NO-WHERE...
...IT REALLY *ISN'T* HERE!

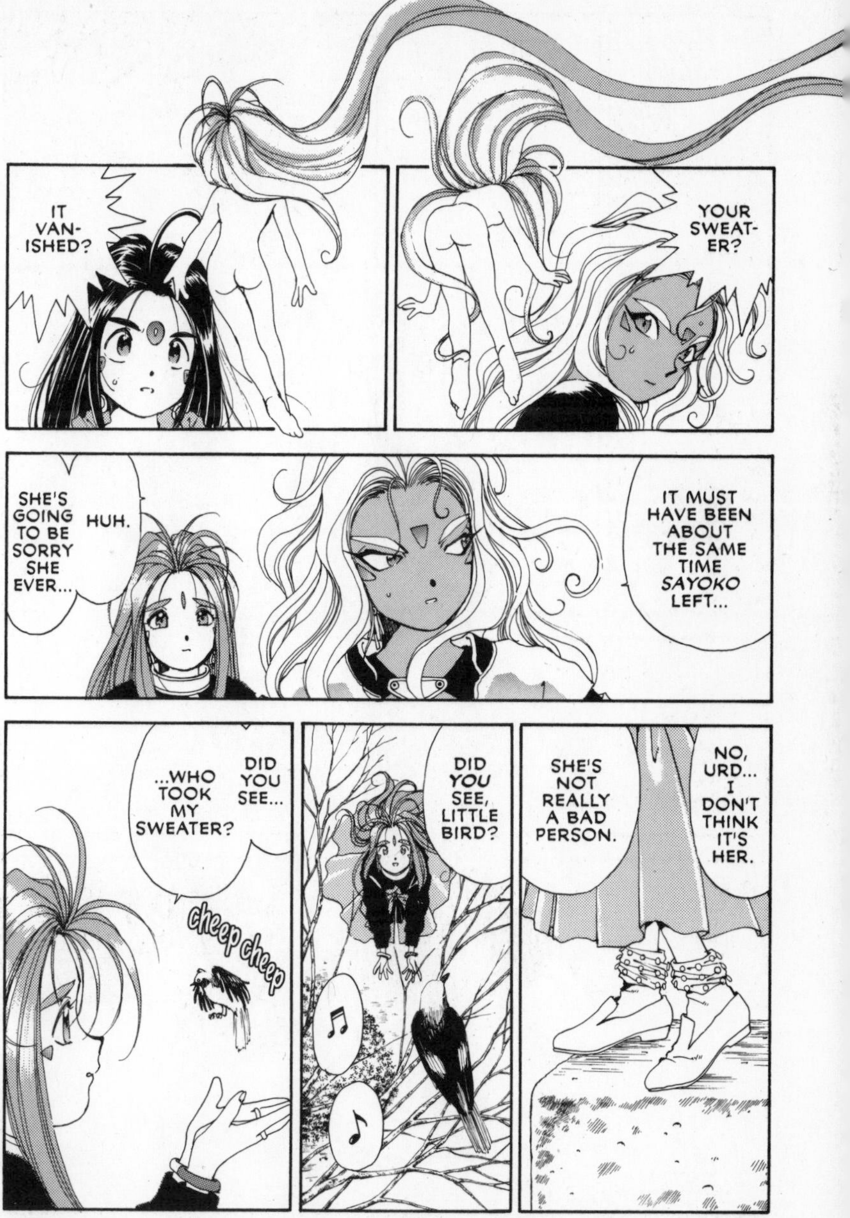
YOUR SWEATER?
IT VANISHED?
IT MUST HAVE BEEN ABOUT THE SAME TIME *SAYOKO* LEFT...
HUH.
SHE'S GOING TO BE SORRY SHE EVER...
NO, URD... I DON'T THINK IT'S HER.
SHE'S NOT REALLY A BAD PERSON.
DID *YOU* SEE, LITTLE BIRD?
DID YOU SEE...
...WHO TOOK MY SWEATER?
cheep cheep

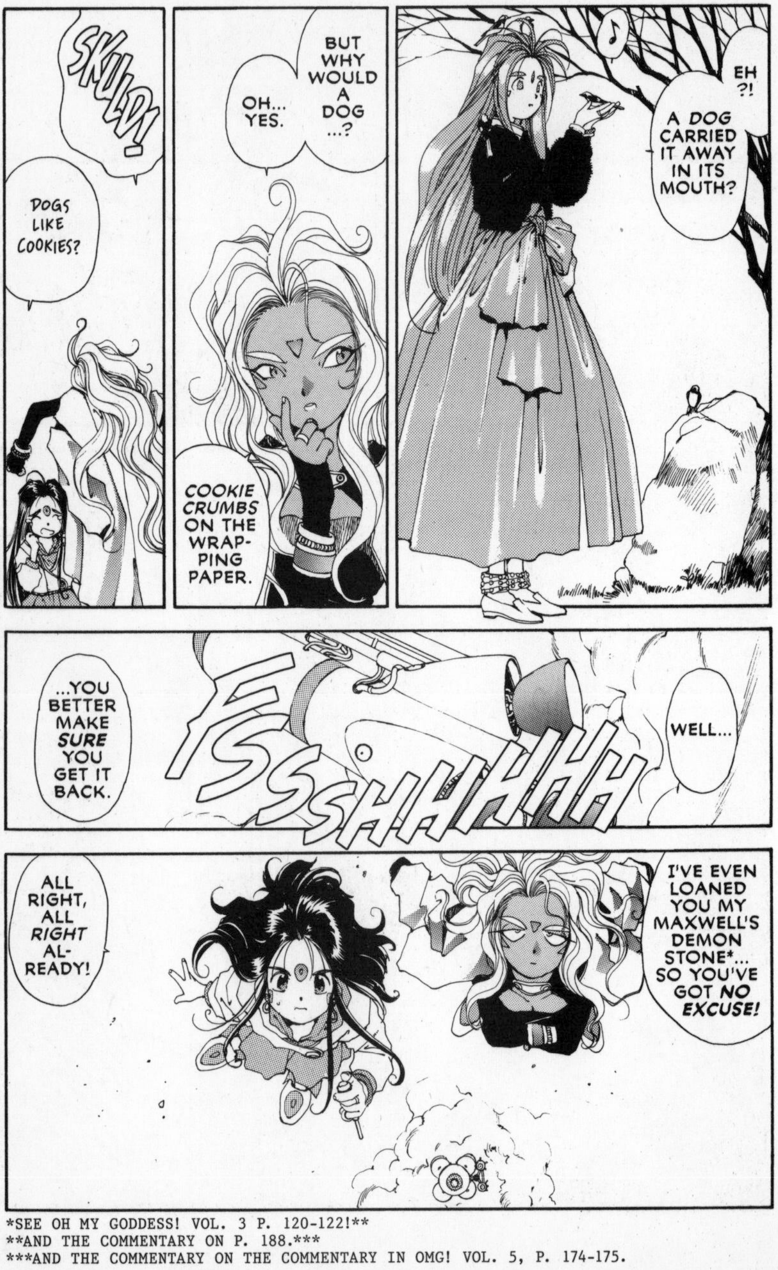
EH ?! A DOG CARRIED IT AWAY IN ITS MOUTH?
BUT WHY WOULD A DOG ...?
OH... YES.
COOKIE CRUMBS ON THE WRAP-PING PAPER.
SKULD!
DOGS LIKE COOKIES?
WELL...
FSSHHHHHH
...YOU BETTER MAKE *SURE* YOU GET IT BACK.
I'VE EVEN LOANED YOU MY MAXWELL'S DEMON STONE*... SO YOU'VE GOT *NO EXCUSE!*
ALL RIGHT, ALL *RIGHT* AL-READY!

*SEE OH MY GODDESS! VOL. 3 P. 120-122!**
AND THE COMMENTARY ON P. 188.*
***AND THE COMMENTARY ON THE COMMENTARY IN OMG! VOL. 5, P. 174-175.

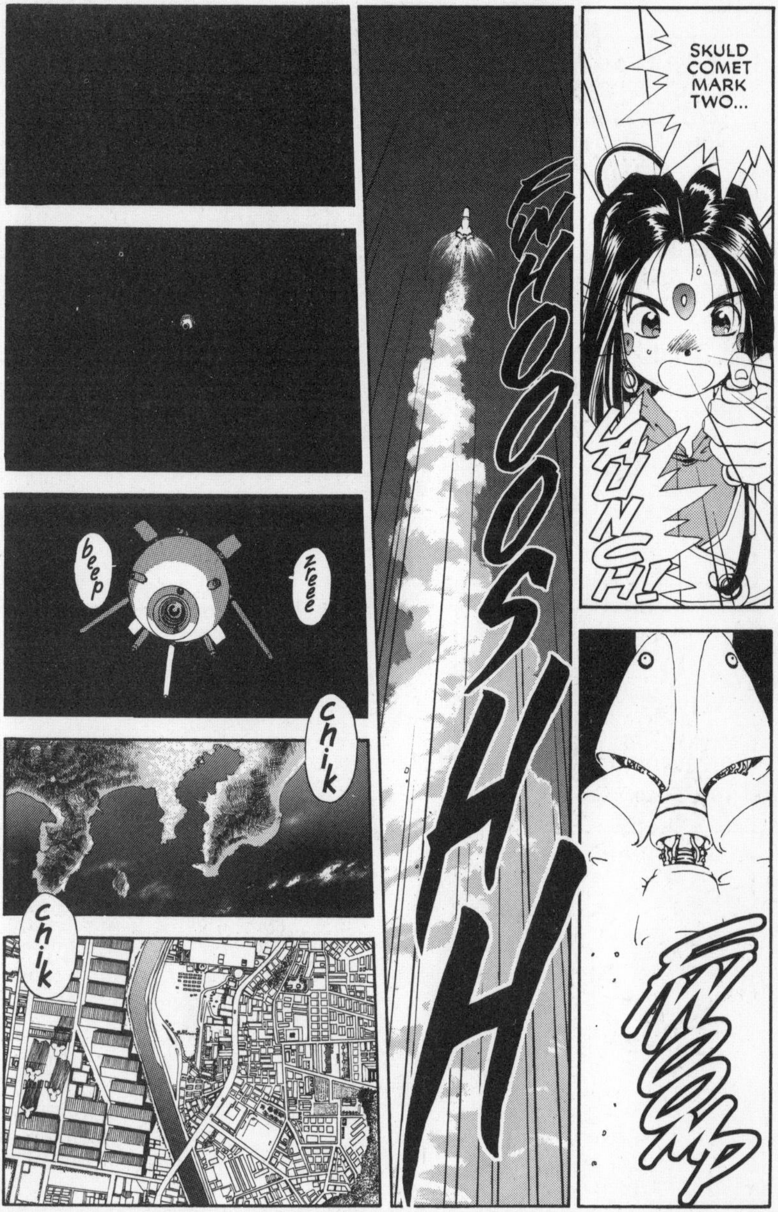
SKULD COMET MARK TWO...
LAUNCH!
FWOOMP
WHOOOOOSHHH
beep
zreee
chik
chik

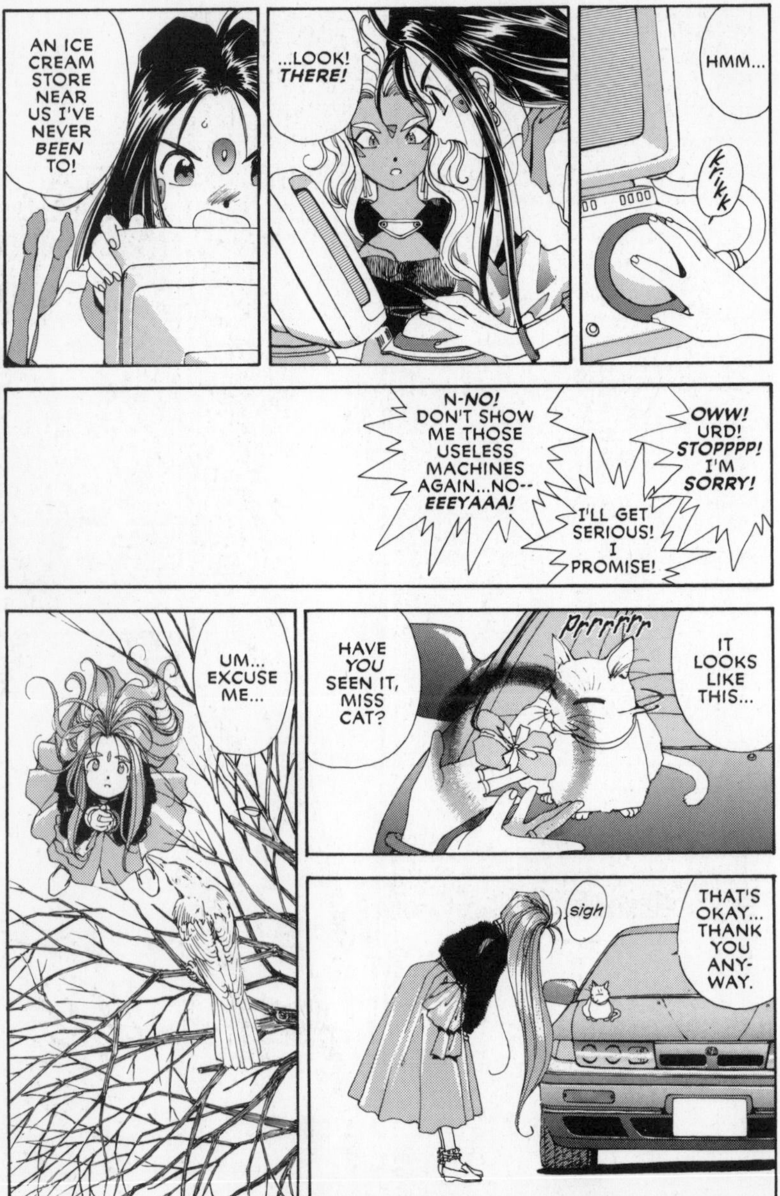
HMM...
krikk
...LOOK! THERE!
AN ICE CREAM STORE NEAR US I'VE NEVER BEEN TO!
OWW! URD! STOPPPP! I'M SORRY!
N-NO! DON'T SHOW ME THOSE USELESS MACHINES AGAIN...NO-- EEEYAAA!
I'LL GET SERIOUS! I PROMISE!
IT LOOKS LIKE THIS...
Prrrrrr
HAVE YOU SEEN IT, MISS CAT?
THAT'S OKAY... THANK YOU ANY-WAY.
sigh
UM... EXCUSE ME...

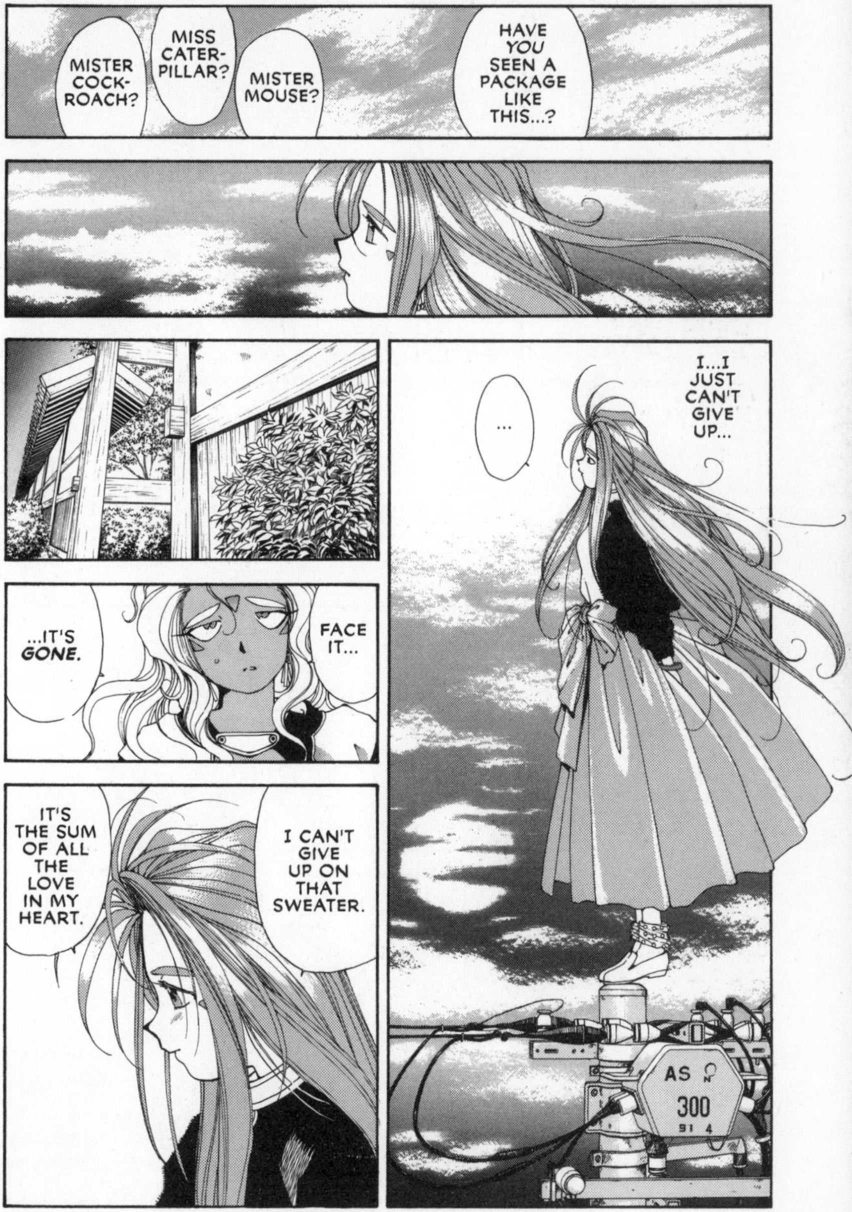
HAVE YOU SEEN A PACKAGE LIKE THIS...?
MISTER MOUSE?
MISS CATER-PILLAR?
MISTER COCK-ROACH?
I...I JUST CAN'T GIVE UP...
...
FACE IT...
...IT'S GONE.
I CAN'T GIVE UP ON THAT SWEATER.
IT'S THE SUM OF ALL THE LOVE IN MY HEART.

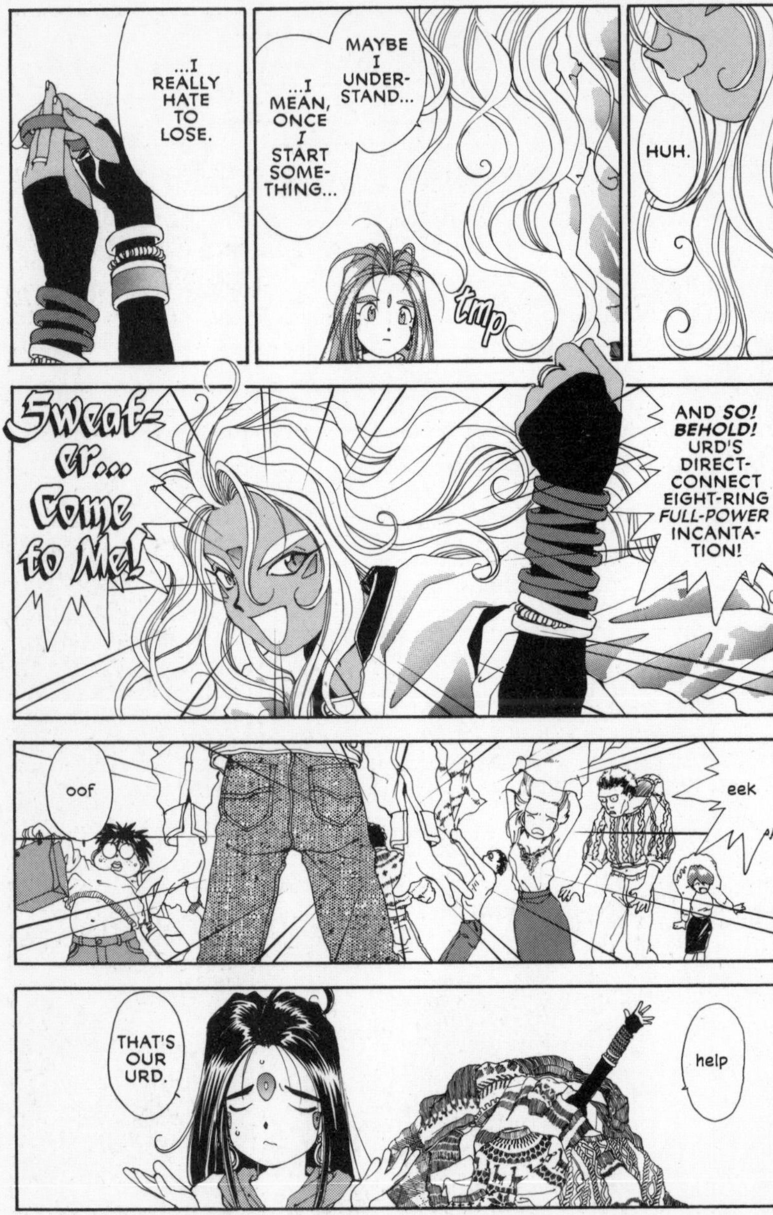
HUH.
MAYBE I UNDERSTAND...
...I MEAN, ONCE I START SOMETHING...
tmp
...I REALLY HATE TO LOSE.
AND SO! BEHOLD! URD'S DIRECT-CONNECT EIGHT-RING FULL-POWER INCANTATION!
Sweat-er... Come to Me!
eek
oof
help
THAT'S OUR URD.

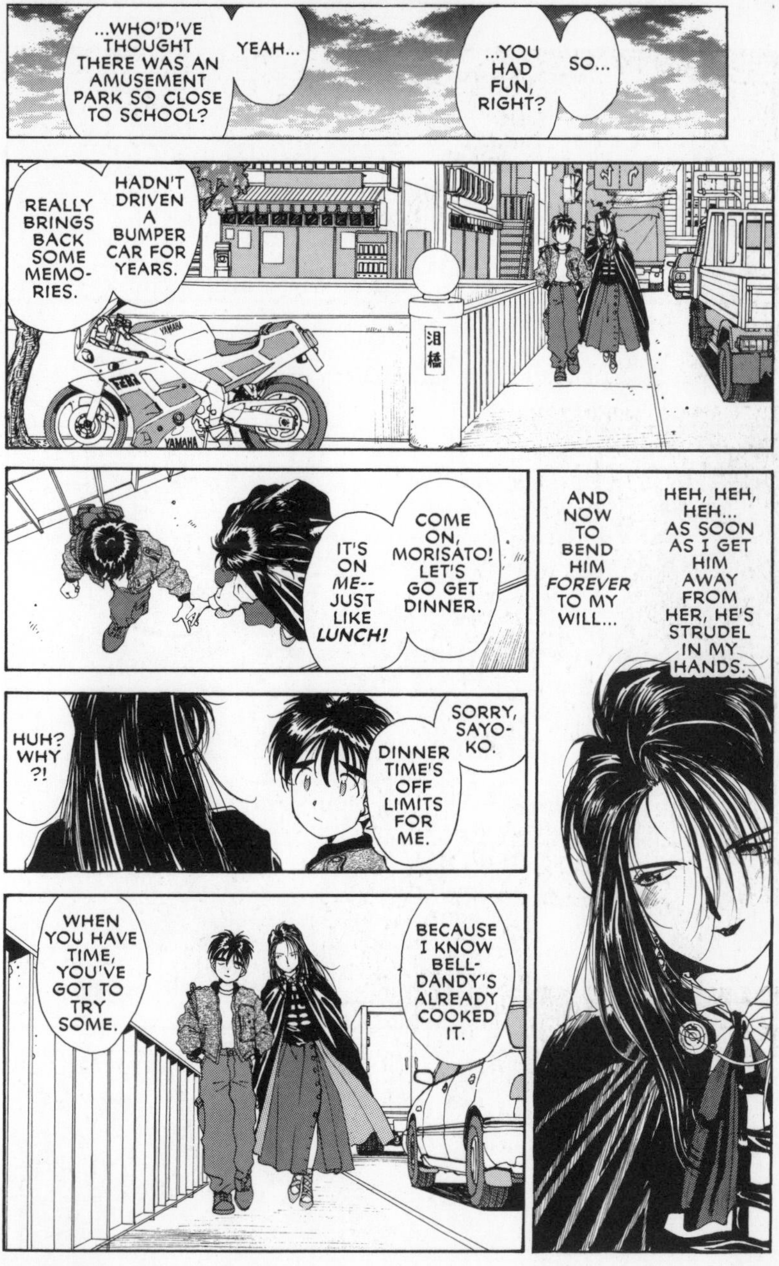
SO...
...YOU HAD FUN, RIGHT?
YEAH...
...WHO'D'VE THOUGHT THERE WAS AN AMUSEMENT PARK SO CLOSE TO SCHOOL?
HADN'T DRIVEN A BUMPER CAR FOR YEARS.
REALLY BRINGS BACK SOME MEMORIES.
HEH, HEH, HEH... AS SOON AS I GET HIM AWAY FROM HER, HE'S STRUDEL IN MY HANDS.
AND NOW TO BEND HIM *FOREVER* TO MY WILL...
COME ON, MORISATO! LET'S GO GET DINNER.
IT'S ON *ME*--JUST LIKE *LUNCH!*
SORRY, SAYOKO.
DINNER TIME'S OFF LIMITS FOR ME.
HUH? WHY?!
BECAUSE I KNOW BELLDANDY'S ALREADY COOKED IT.
WHEN YOU HAVE TIME, YOU'VE GOT TO TRY SOME.

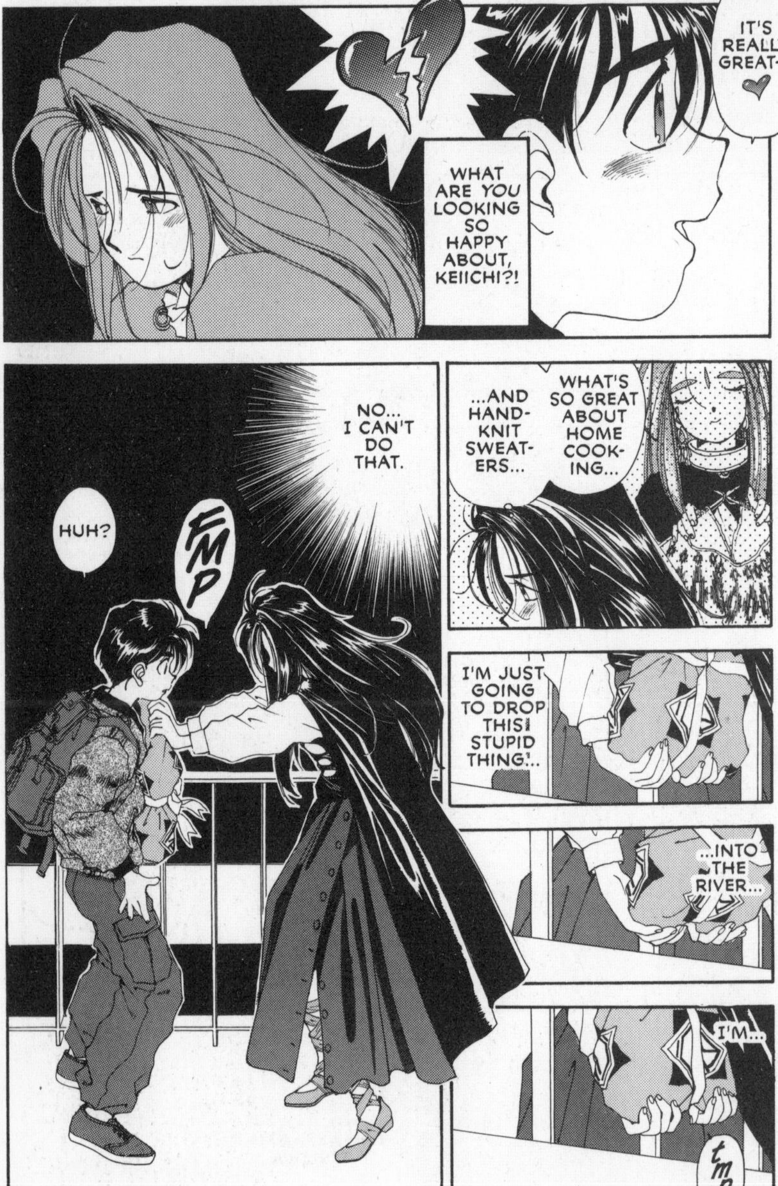
IT'S REALLY GREAT--! ♥
WHAT ARE YOU LOOKING SO HAPPY ABOUT, KEIICHI?!
WHAT'S SO GREAT ABOUT HOME COOKING...
...AND HAND-KNIT SWEATERS...
I'M JUST GOING TO DROP THIS STUPID THING!..
...INTO THE RIVER...
I'M...
tmp
NO... I CAN'T DO THAT.
EMP
HUH?

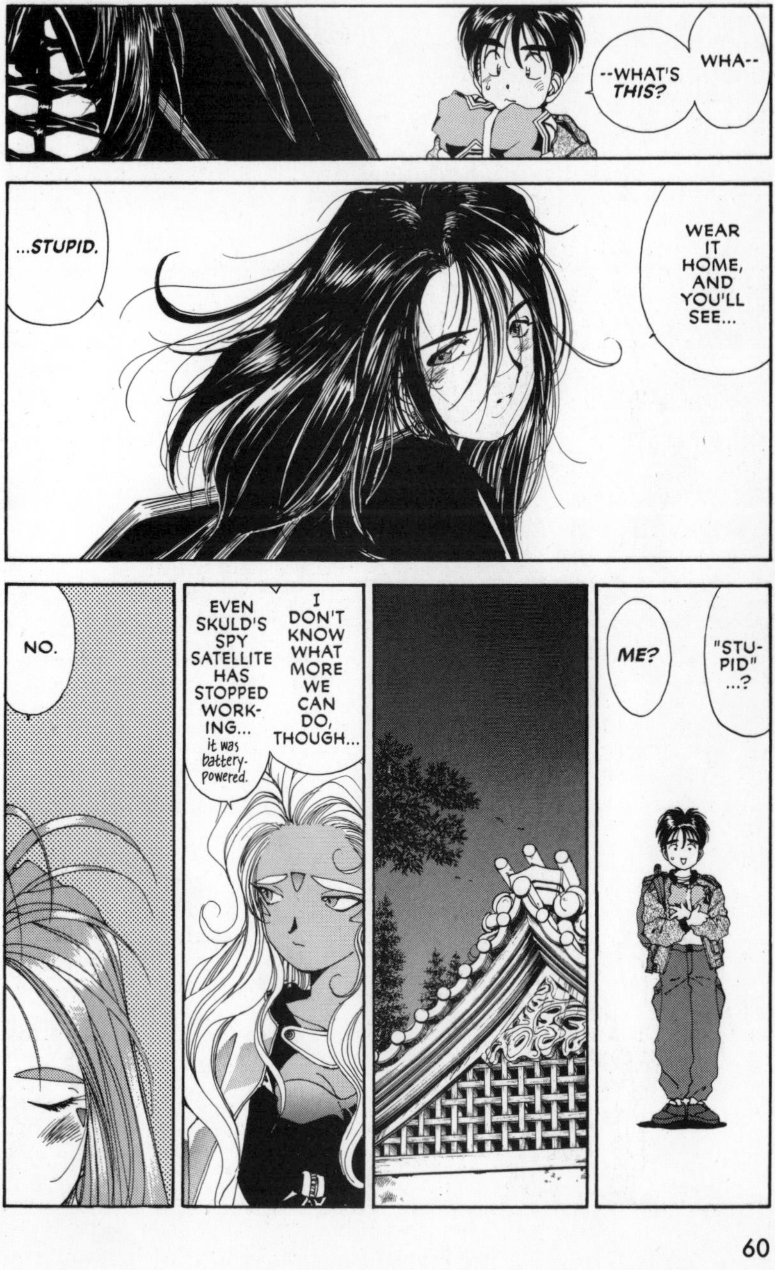
WHA--
--WHAT'S *THIS?*
WEAR IT HOME, AND YOU'LL SEE...
...*STUPID.*
"STU-PID" ...?
ME?
I DON'T KNOW WHAT MORE WE CAN DO, THOUGH...
EVEN SKULD'S SPY SATELLITE HAS STOPPED WORKING-ING... it was battery-powered.
NO.

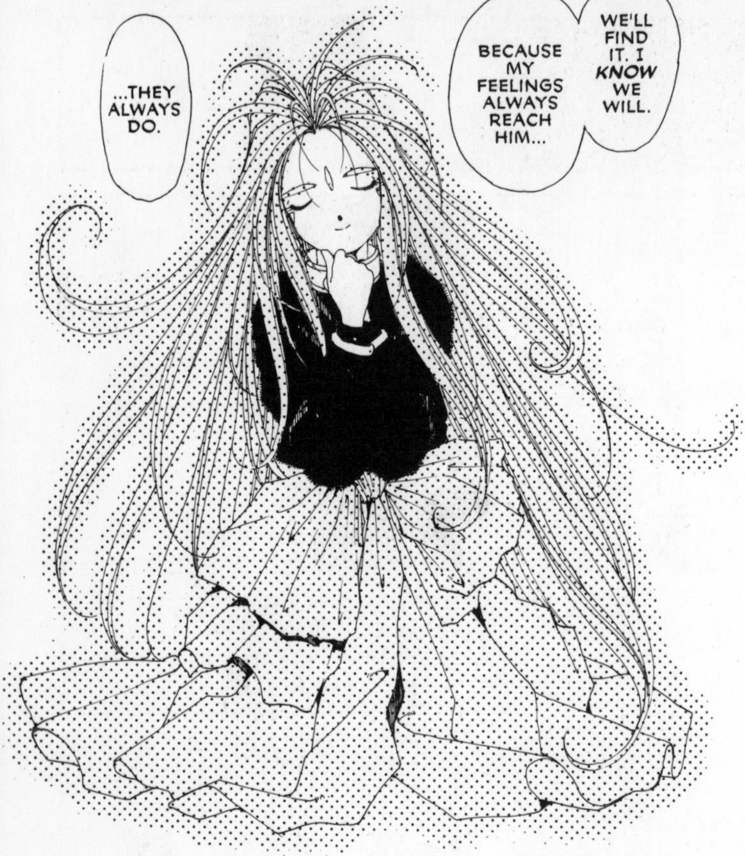
WE'LL FIND IT. I KNOW WE WILL.
BECAUSE MY FEELINGS ALWAYS REACH HIM...
...THEY ALWAYS DO.

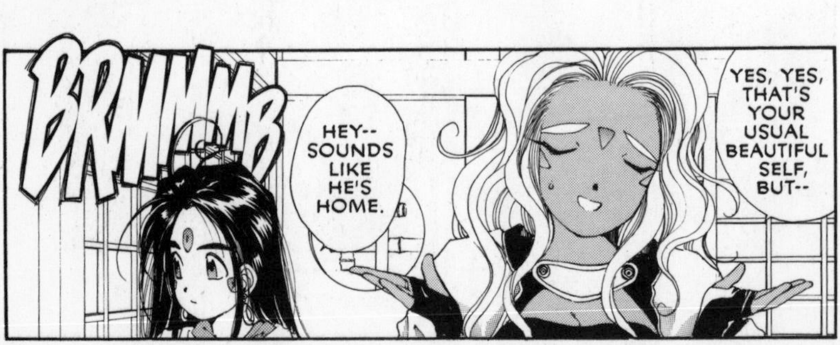
YES, YES, THAT'S YOUR USUAL BEAUTIFUL SELF, BUT--
BRMMMB
HEY-- SOUNDS LIKE HE'S HOME.

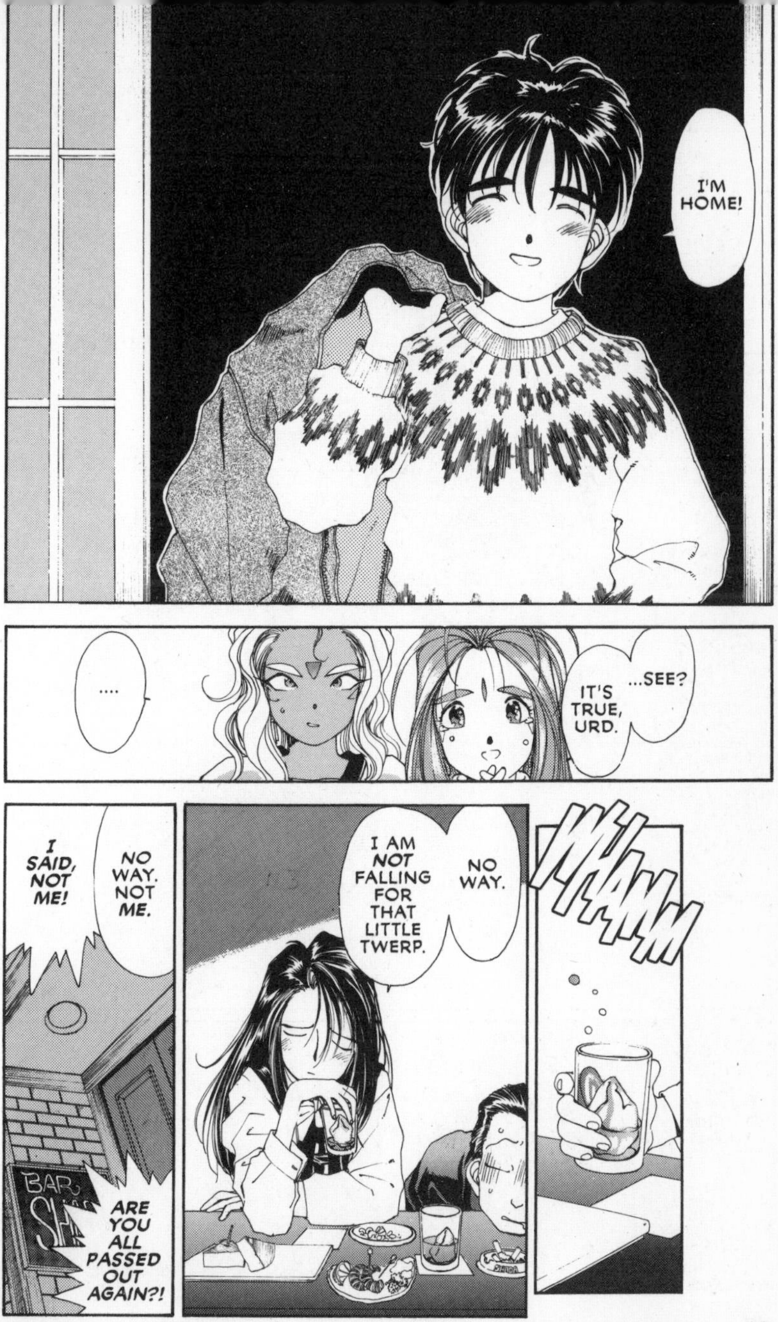
I'M HOME!
...SEE? IT'S TRUE, URD.
....
WHAMM
NO WAY.
I AM *NOT* FALLING FOR THAT LITTLE TWERP.
NO WAY. NOT *ME*.
I SAID, NOT ME!
ARE YOU ALL PASSED OUT AGAIN?!

THE ADVENTURES OF MINI-URD

Now with added MINI-SKULD!

◆ STORMWRACK--A TALE OF BASEBALL ◆

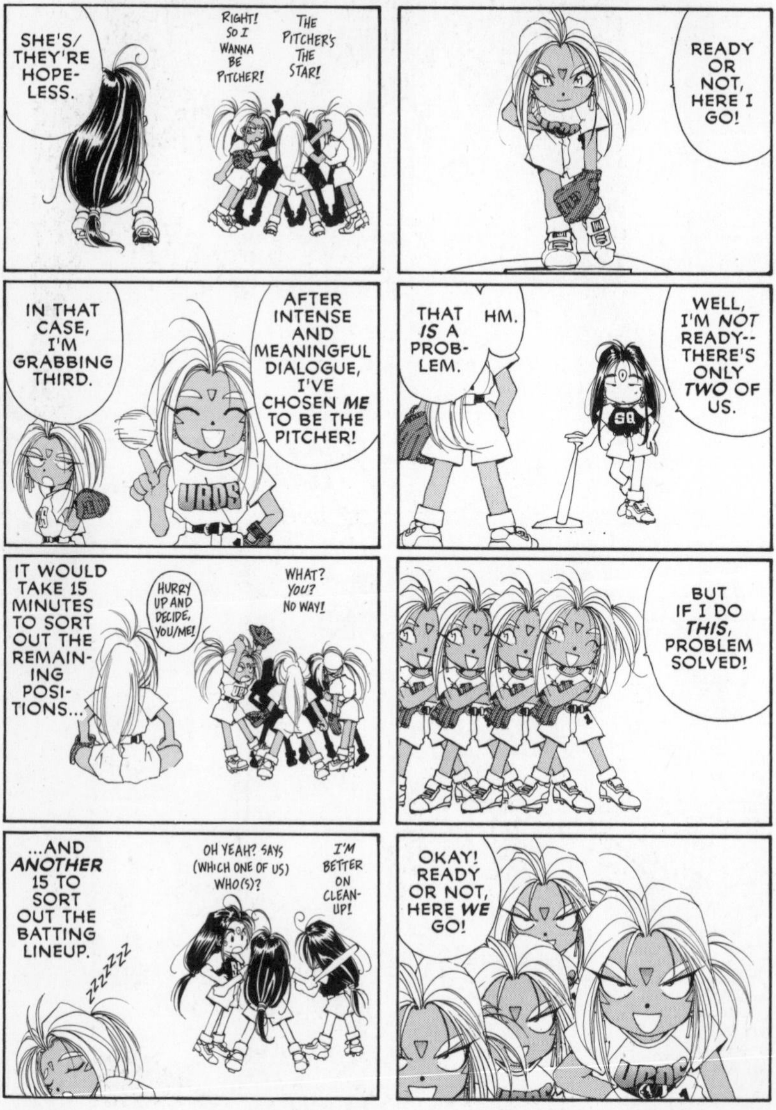
READY OR NOT, HERE I GO!
THE PITCHER'S THE STAR!
RIGHT! SO I WANNA BE PITCHER!
SHE'S/THEY'RE HOPE-LESS.
WELL, I'M *NOT* READY--THERE'S ONLY *TWO* OF US.
HM.
THAT *IS* A PROB-LEM.
AFTER INTENSE AND MEANINGFUL DIALOGUE, I'VE CHOSEN *ME* TO BE THE PITCHER!
IN THAT CASE, I'M GRABBING THIRD.
BUT IF I DO *THIS*, PROBLEM SOLVED!
WHAT? *YOU?* NO WAY!
HURRY UP AND DECIDE, YOU/ME!
IT WOULD TAKE 15 MINUTES TO SORT OUT THE REMAIN-ING POSI-TIONS...
OKAY! READY OR NOT, HERE *WE* GO!
I'M BETTER ON CLEAN-UP!
OH YEAH? SAYS (WHICH ONE OF US) WHO(S)?
...AND ***ANOTHER*** 15 TO SORT OUT THE BATTING LINEUP.

STORMWRACK--A TALE OF BASEBALL (PART DEUX)

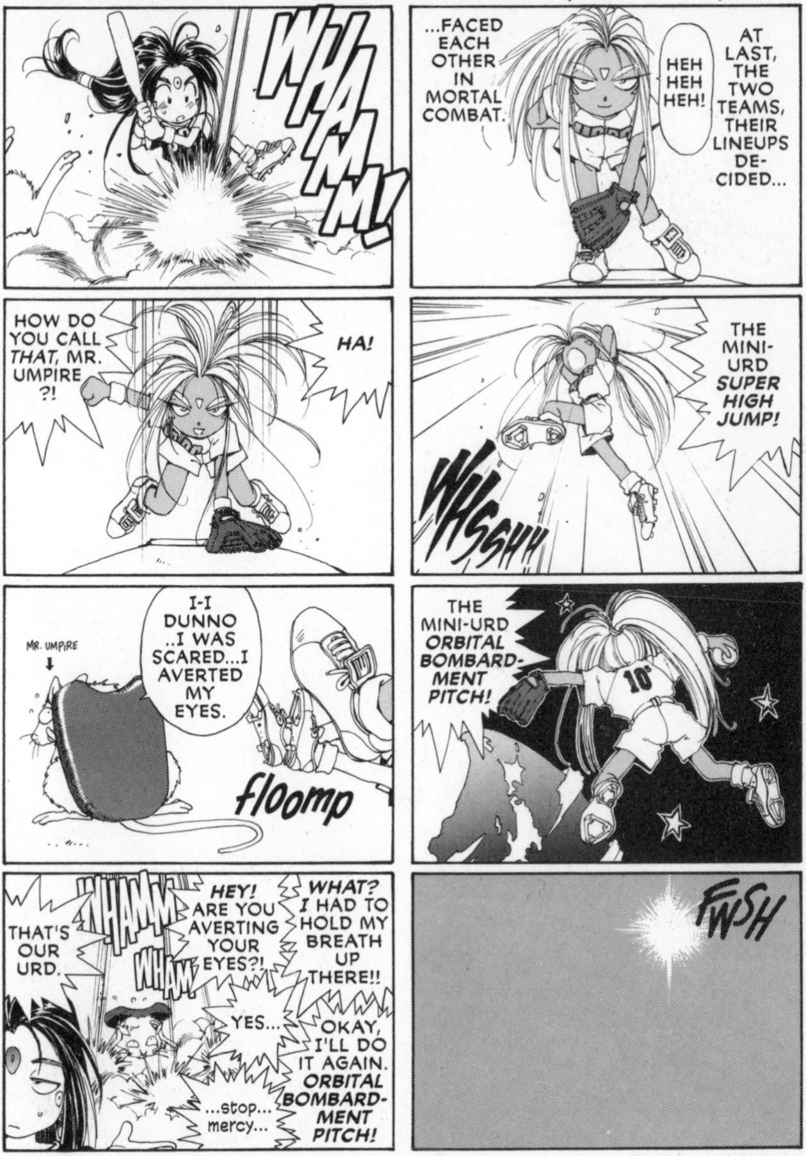
AT LAST, THE TWO TEAMS, THEIR LINEUPS DECIDED...
HEH HEH HEH!
...FACED EACH OTHER IN MORTAL COMBAT.
WHAMM!
THE MINI-URD SUPER HIGH JUMP!
WHSSHH
HA!
HOW DO YOU CALL THAT, MR. UMPIRE ?!
THE MINI-URD ORBITAL BOMBARDMENT PITCH!
I-I DUNNO ..I WAS SCARED...I AVERTED MY EYES.
MR. UMPIRE
floomp
FWSH
WHAT? I HAD TO HOLD MY BREATH UP THERE!!
HEY! ARE YOU AVERTING YOUR EYES?!
WHAMM
WHAM
THAT'S OUR URD.
OKAY, I'LL DO IT AGAIN. ORBITAL BOMBARDMENT PITCH!
YES...
...stop... mercy...

◇STORMWRACK--A TALE OF BASEBALL (PART DER DRITTE)◇

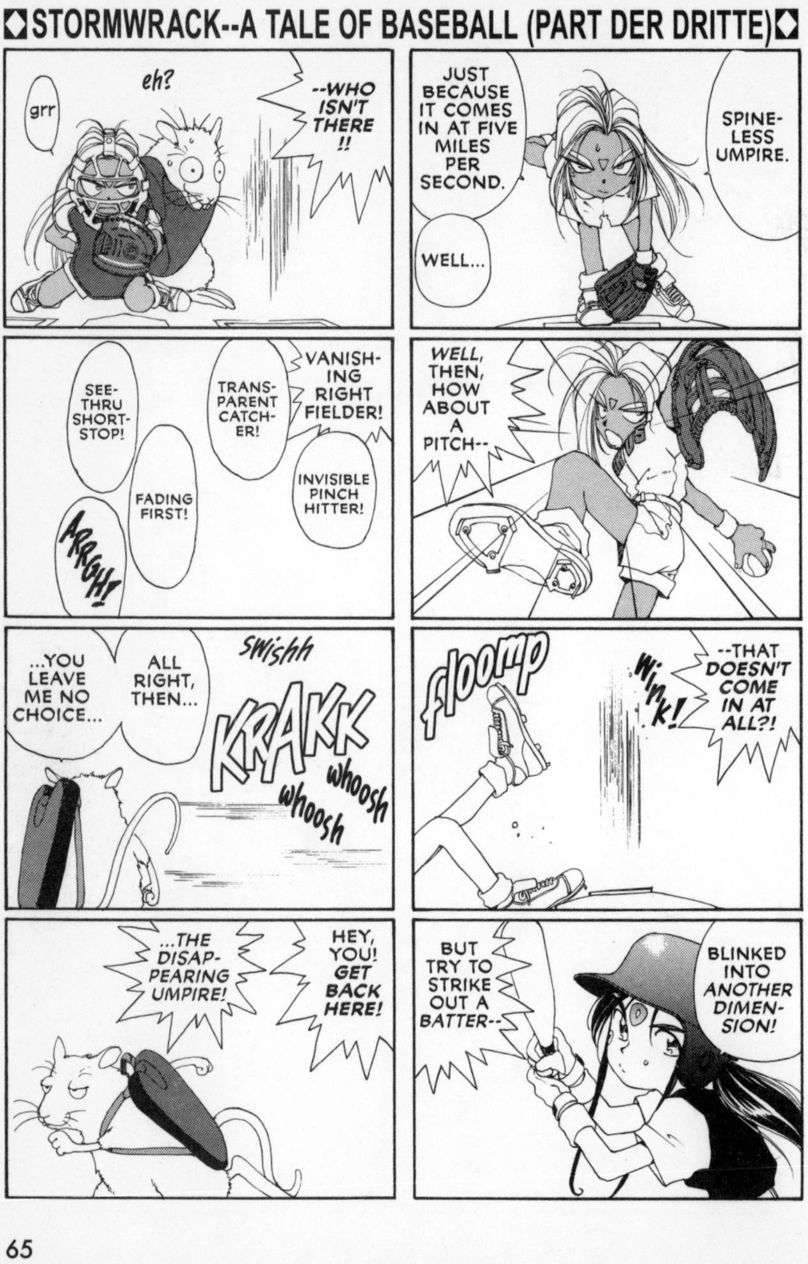

SPINELESS UMPIRE.
JUST BECAUSE IT COMES IN AT FIVE MILES PER SECOND.
WELL...
WELL, THEN, HOW ABOUT A PITCH--
--THAT DOESN'T COME IN AT ALL?!
wink!
floomp
BLINKED INTO ANOTHER DIMENSION!
BUT TRY TO STRIKE OUT A BATTER--
--WHO ISN'T THERE !!
eh?
grr
VANISHING RIGHT FIELDER!
TRANSPARENT CATCHER!
INVISIBLE PINCH HITTER!
SEE-THRU SHORTSTOP!
FADING FIRST!
ARRGH!
swishh
ALL RIGHT, THEN...
...YOU LEAVE ME NO CHOICE...
KRAKK
whoosh
whoosh
HEY, YOU! GET BACK HERE!
...THE DISAPPEARING UMPIRE!

STORMWRACK--A TALE OF BASEBALL
◆ (WHATEVER COMES AFTER THAT) ◆

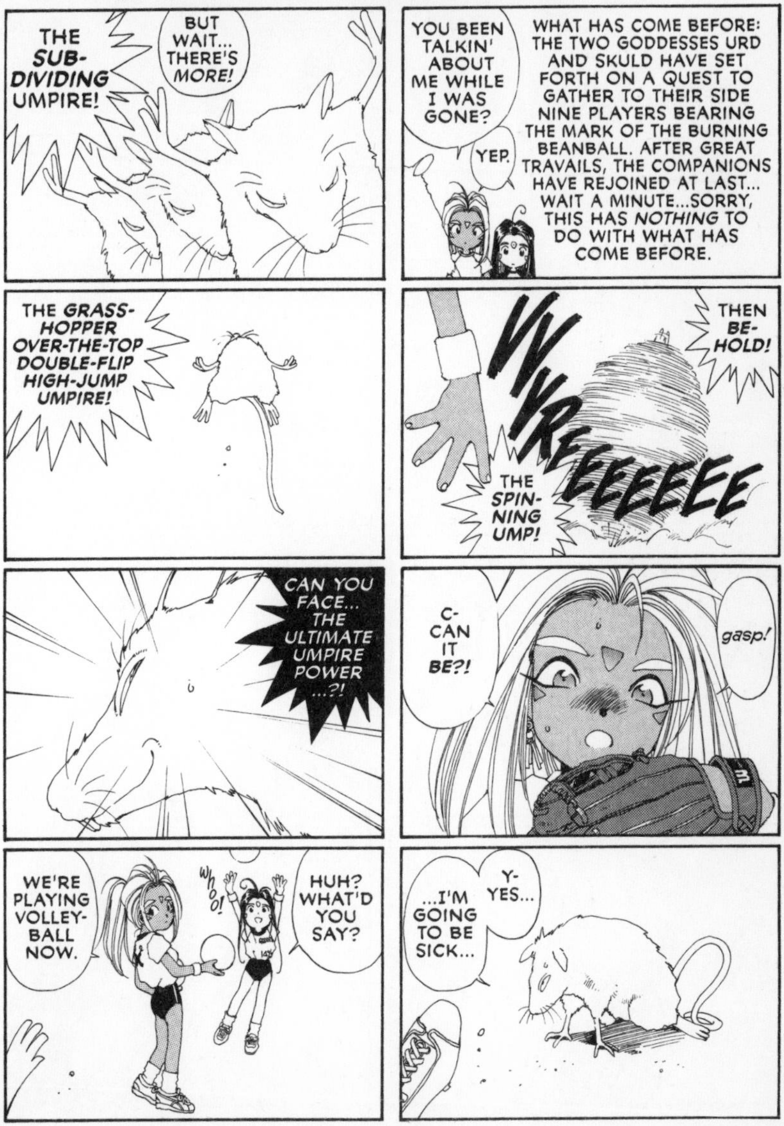

WHAT HAS COME BEFORE: THE TWO GODDESSES URD AND SKULD HAVE SET FORTH ON A QUEST TO GATHER TO THEIR SIDE NINE PLAYERS BEARING THE MARK OF THE BURNING BEANBALL. AFTER GREAT TRAVAILS, THE COMPANIONS HAVE REJOINED AT LAST... WAIT A MINUTE...SORRY, THIS HAS NOTHING TO DO WITH WHAT HAS COME BEFORE.
YOU BEEN TALKIN' ABOUT ME WHILE I WAS GONE?
YEP.
BUT WAIT... THERE'S MORE!
THE SUB-DIVIDING UMPIRE!
THEN BEHOLD!
VVVREEEEEE
THE SPINNING UMP!
THE GRASSHOPPER OVER-THE-TOP DOUBLE-FLIP HIGH-JUMP UMPIRE!
gasp!
C-CAN IT BE?!
CAN YOU FACE... THE ULTIMATE UMPIRE POWER ...?!
Y-YES...
...I'M GOING TO BE SICK...
HUH? WHAT'D YOU SAY?
whoo!
WE'RE PLAYING VOLLEYBALL NOW.

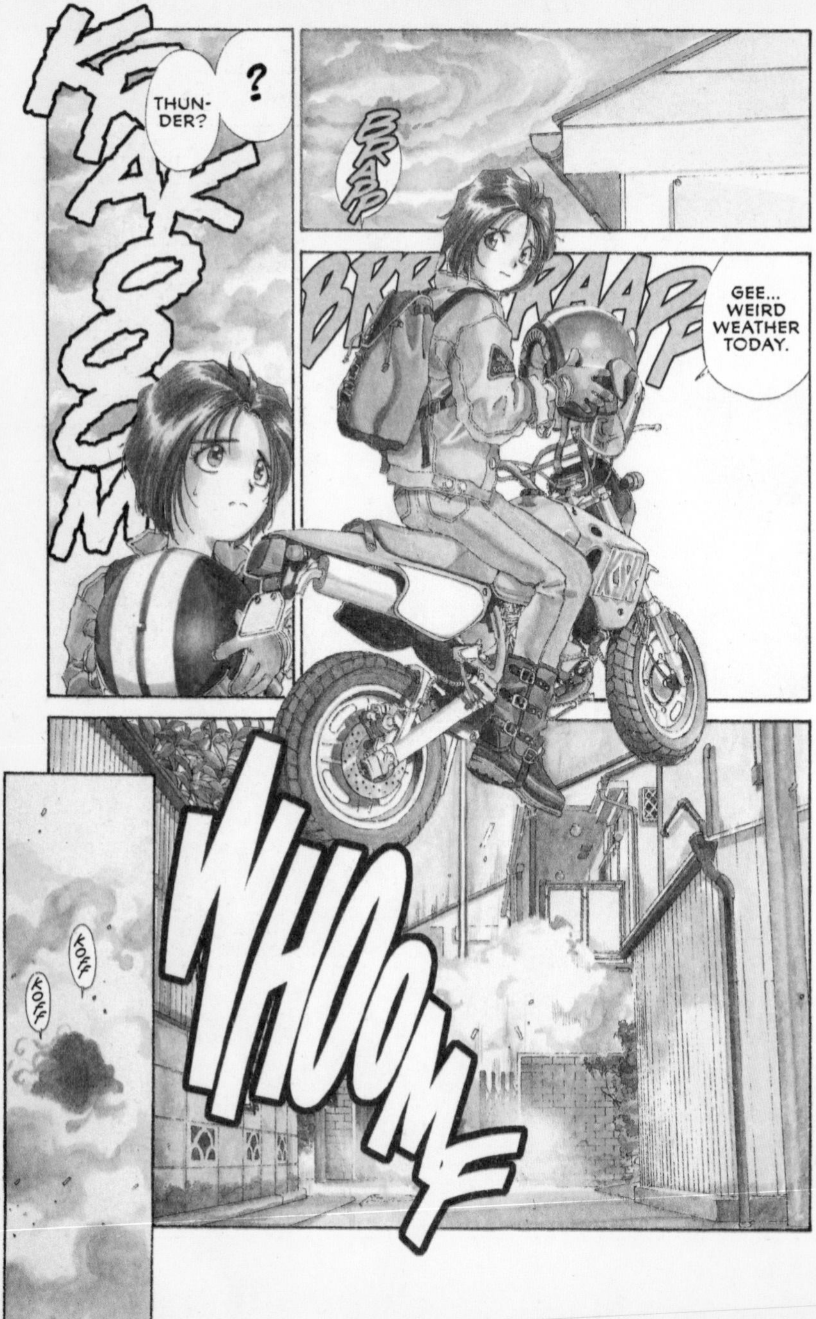
BRAP
BRRRAAPP
GEE... WEIRD WEATHER TODAY.
KAKOOOOM
?
THUNDER?
WHOOMF
KOFF
KOFF

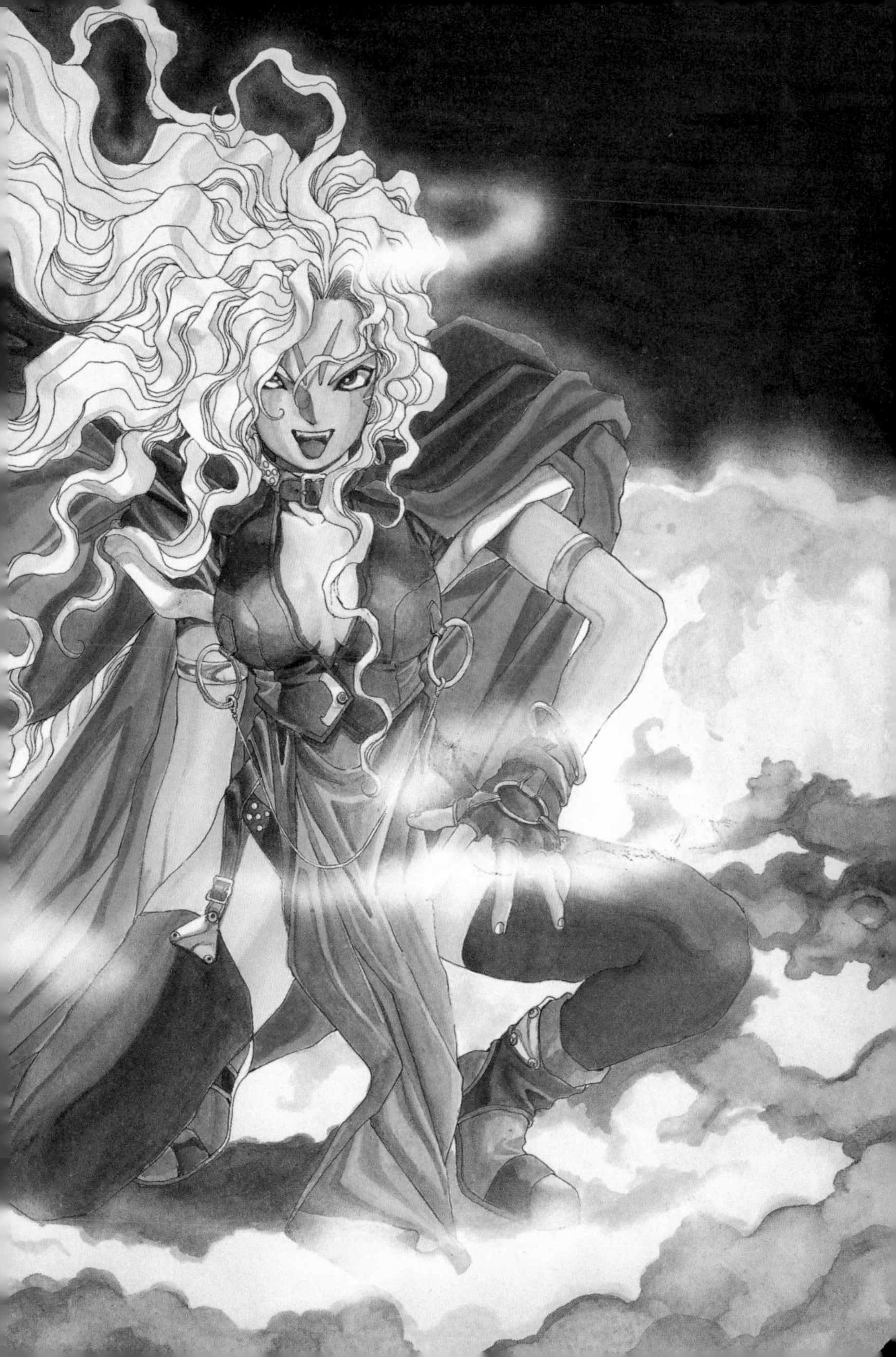

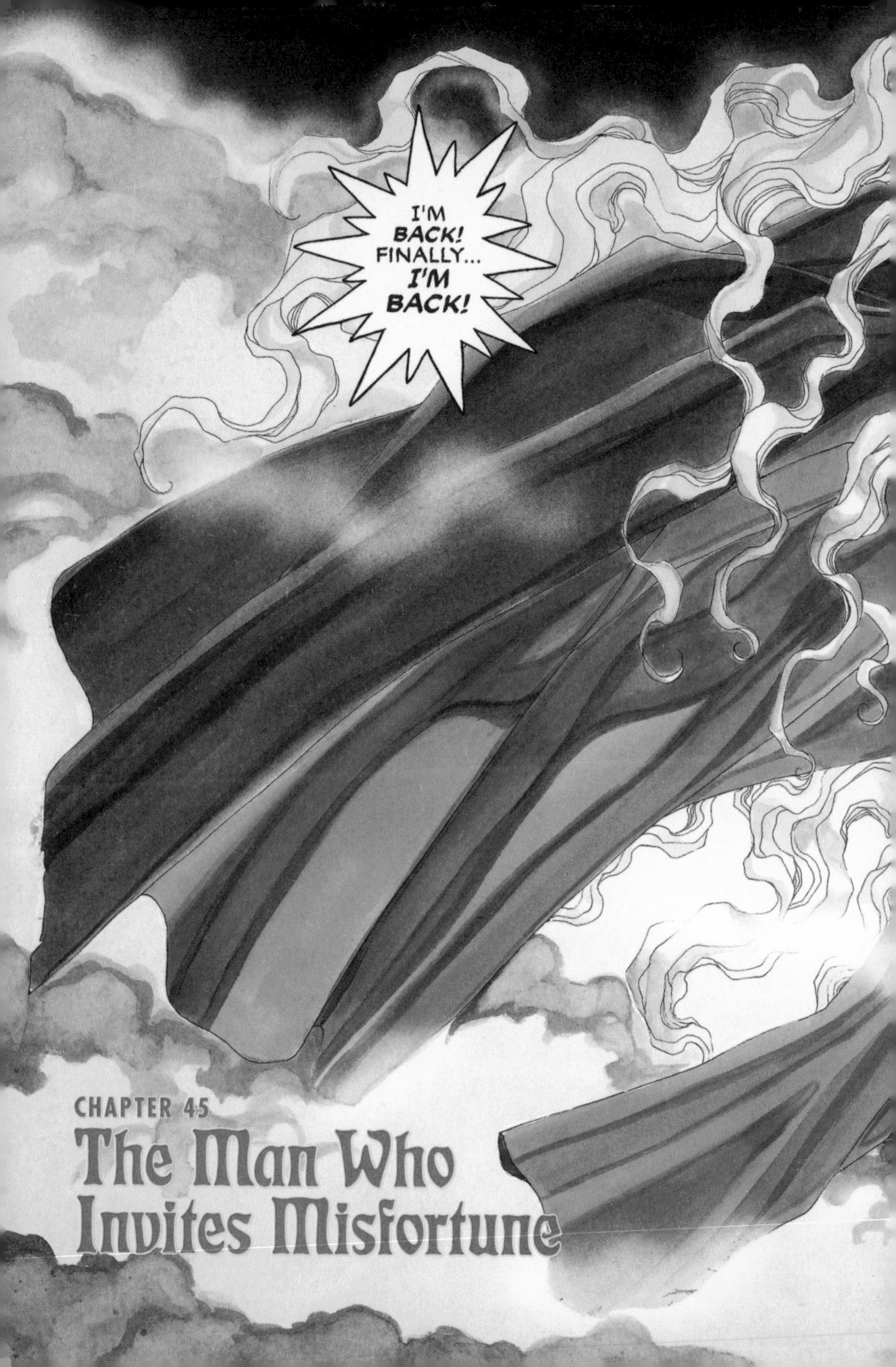

CHAPTER 45

The Man Who Invites Misfortune

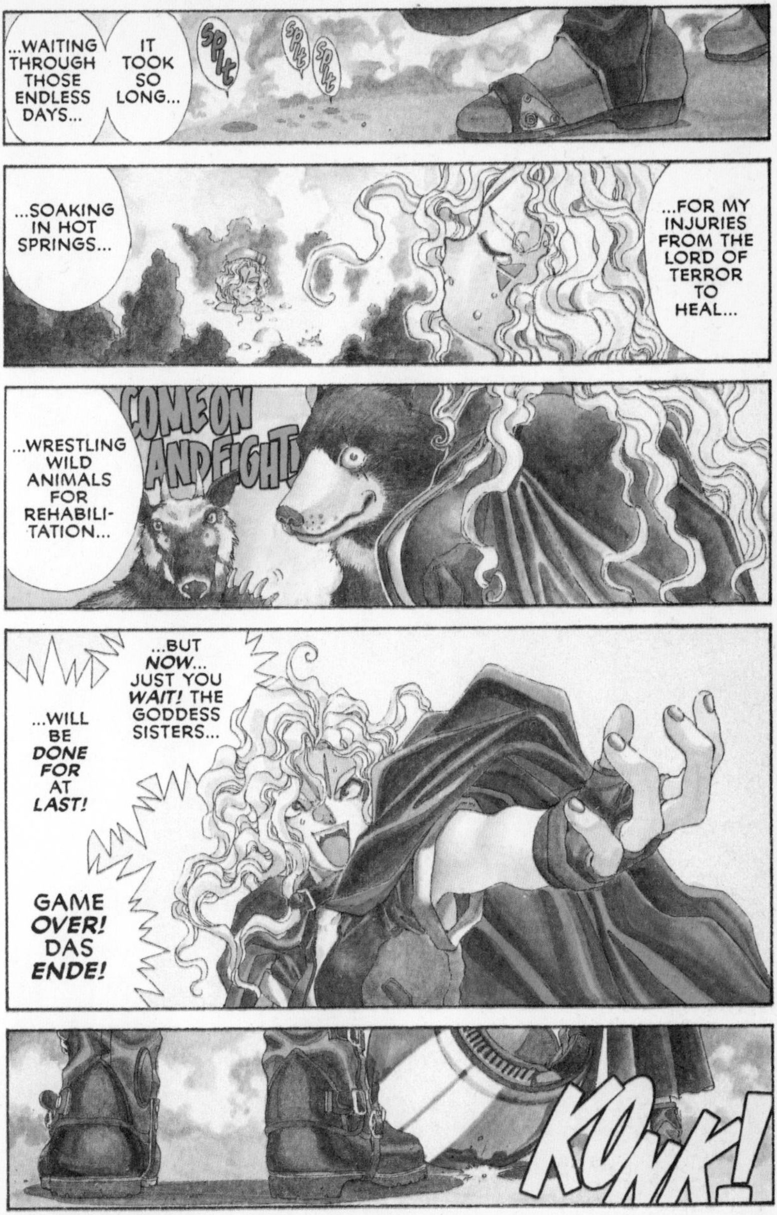
spit
spit
spit
IT TOOK SO LONG...
...WAITING THROUGH THOSE ENDLESS DAYS...
...FOR MY INJURIES FROM THE LORD OF TERROR TO HEAL...
...SOAKING IN HOT SPRINGS...
COME ON AND FIGHT!
...WRESTLING WILD ANIMALS FOR REHABILI- TATION...
...BUT *NOW*... JUST YOU *WAIT!* THE GODDESS SISTERS...
...WILL BE *DONE FOR* AT *LAST!*
GAME *OVER!* DAS *ENDE!*
KONK!

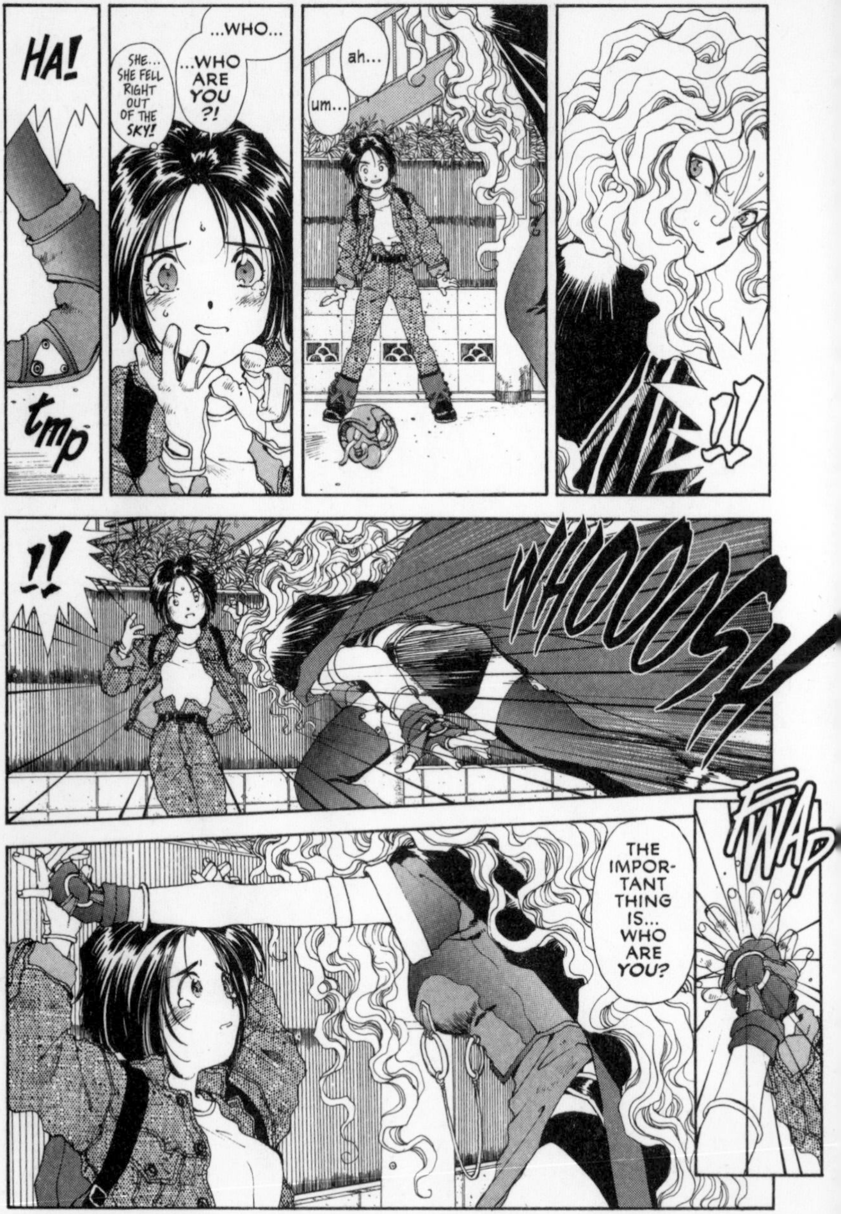
!!
ah...
um...
...WHO...
...WHO ARE YOU?!
SHE... SHE FELL RIGHT OUT OF THE SKY!
HA!
tmp
WHOOOSH
!!
FWAP
THE IMPOR-TANT THING IS... WHO ARE YOU?

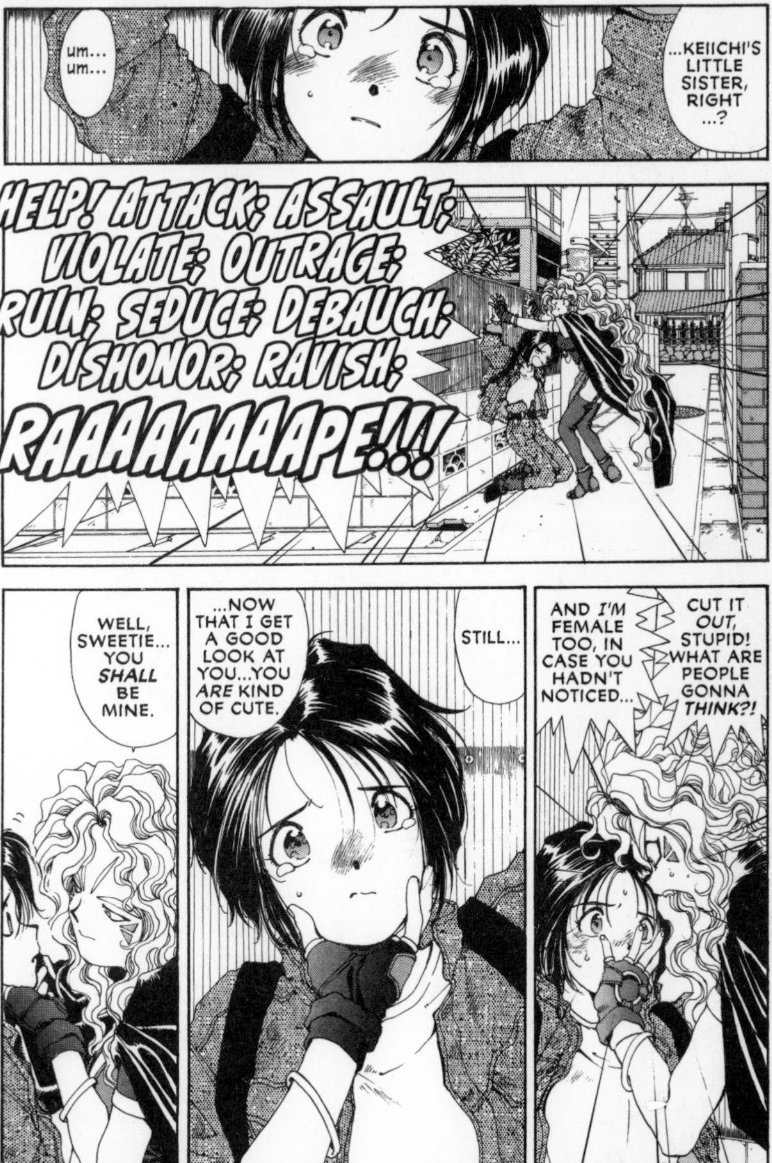
...KEIICHI'S LITTLE SISTER, RIGHT ...?
um... um...
HELP! ATTACK; ASSAULT; VIOLATE; OUTRAGE; RUIN; SEDUCE; DEBAUCH; DISHONOR; RAVISH;
RAAAAAAAAAPE!!!
CUT IT *OUT*, STUPID! WHAT ARE PEOPLE GONNA *THINK?!*
AND *I'M* FEMALE TOO, IN CASE YOU HADN'T NOTICED...
STILL...
...NOW THAT I GET A GOOD LOOK AT YOU...YOU *ARE* KIND OF CUTE.
WELL, SWEETIE... YOU *SHALL* BE MINE.

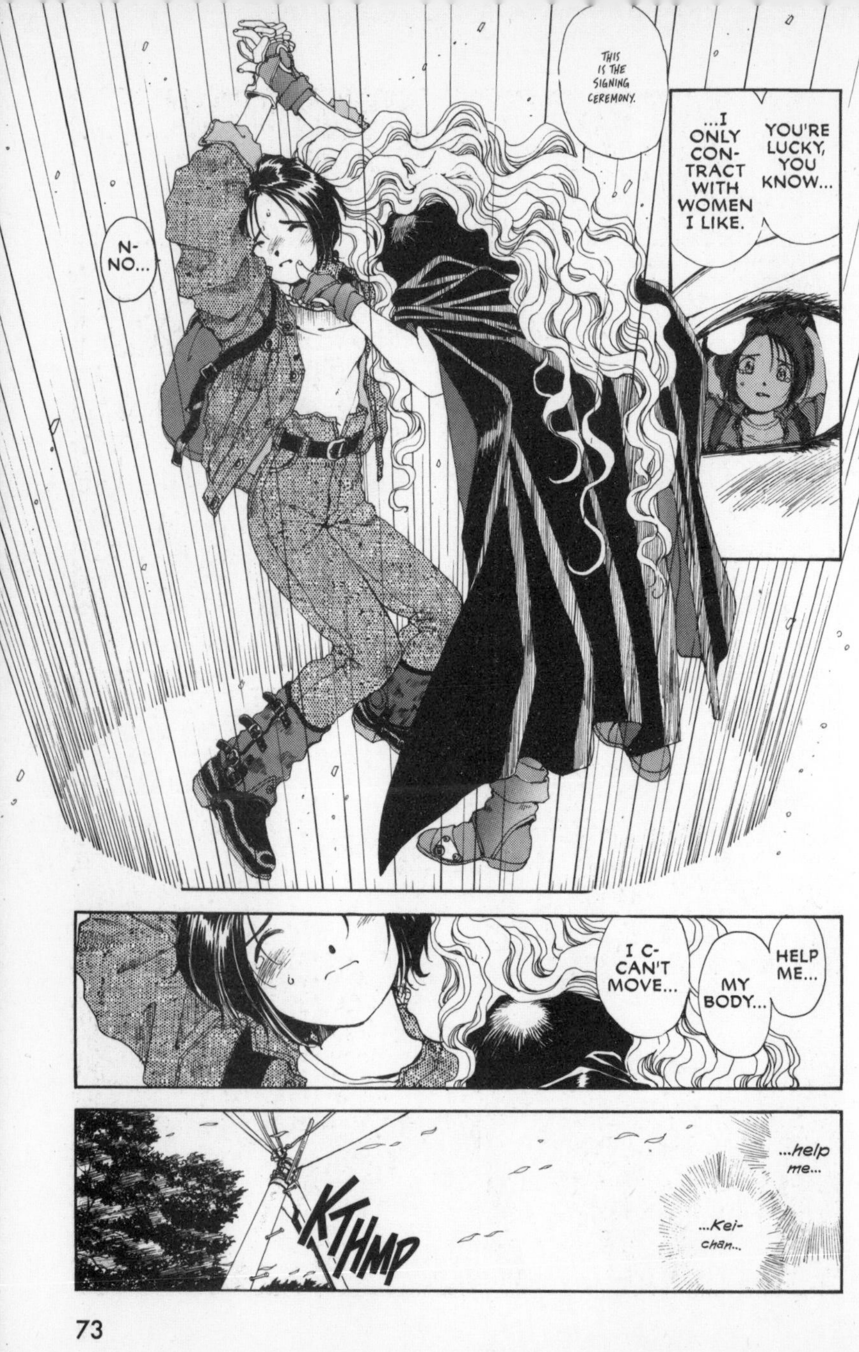
YOU'RE LUCKY, YOU KNOW...
...I ONLY CONTRACT WITH WOMEN I LIKE.
THIS IS THE SIGNING CEREMONY.
N-NO...
HELP ME...
MY BODY...
I C-CAN'T MOVE...
...help me...
...Kei-chan...
KTHMP

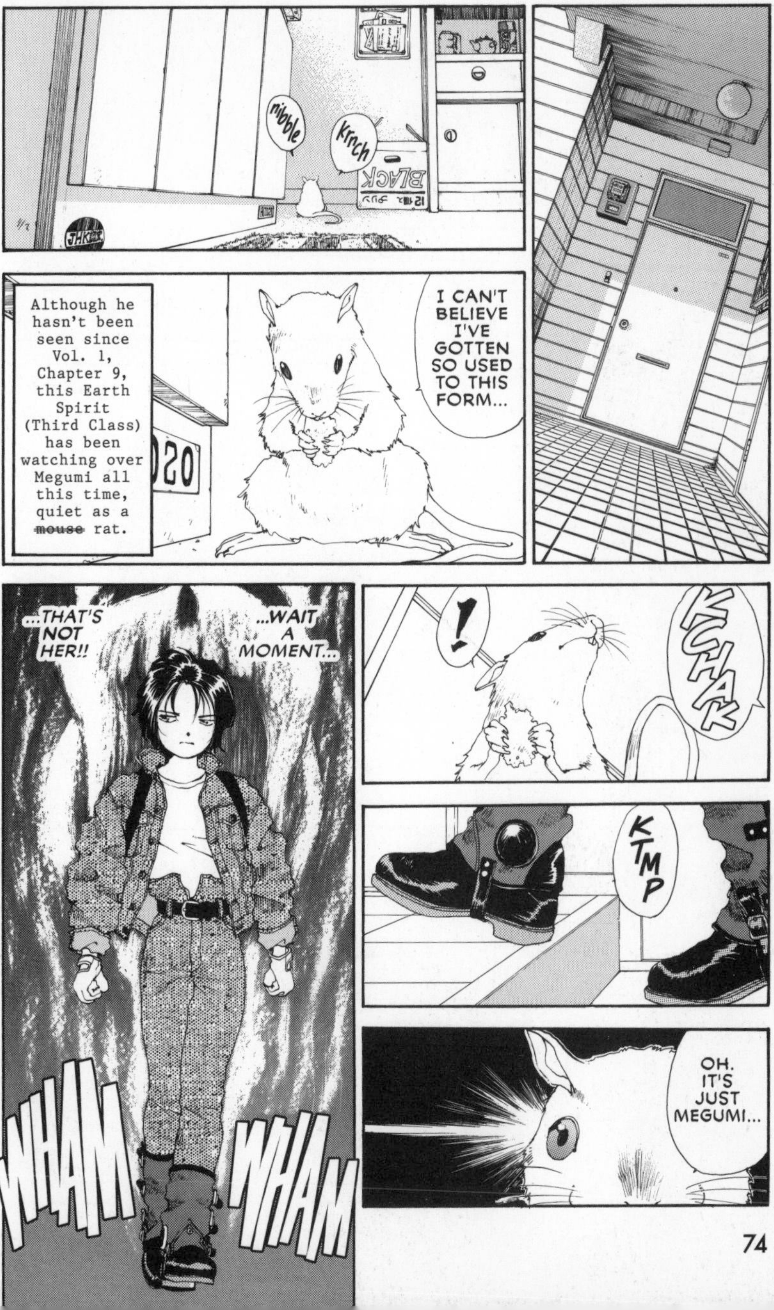
nibble
krrch
BLACK
I CAN'T BELIEVE I'VE GOTTEN SO USED TO THIS FORM...
Although he hasn't been seen since Vol. 1, Chapter 9, this Earth Spirit (Third Class) has been watching over Megumi all this time, quiet as a ~~mouse~~ rat.
KCHAK
!
KTMP
OH. IT'S JUST MEGUMI...
...WAIT A MOMENT...
...THAT'S NOT HER!!
WHAM
WHAM

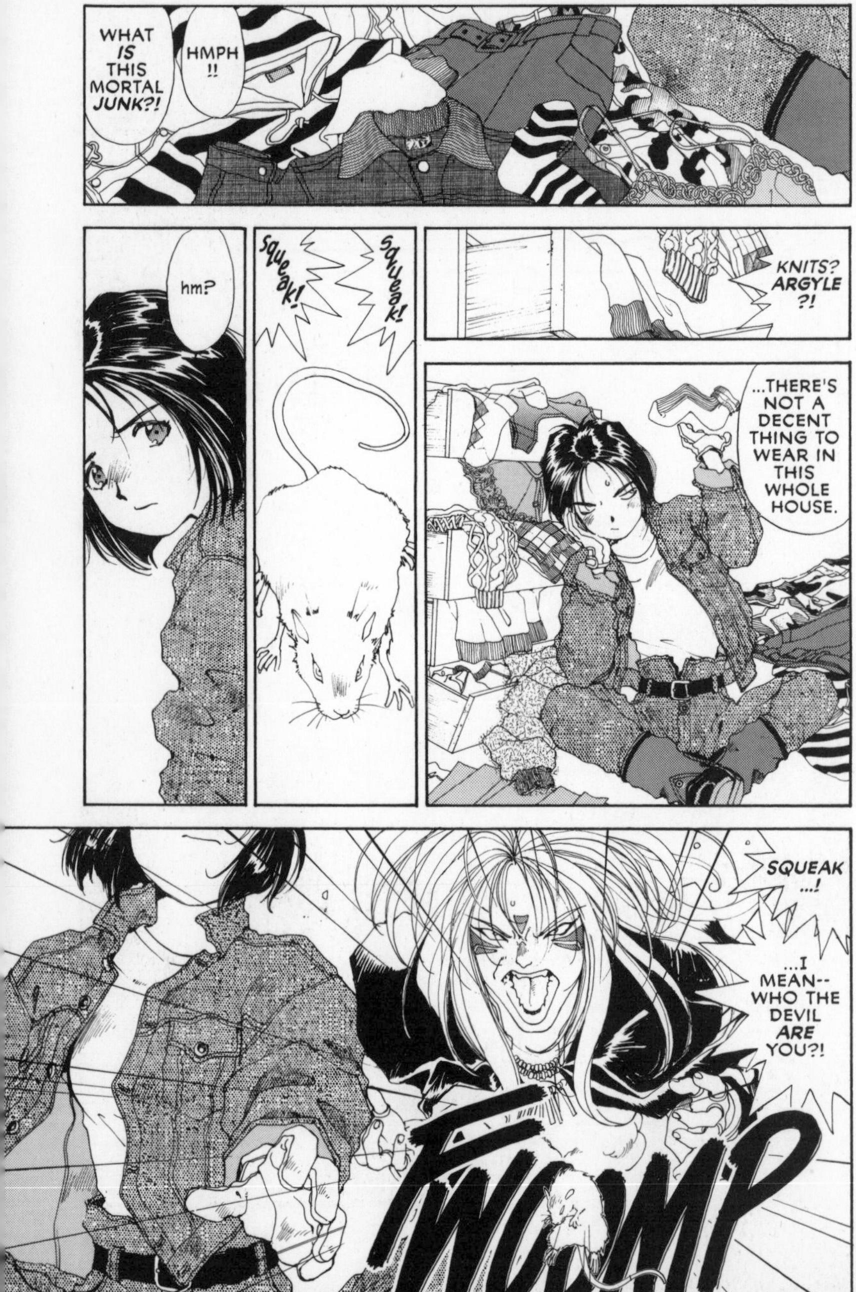
HMPH !!
WHAT IS THIS MORTAL JUNK?!
KNITS? ARGYLE ?!
...THERE'S NOT A DECENT THING TO WEAR IN THIS WHOLE HOUSE.
squeak!
squeak!
hm?
SQUEAK ...!
...I MEAN-- WHO THE DEVIL ARE YOU?!
THOMP

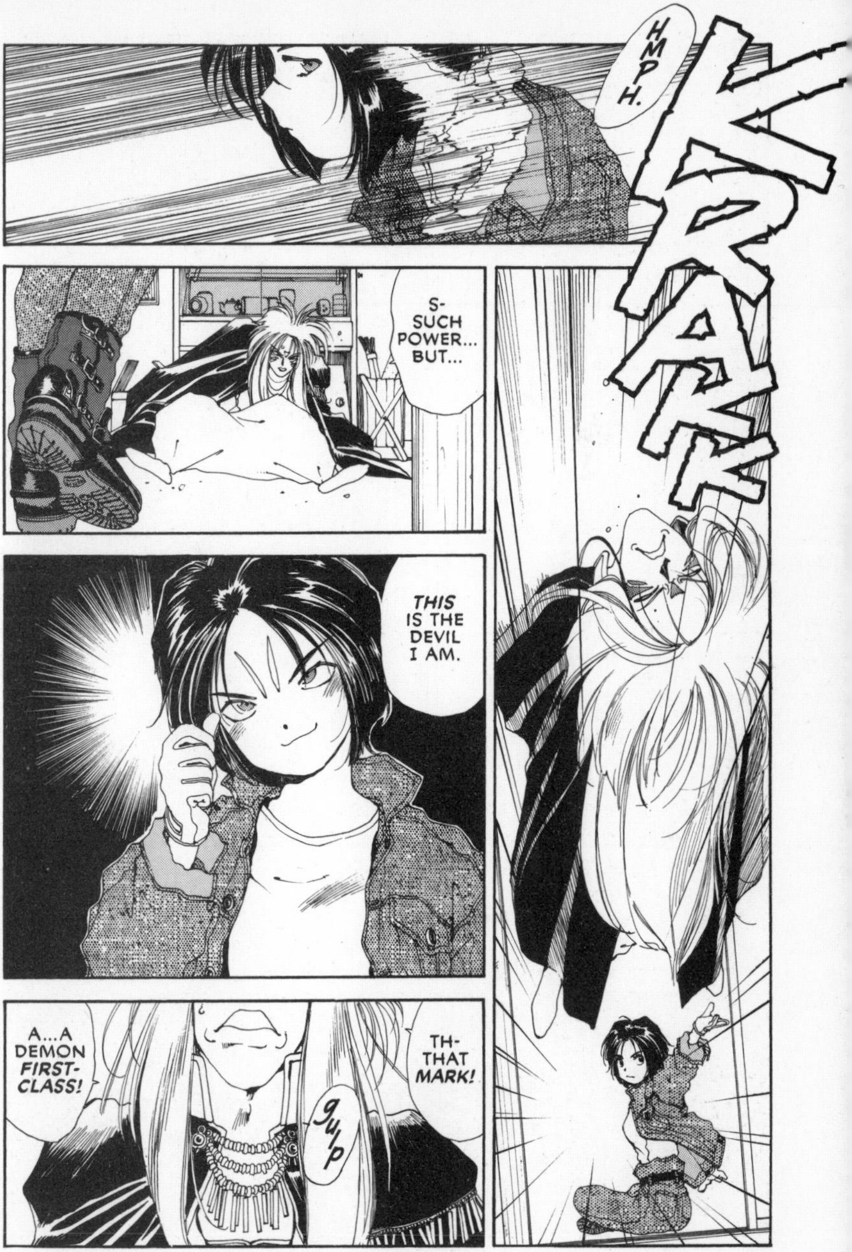
HMPH.
KRAK
S-SUCH POWER... BUT...
THIS IS THE DEVIL I AM.
TH-THAT MARK!
gulp
A...A DEMON FIRST-CLASS!

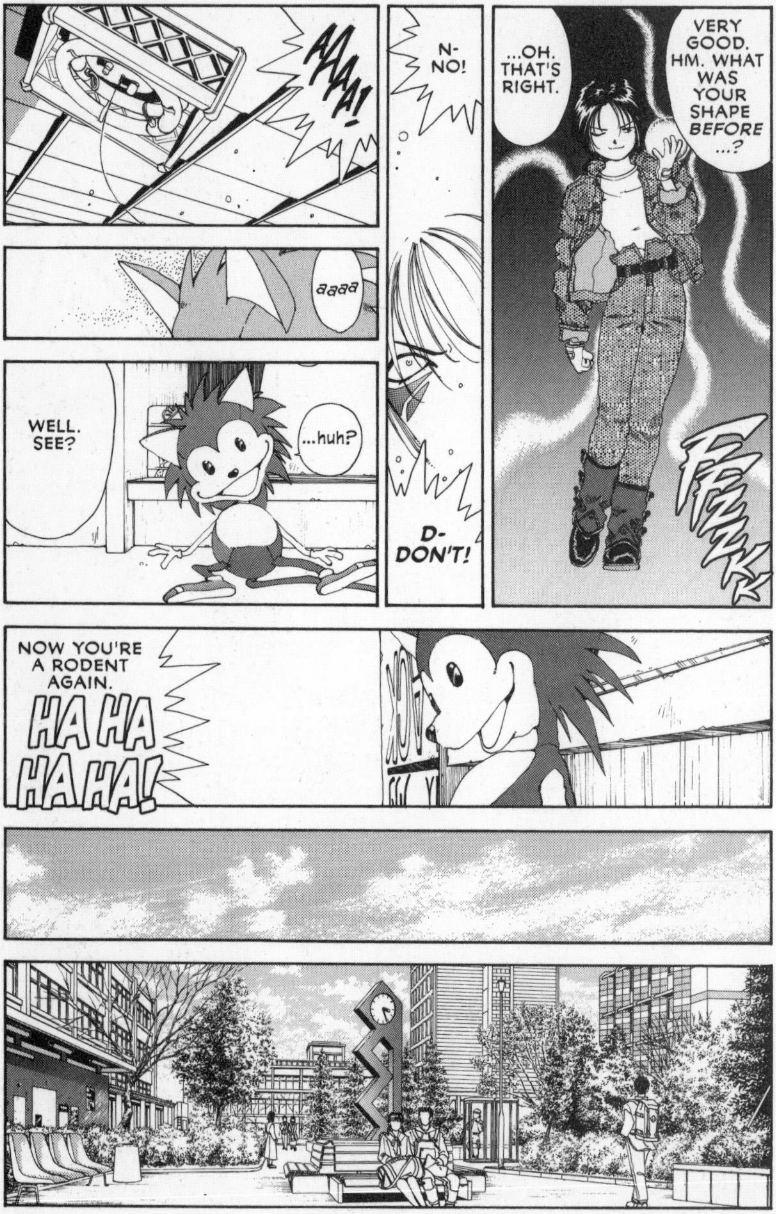

VERY GOOD. HM. WHAT WAS YOUR SHAPE BEFORE ...?
...OH. THAT'S RIGHT.
N- NO!
D- DON'T!
aaaa
...huh?
WELL. SEE?
NOW YOU'RE A RODENT AGAIN.
HA HA HA HA!

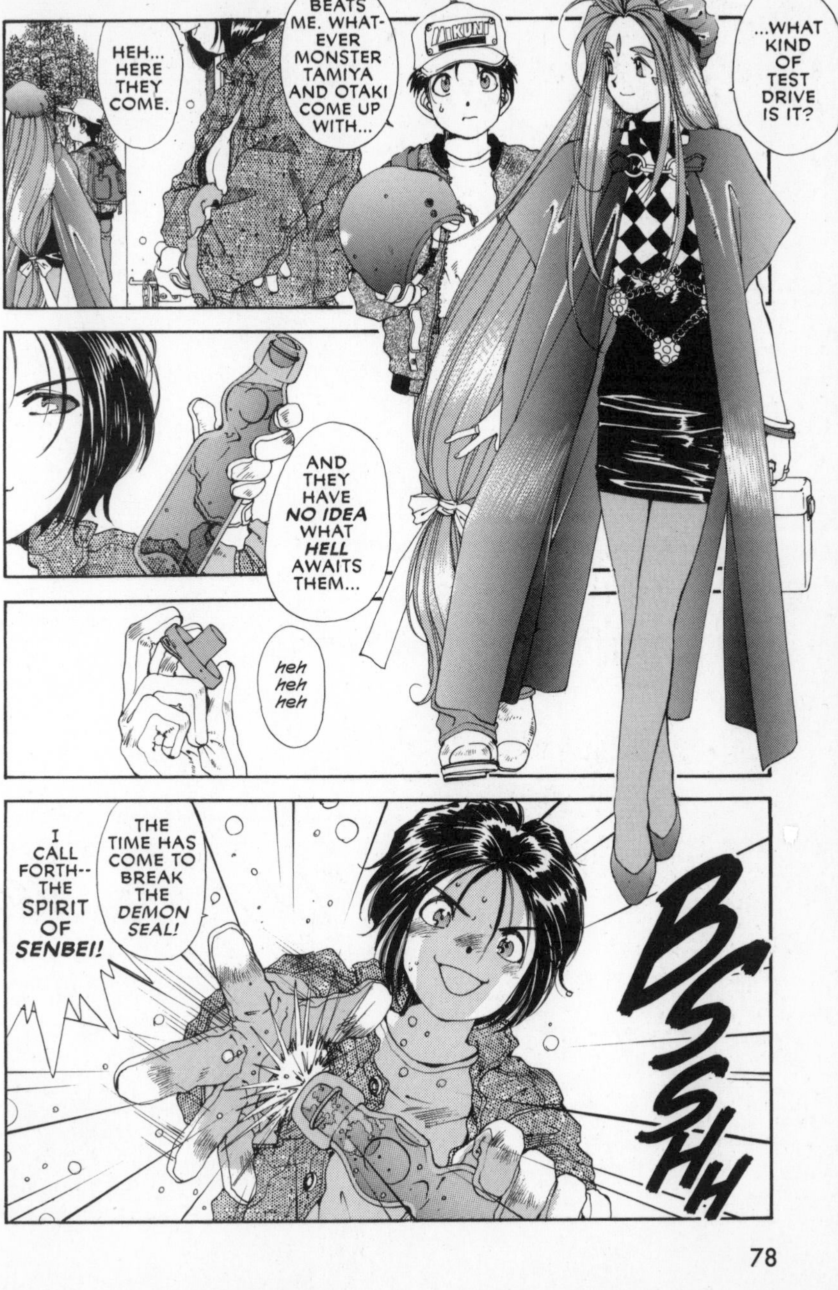
...WHAT KIND OF TEST DRIVE IS IT?
BEATS ME. WHAT-EVER MONSTER TAMIYA AND OTAKI COME UP WITH...
HEH... HERE THEY COME.
AND THEY HAVE *NO IDEA* WHAT *HELL* AWAITS THEM...
heh heh heh
THE TIME HAS COME TO BREAK THE *DEMON SEAL!*
I CALL FORTH-- THE SPIRIT OF *SENBEI!*
BSSHH

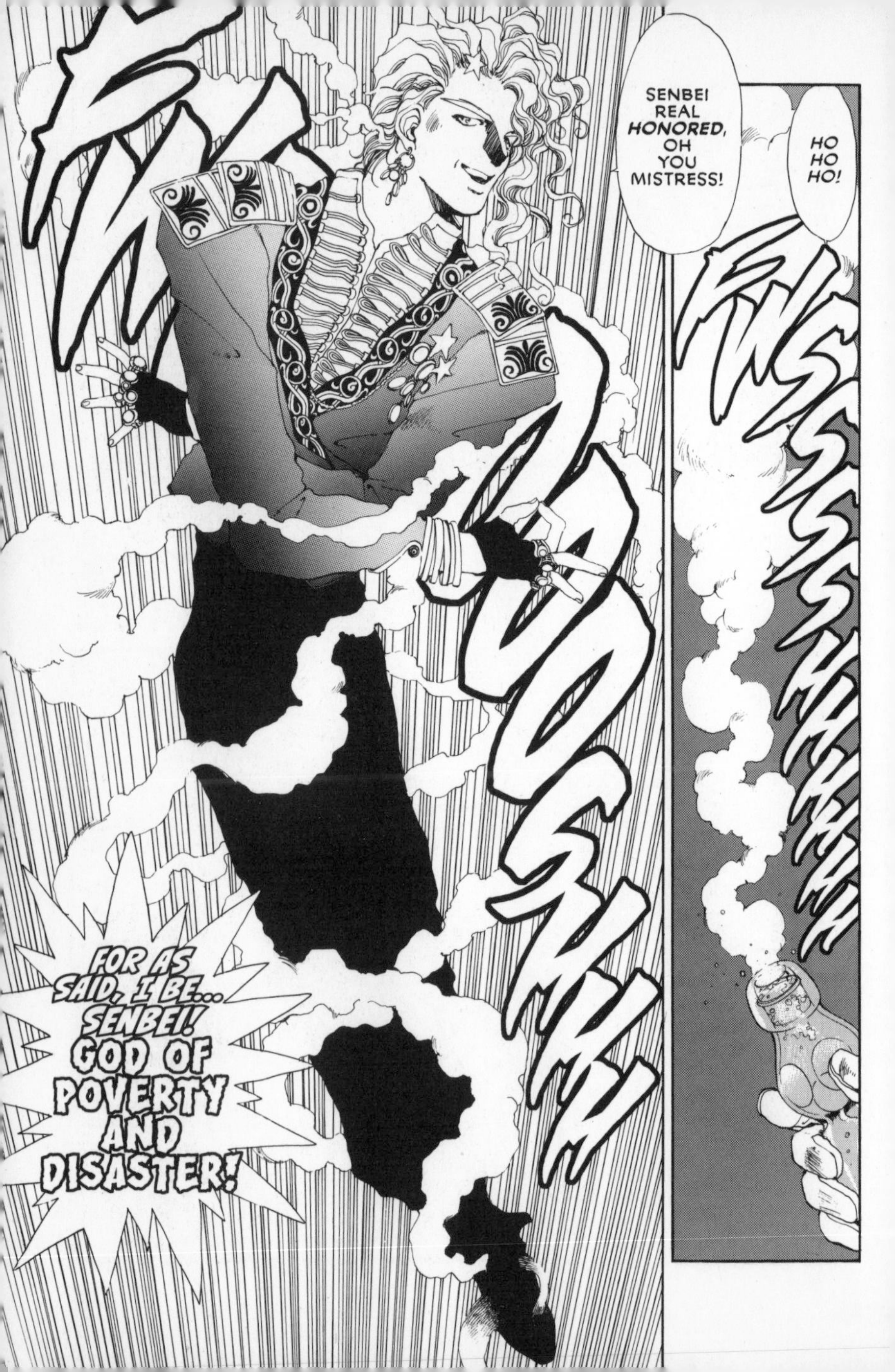
HO HO HO!
SENBEI REAL HONORED, OH YOU MISTRESS!
FOR AS SAID, I BE... SENBEI! GOD OF POVERTY AND DISASTER!

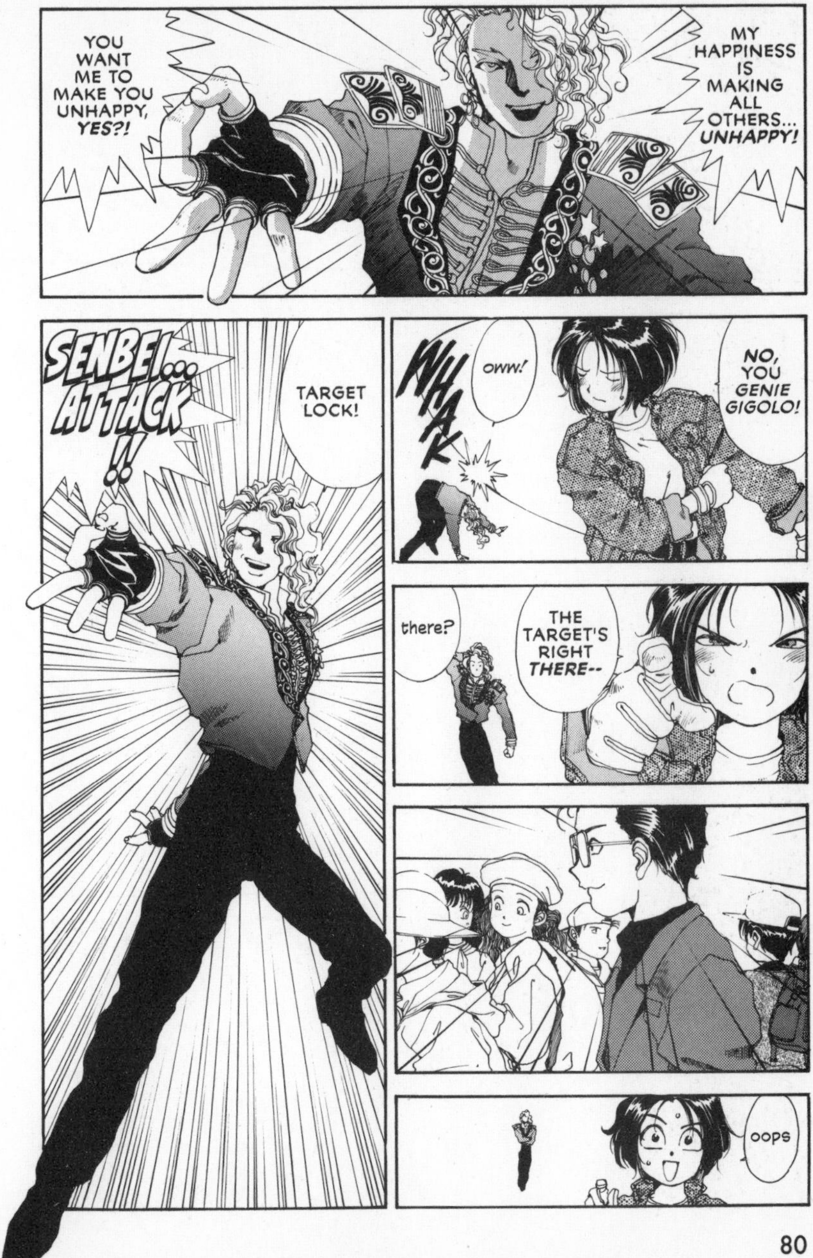
MY HAPPINESS IS MAKING ALL OTHERS... *UNHAPPY!*
YOU WANT ME TO MAKE YOU UNHAPPY, *YES?!*
NO, YOU *GENIE GIGOLO!*
OWW!
WHAK
THE TARGET'S RIGHT *THERE--*
there?
oops
TARGET LOCK!
SENBEI... ATTACK !!

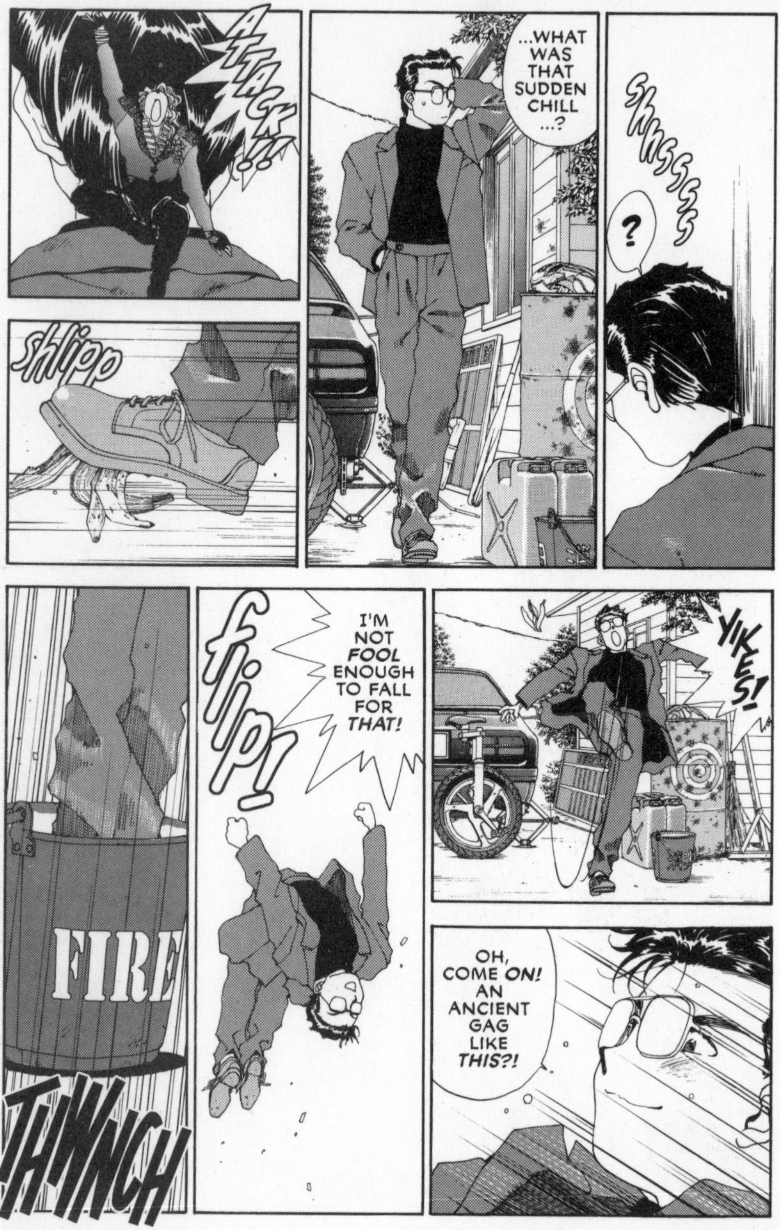
SHHSSSS
?
...WHAT WAS THAT SUDDEN CHILL ...?
ATTACK!!
shlipp
YIKES!
OH, COME ON! AN ANCIENT GAG LIKE THIS?!
flip!
I'M NOT FOOL ENOUGH TO FALL FOR THAT!
FIRE
THWNCH

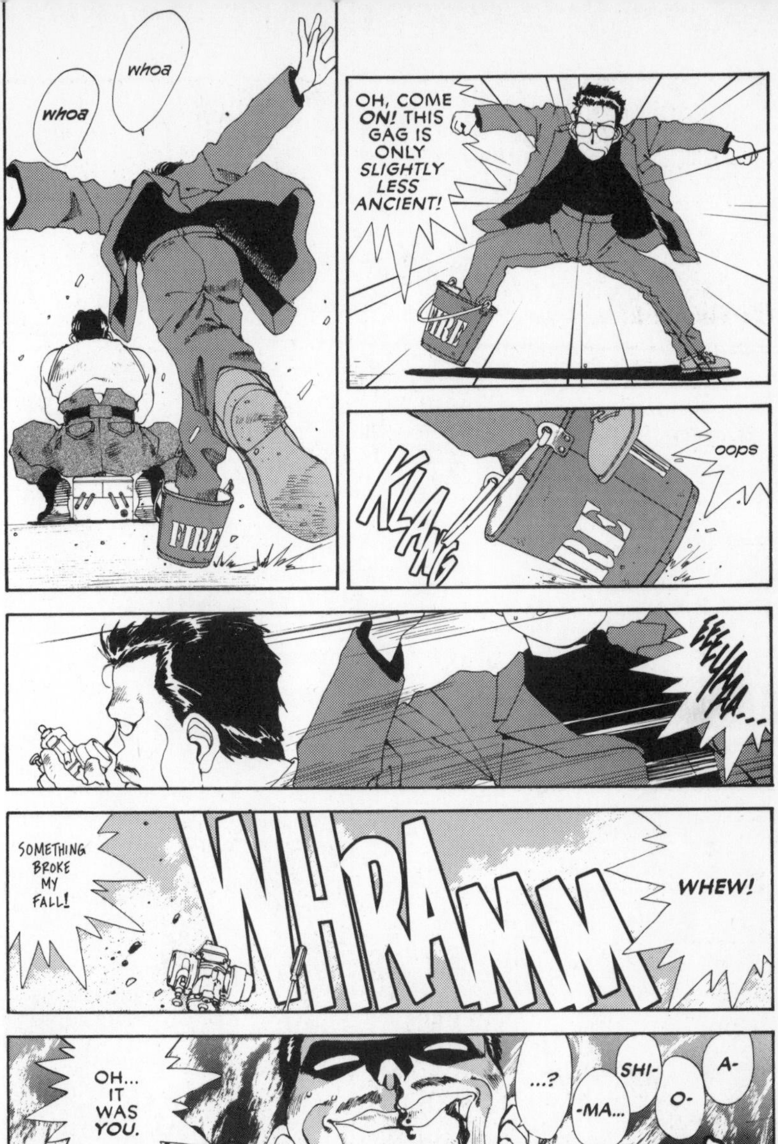
OH, COME ON! THIS GAG IS ONLY SLIGHTLY LESS ANCIENT!
oops
KLANG
whoa
whoa
EEEYAAA...
WHEW!
WHRAMM
SOMETHING BROKE MY FALL!
A-
O-
SHI-
-MA...
...?
KRAKKLE
OH... IT WAS YOU.
RUAHRA

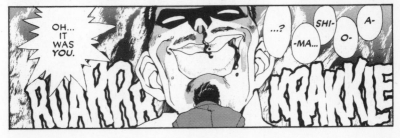

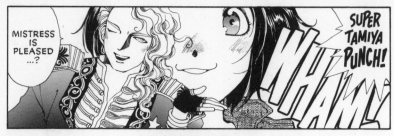

SUPER TAMIYA PUNCH!
WHAM!
MISTRESS IS PLEASED ...?
YOU SEE... VOLUME OF HAPPINESS IN UNIVERSE IS FINITE!
BY BRING THE MISFORTUNE TO HIM...
...SENBEI'S HAPPINESS GO UP, UP, UP!
SUCH IS FIRST LAW OF CONSERVATION OF HAPPINESS!
IF YOU DESIRE...
...SENBEI MAKE HIM EVEN UNHAPPY MORE, OKAY?!
AWE-SOME!
WITH HIM ON MY SIDE, I CAN FINALLY WIN!
AND AS SPECIAL SERVICE, SENBEI DOES SONG NOT ABOUT WHALE, BUT ABOUT BEING HAPPY!
...OR MAYBE LOSE...
Happy Happy
Joy Joy
this guy is a complete moron
tap tap

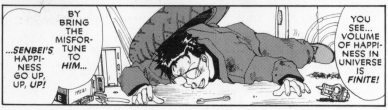

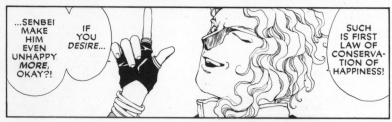

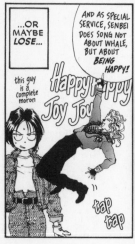

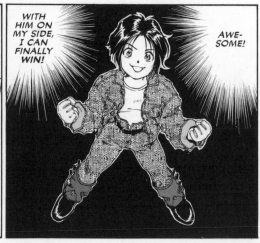

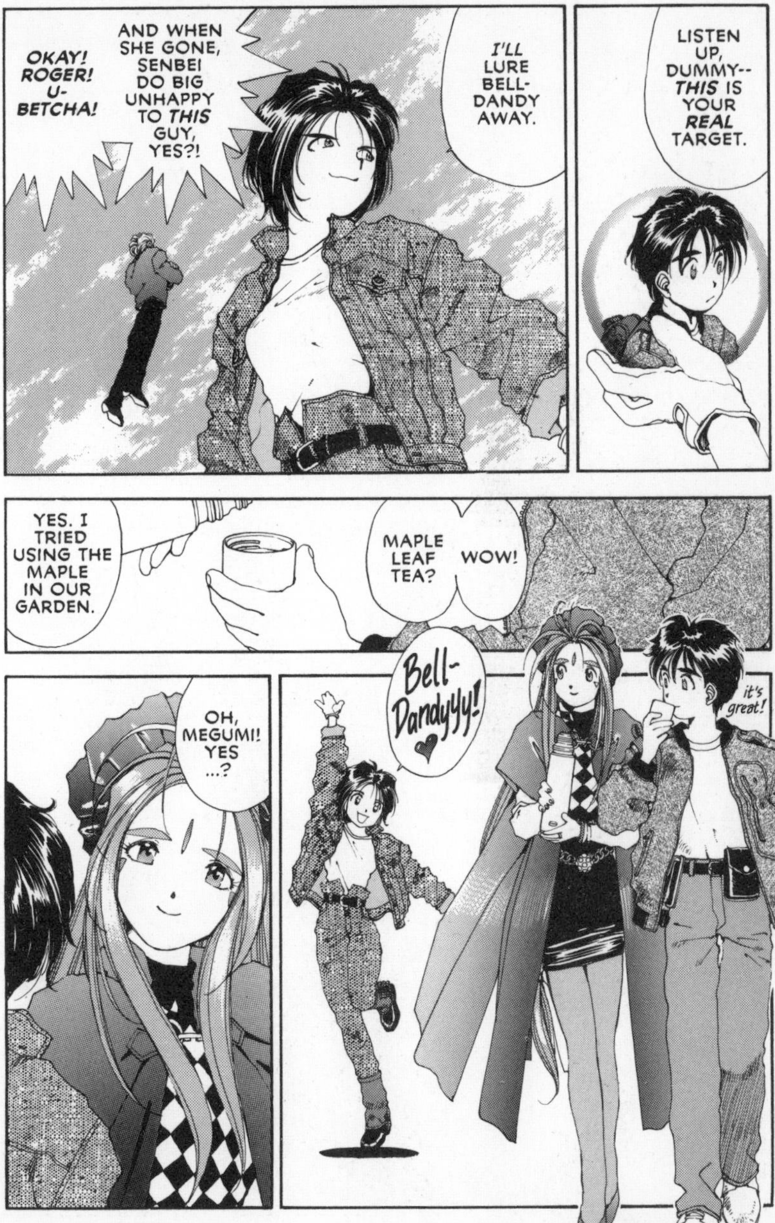
LISTEN UP, DUMMY-- THIS IS YOUR REAL TARGET.
I'LL LURE BELL-DANDY AWAY.
AND WHEN SHE GONE, SENBEI DO BIG UNHAPPY TO THIS GUY, YES?!
OKAY! ROGER! U-BETCHA!
WOW!
MAPLE LEAF TEA?
YES. I TRIED USING THE MAPLE IN OUR GARDEN.
it's great!
Bell-Dandyyy!
OH, MEGUMI! YES ...?

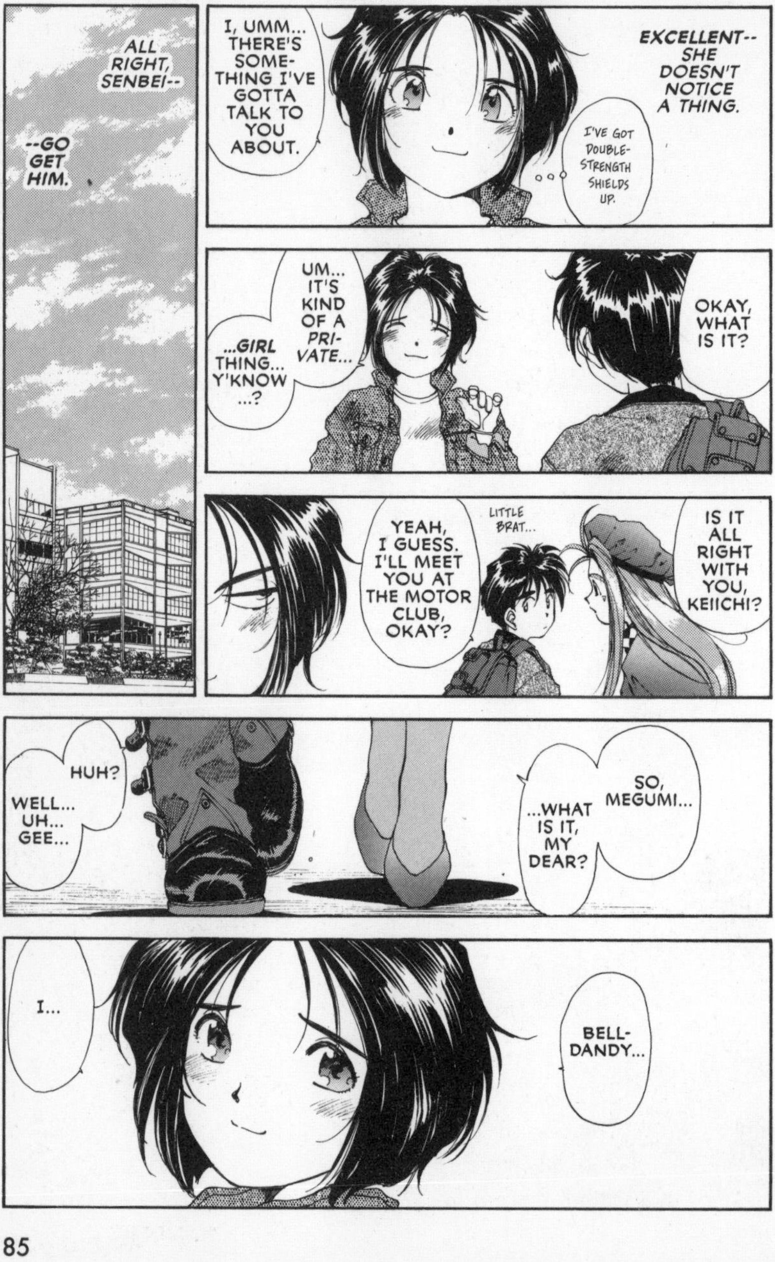
EXCELLENT-- SHE DOESN'T NOTICE A THING.
I'VE GOT DOUBLE-STRENGTH SHIELDS UP.
I, UMM... THERE'S SOME-THING I'VE GOTTA TALK TO YOU ABOUT.
OKAY, WHAT IS IT?
UM... IT'S KIND OF A PRI-VATE...
...GIRL THING... Y'KNOW ...?
IS IT ALL RIGHT WITH YOU, KEIICHI?
LITTLE BRAT...
YEAH, I GUESS. I'LL MEET YOU AT THE MOTOR CLUB, OKAY?
ALL RIGHT, SENBEI--
--GO GET HIM.
SO, MEGUMI...
...WHAT IS IT, MY DEAR?
HUH?
WELL... UH... GEE...
BELL-DANDY...
I...

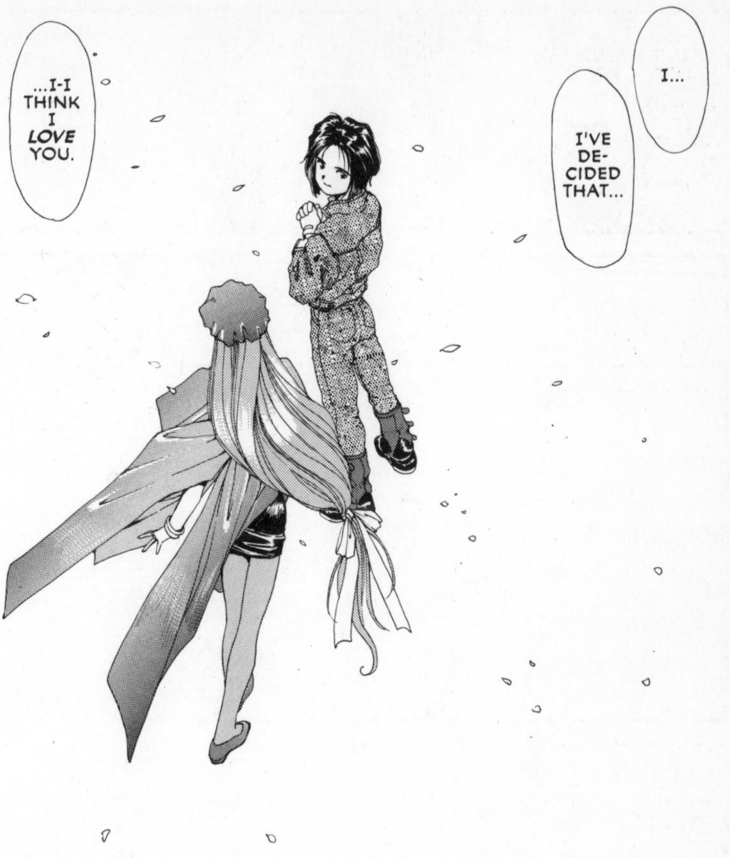
I...
I'VE DE-CIDED THAT...
...I-I THINK I *LOVE* YOU.

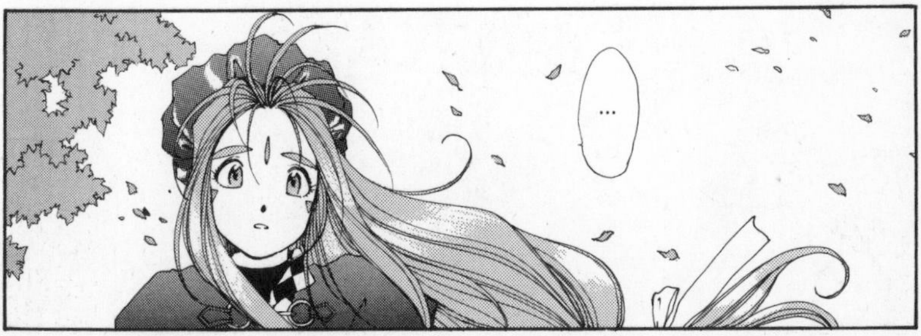
...

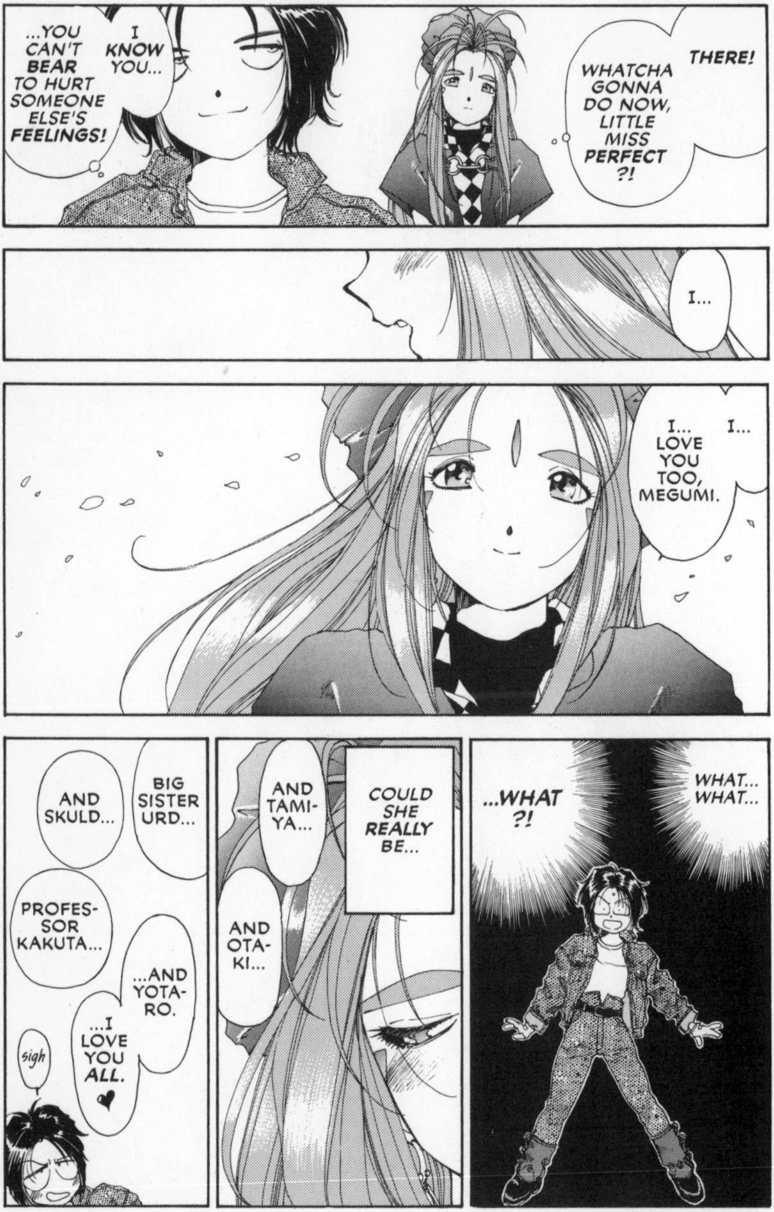
THERE!
WHATCHA GONNA DO NOW, LITTLE MISS PERFECT?!
I KNOW YOU...
...YOU CAN'T BEAR TO HURT SOMEONE ELSE'S FEELINGS!
I...
I... I... LOVE YOU TOO, MEGUMI.
WHAT... WHAT...
...WHAT?!
COULD SHE REALLY BE...
AND TAMIYA...
AND OTAKI...
BIG SISTER URD...
AND SKULD...
PROFESSOR KAKUTA...
...AND YOTARO.
...I LOVE YOU ALL. ♥
sigh

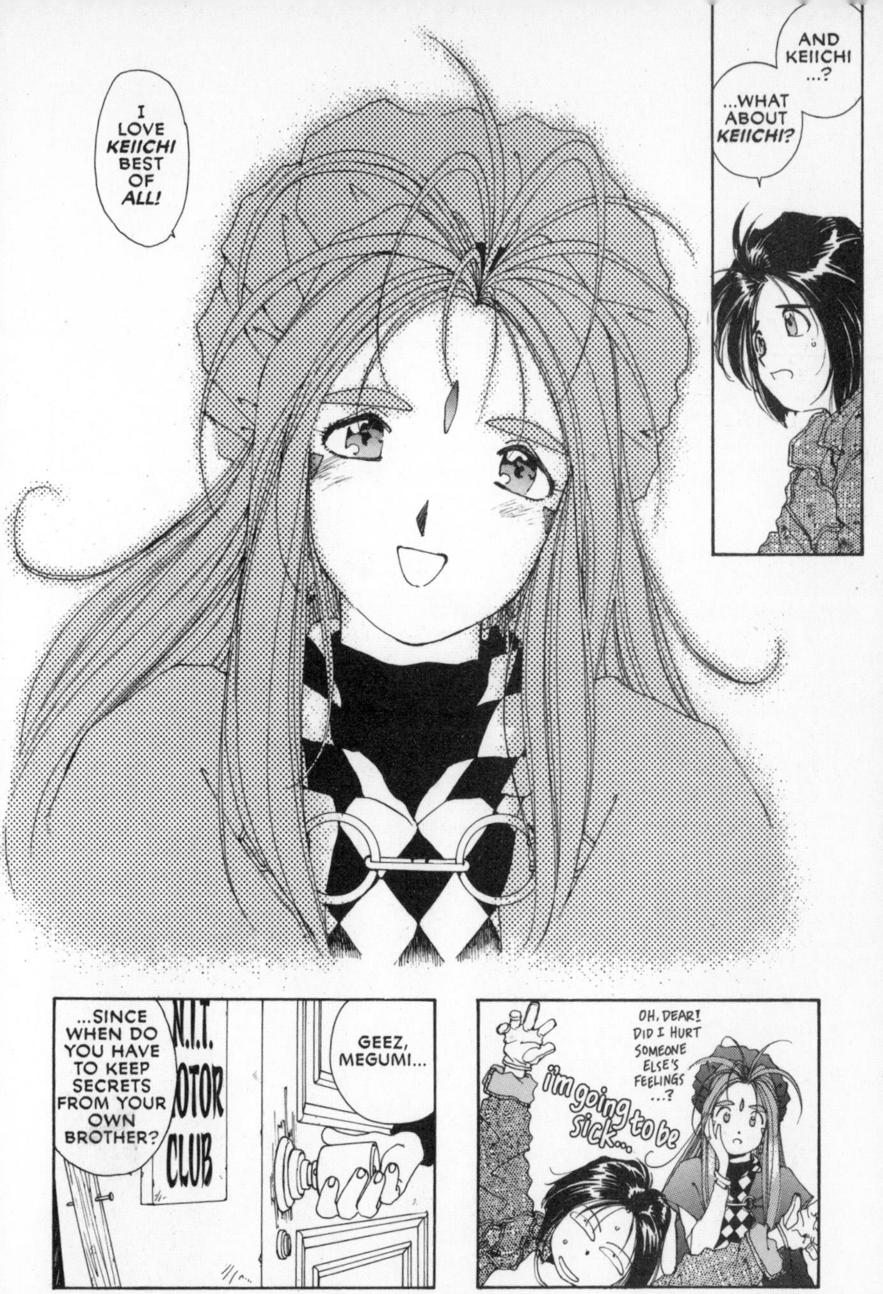
AND KEIICHI ...?
...WHAT ABOUT KEIICHI?
I LOVE KEIICHI BEST OF ALL!
OH, DEAR! DID I HURT SOMEONE ELSE'S FEELINGS ...?
i'm going to be sick...
GEEZ, MEGUMI...
...SINCE WHEN DO YOU HAVE TO KEEP SECRETS FROM YOUR OWN BROTHER?
N.I.T.
OTOR
CLUB

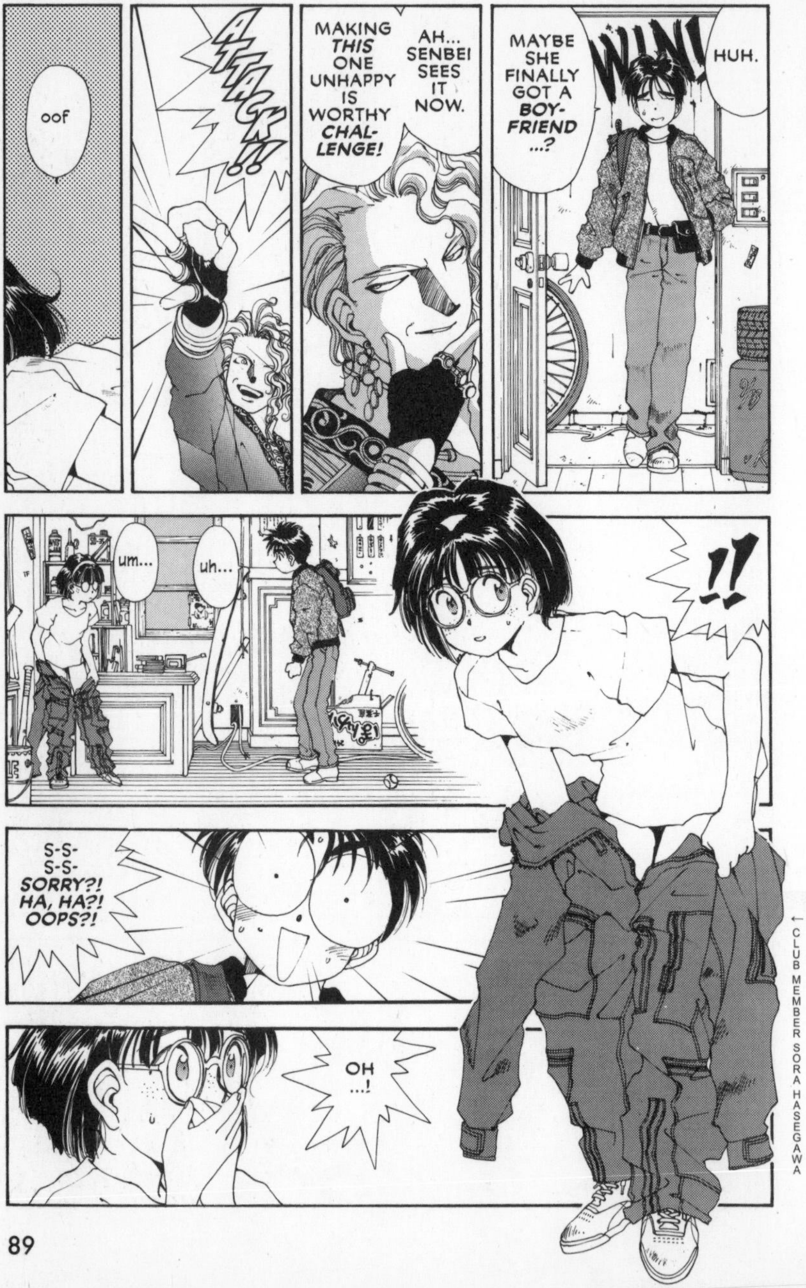
HUH.
WIN!
MAYBE SHE FINALLY GOT A BOY-FRIEND ...?
AH... SENBEI SEES IT NOW.
MAKING THIS ONE UNHAPPY IS WORTHY CHAL-LENGE!
ATTACK!!
oof
!!
← CLUB MEMBER SORA HASEGAWA
uh...
um...
S-S-S-S-SORRY?! HA, HA?! OOPS?!
OH ...!

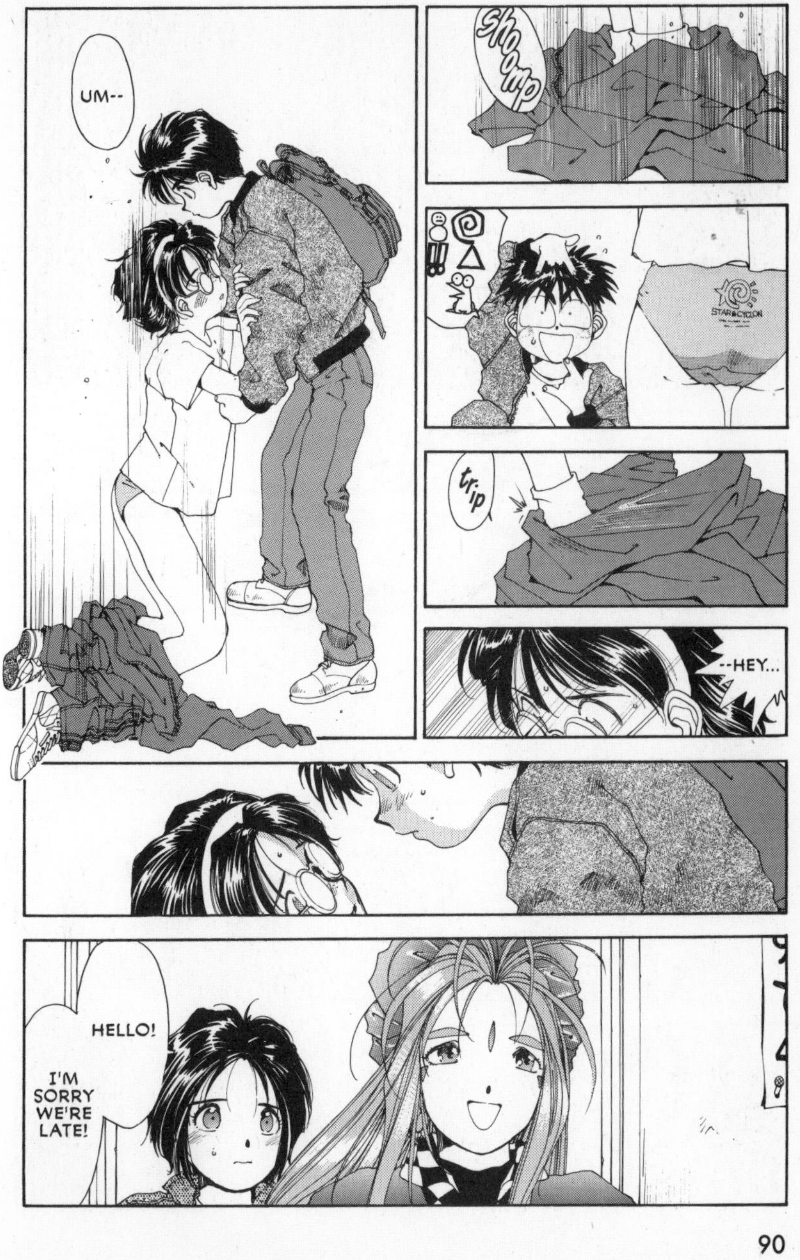
shoomp
trip
--HEY...
UM--
HELLO!
I'M SORRY WE'RE LATE!

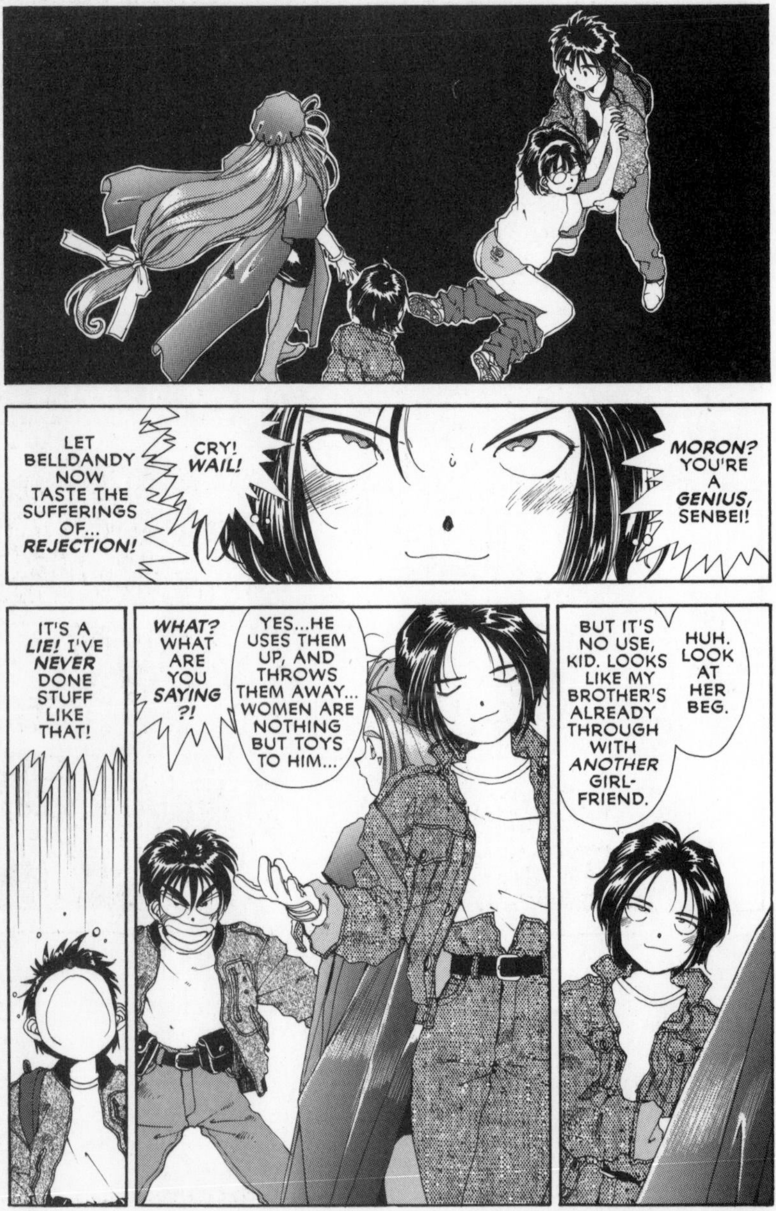
MORON? YOU'RE A GENIUS, SENBEI!
CRY! WAIL!
LET BELLDANDY NOW TASTE THE SUFFERINGS OF... REJECTION!
HUH. LOOK AT HER BEG.
BUT IT'S NO USE, KID. LOOKS LIKE MY BROTHER'S ALREADY THROUGH WITH ANOTHER GIRL-FRIEND.
YES...HE USES THEM UP, AND THROWS THEM AWAY... WOMEN ARE NOTHING BUT TOYS TO HIM...
WHAT? WHAT ARE YOU SAYING?!
IT'S A LIE! I'VE NEVER DONE STUFF LIKE THAT!

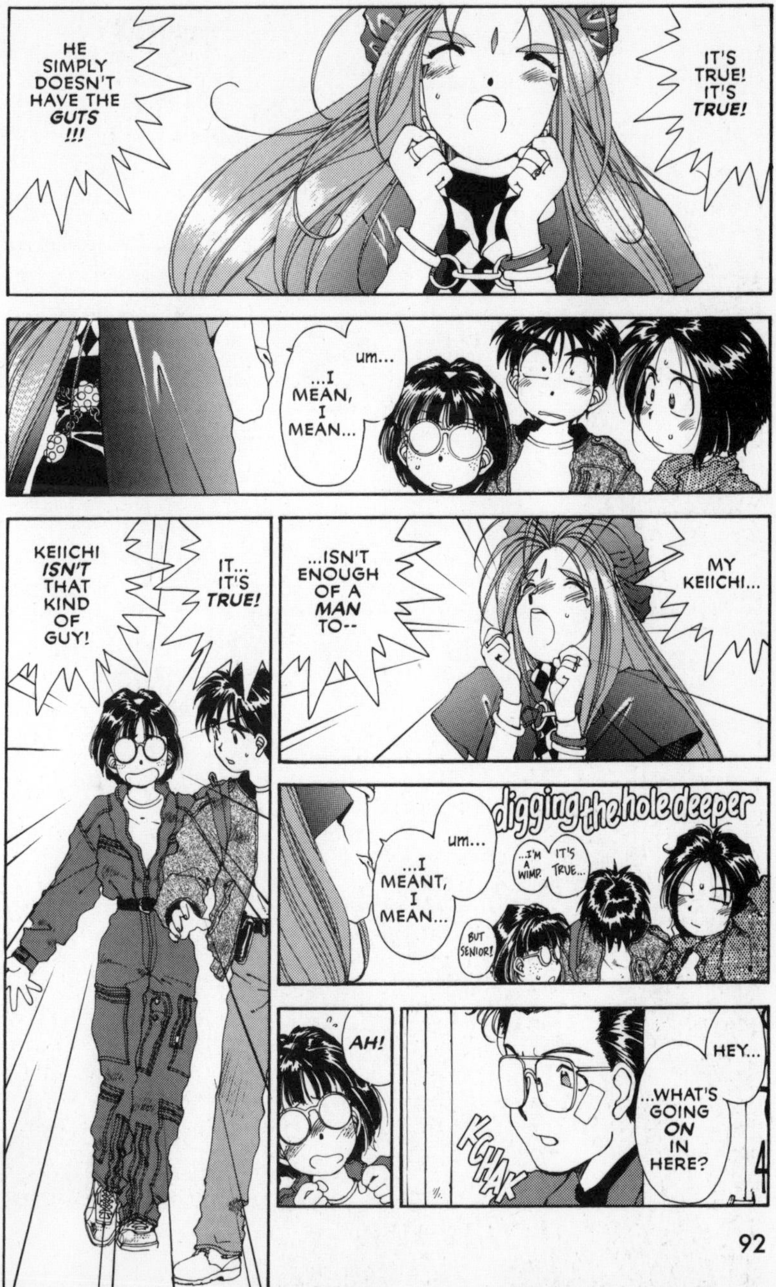
IT'S TRUE! IT'S TRUE!
HE SIMPLY DOESN'T HAVE THE GUTS !!!
um...
...I MEAN, I MEAN...
MY KEIICHI...
...ISN'T ENOUGH OF A MAN TO--
digging the hole deeper
um...
...I MEANT, I MEAN...
IT'S TRUE...
...I'M A WIMP.
BUT SENIOR!
HEY...
...WHAT'S GOING ON IN HERE?
KCHAK
AH!
IT... IT'S TRUE!
KEIICHI ISN'T THAT KIND OF GUY!

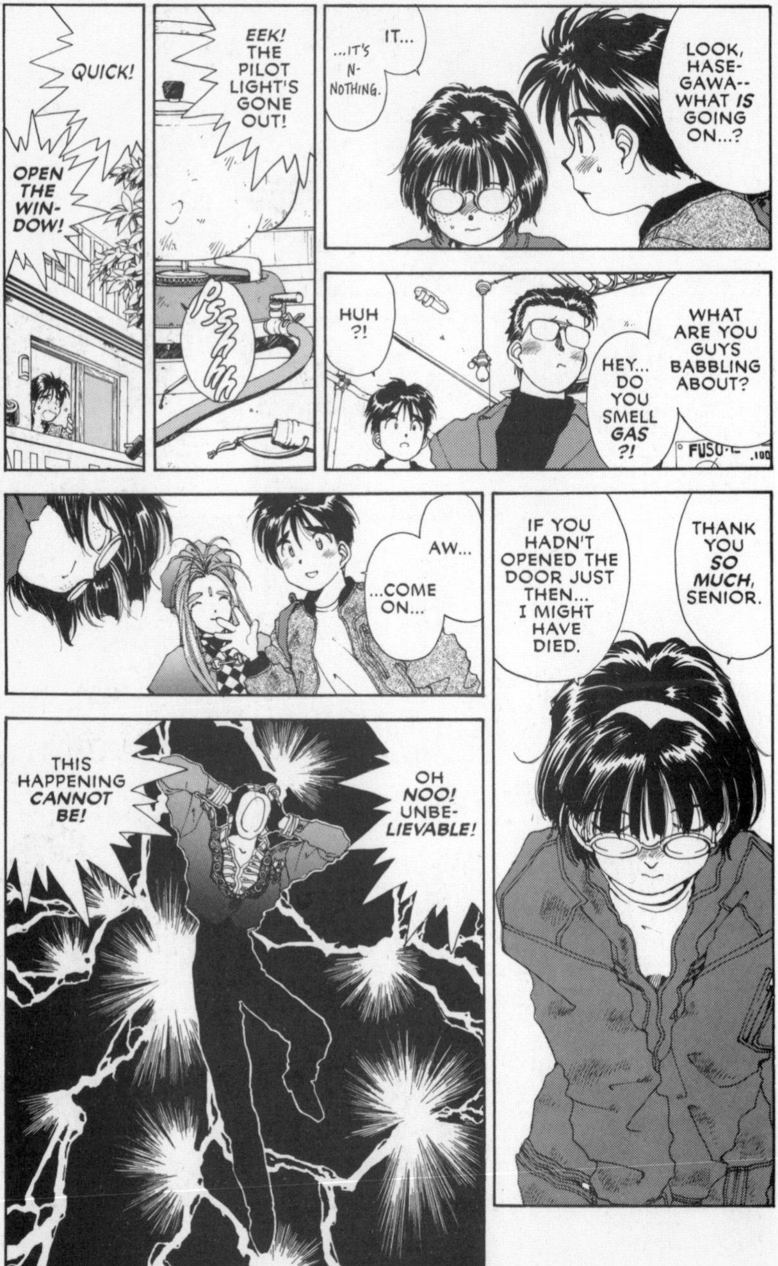
LOOK, HASEGAWA-- WHAT IS GOING ON...?
IT...
...IT'S N-NOTHING.
WHAT ARE YOU GUYS BABBLING ABOUT?
HEY... DO YOU SMELL GAS?!
HUH ?!
FUSO
EEK! THE PILOT LIGHT'S GONE OUT!
PSSHHH
QUICK!
OPEN THE WIN-DOW!
THANK YOU SO MUCH, SENIOR.
IF YOU HADN'T OPENED THE DOOR JUST THEN... I MIGHT HAVE DIED.
AW...
...COME ON...
OH NOO! UNBE-LIEVABLE!
THIS HAPPENING CANNOT BE!

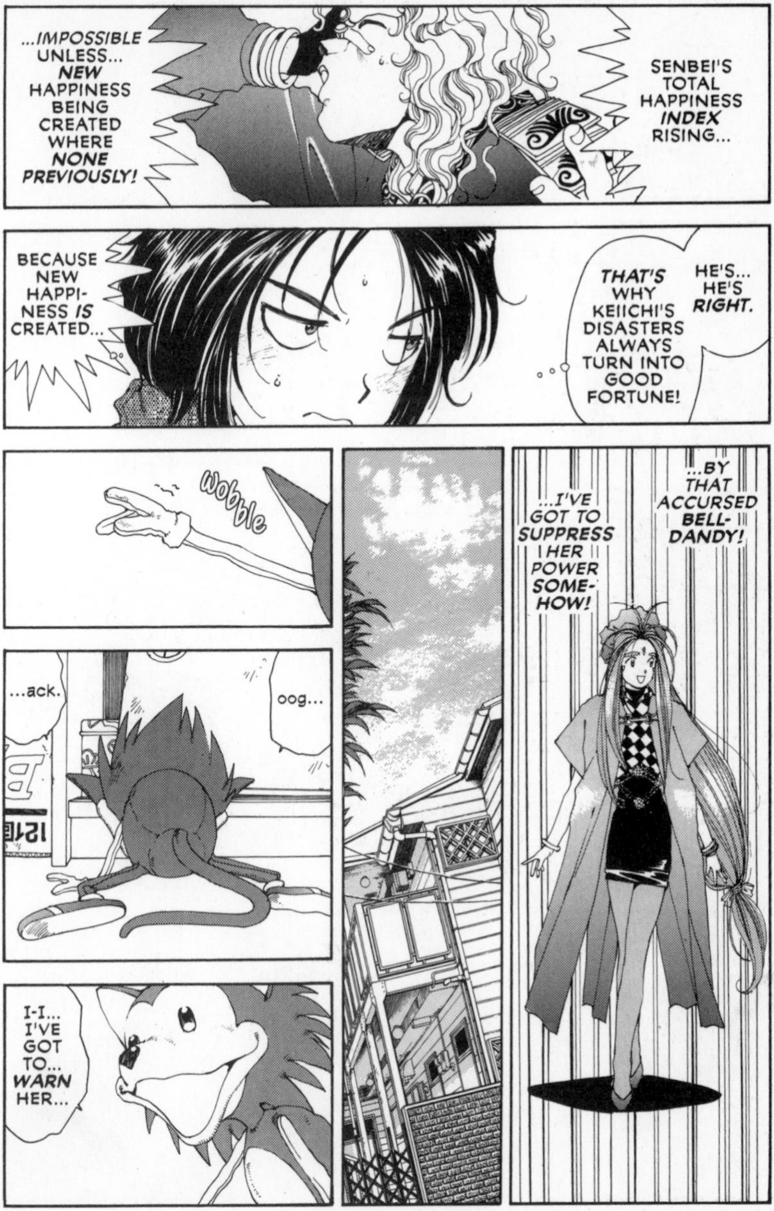
SENBEI'S TOTAL HAPPINESS INDEX RISING...
...IMPOSSIBLE UNLESS... NEW HAPPINESS BEING CREATED WHERE NONE PREVIOUSLY!
HE'S... HE'S RIGHT.
THAT'S WHY KEIICHI'S DISASTERS ALWAYS TURN INTO GOOD FORTUNE!
BECAUSE NEW HAPPINESS IS CREATED...
...BY THAT ACCURSED BELL-DANDY!
...I'VE GOT TO SUPPRESS HER POWER SOME-HOW!
wobble
oog...
...ack.
I-I... I'VE GOT TO... WARN HER...

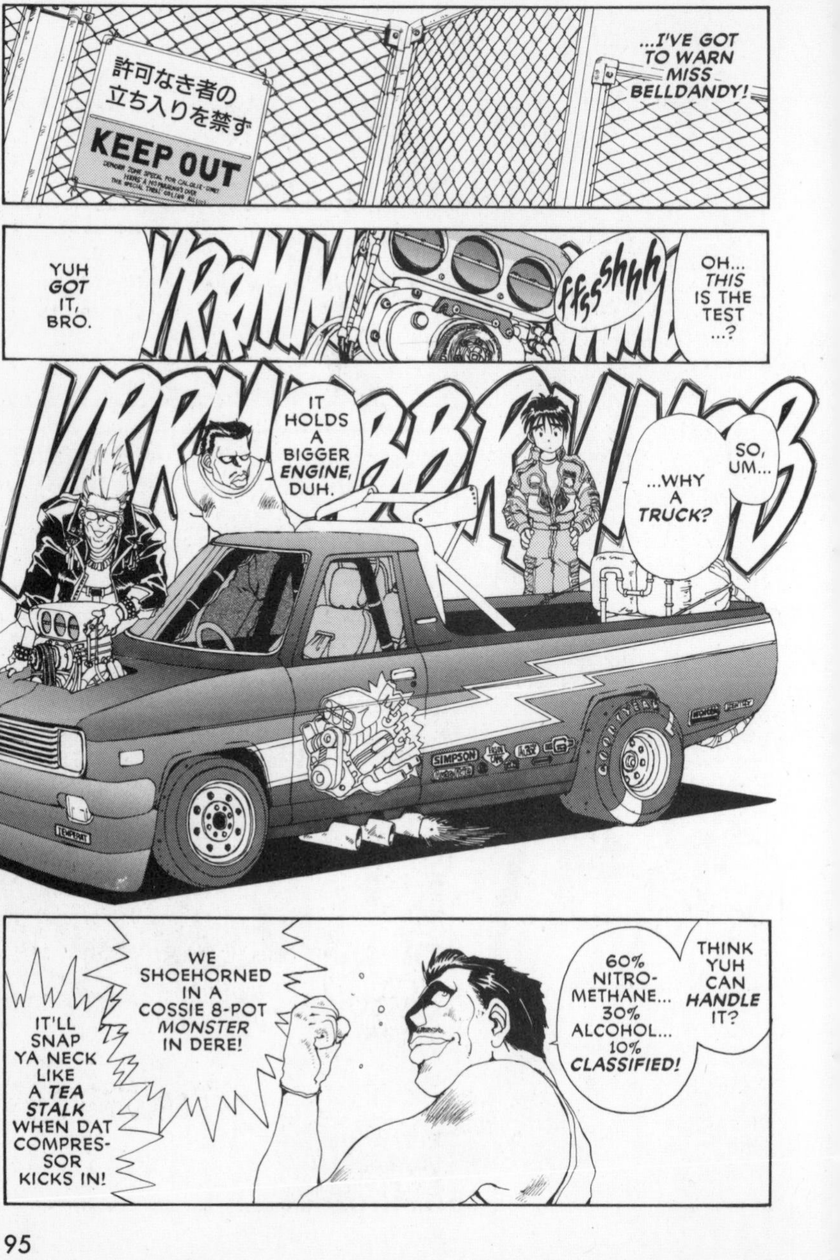
許可なき者の
立ち入りを禁ず
KEEP OUT
...I'VE GOT TO WARN MISS BELLDANDY!
OH... THIS IS THE TEST ...?
ffssshhh
VRRMM
YUH GOT IT, BRO.
SO, UM...
...WHY A TRUCK?
IT HOLDS A BIGGER ENGINE, DUH.
SIMPSON
THINK YUH CAN HANDLE IT?
60% NITRO-METHANE... 30% ALCOHOL... 10% CLASSIFIED!
WE SHOEHORNED IN A COSSIE 8-POT MONSTER IN DERE!
IT'LL SNAP YA NECK LIKE A TEA STALK WHEN DAT COMPRES-SOR KICKS IN!

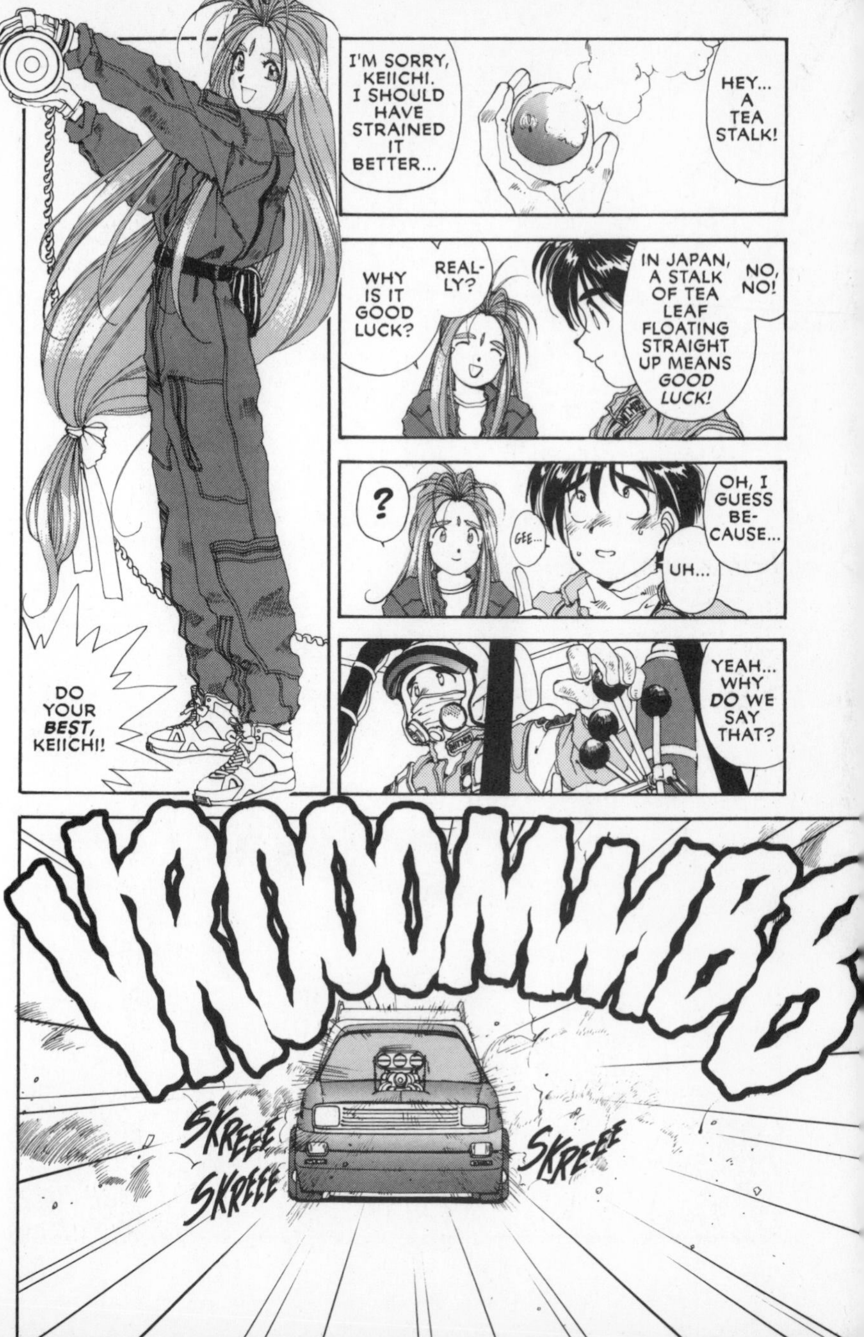
HEY... A TEA STALK!
I'M SORRY, KEIICHI. I SHOULD HAVE STRAINED IT BETTER...
NO, NO!
IN JAPAN, A STALK OF TEA LEAF FLOATING STRAIGHT UP MEANS *GOOD LUCK!*
REAL-LY?
WHY IS IT GOOD LUCK?
OH, I GUESS BE-CAUSE...
UH...
GEE...
?
YEAH... WHY *DO* WE SAY THAT?
DO YOUR *BEST*, KEIICHI!
VROOMMB
SKREEE
SKREEE
SKREEE

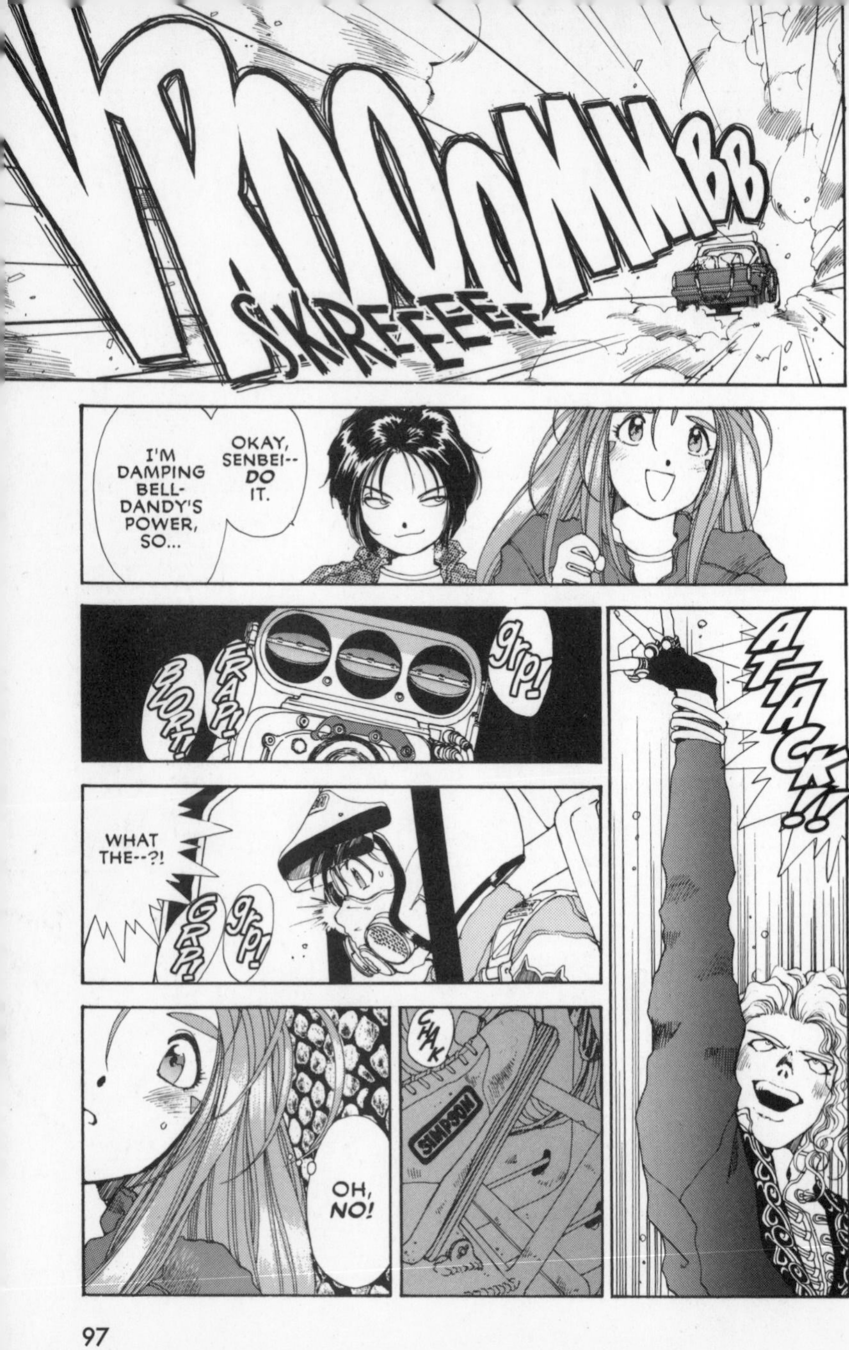
VROOMMBB
SKREEEEE
OKAY, SENBEI-- *DO* IT.
I'M DAMPING BELL-DANDY'S POWER, SO...
ATTACK!!
grp!
FRAP!
BLORP!
WHAT THE--?!
grp!
GRP!
CHAK
SIMPSON
OH, NO!

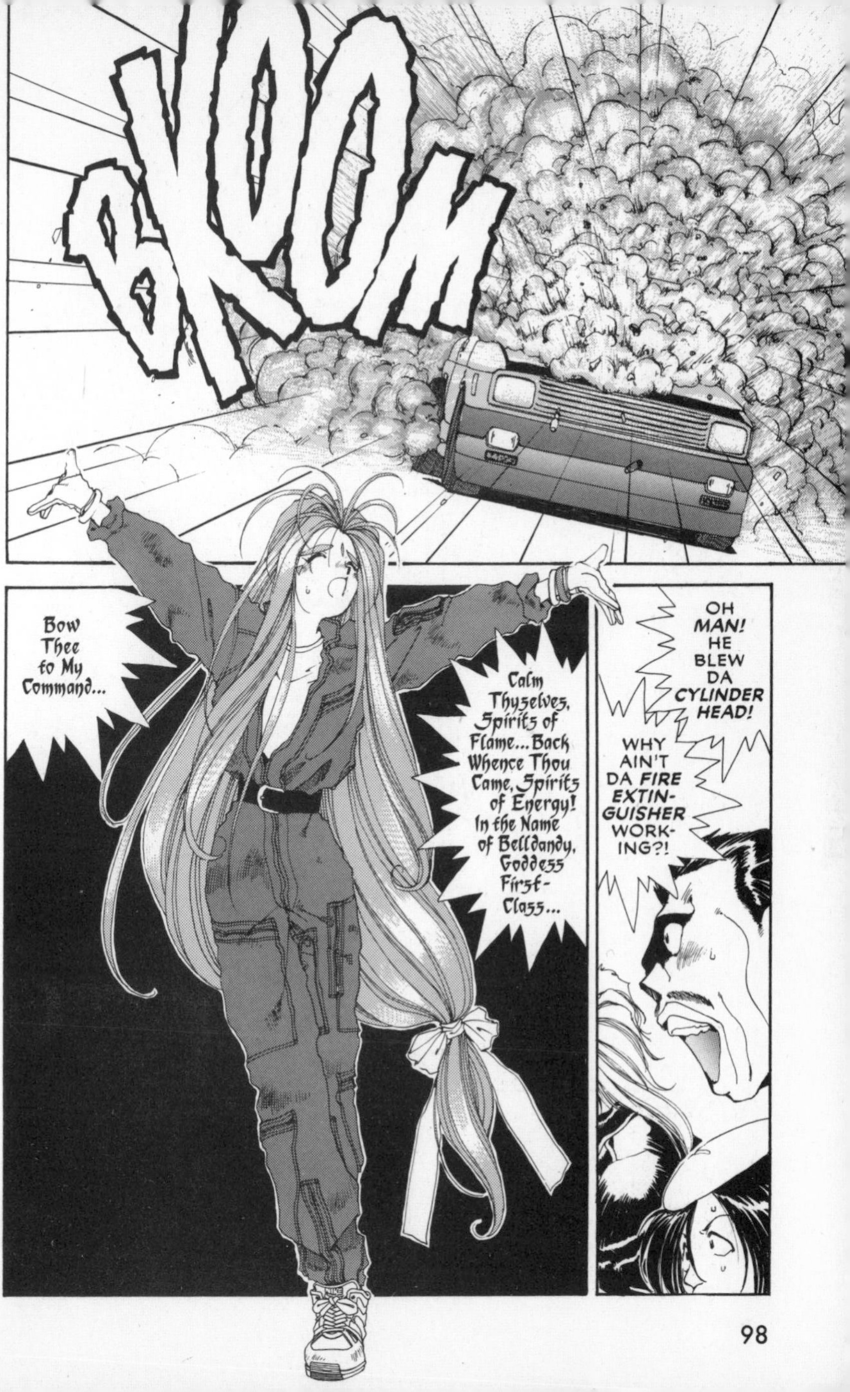
BKOOM
OH MAN! HE BLEW DA CYLINDER HEAD!
WHY AIN'T DA FIRE EXTIN-GUISHER WORKING?!
Calm Thyselves, Spirits of Flame... Back Whence Thou Came, Spirits of Energy! In the Name of Belldandy, Goddess First-Class...
Bow Thee to My Command...

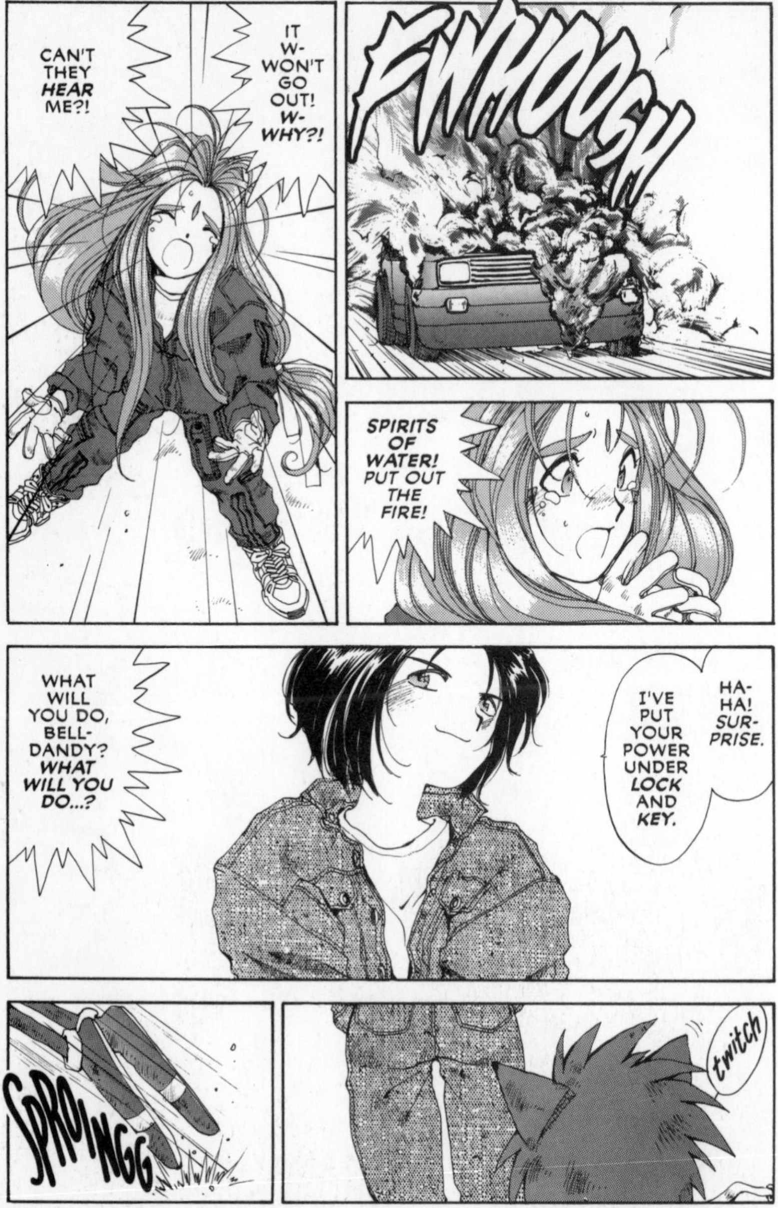
FWHOOSH
SPIRITS OF WATER! PUT OUT THE FIRE!
IT W-WON'T GO OUT! W-WHY?!
CAN'T THEY HEAR ME?!
HA-HA! SUR-PRISE.
I'VE PUT YOUR POWER UNDER LOCK AND KEY.
WHAT WILL YOU DO, BELL-DANDY? WHAT WILL YOU DO...?
twitch
SPROINGG

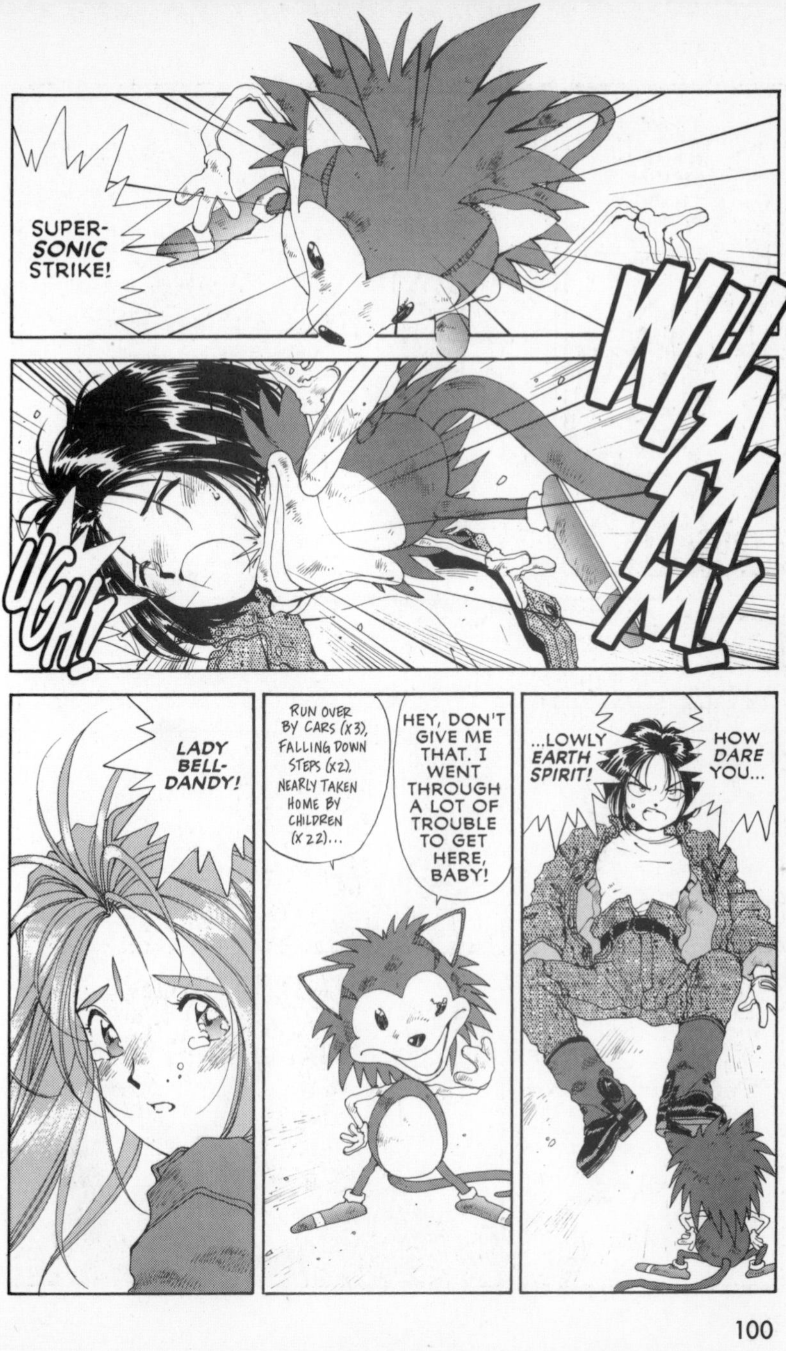
SUPER-SONIC STRIKE!
WHAMMM!
UGH!
HOW DARE YOU...
...LOWLY EARTH SPIRIT!
HEY, DON'T GIVE ME THAT. I WENT THROUGH A LOT OF TROUBLE TO GET HERE, BABY!
RUN OVER BY CARS (X3), FALLING DOWN STEPS (X2), NEARLY TAKEN HOME BY CHILDREN (X22)...
LADY BELL-DANDY!

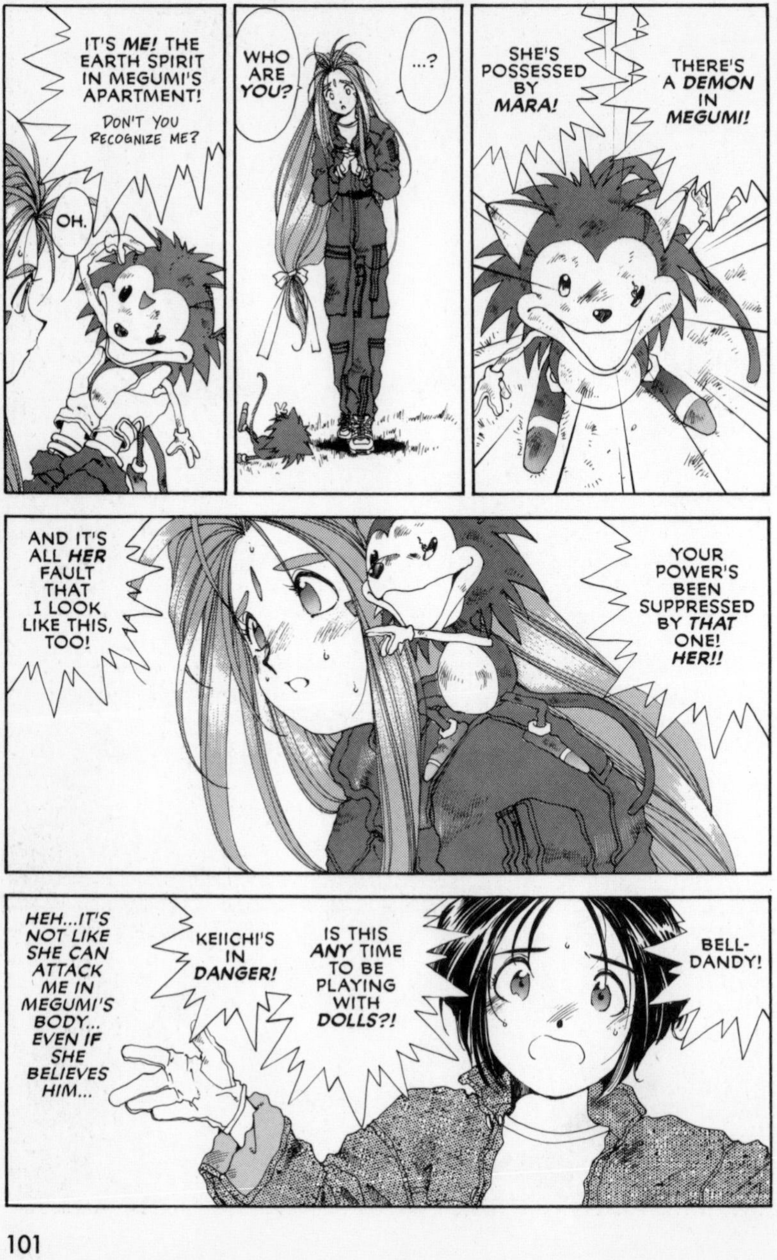
THERE'S A DEMON IN MEGUMI!
SHE'S POSSESSED BY MARA!
...?
WHO ARE YOU?
IT'S ME! THE EARTH SPIRIT IN MEGUMI'S APARTMENT!
DON'T YOU RECOGNIZE ME?
OH.
YOUR POWER'S BEEN SUPPRESSED BY THAT ONE! HER!!
AND IT'S ALL HER FAULT THAT I LOOK LIKE THIS, TOO!
BELL-DANDY!
IS THIS ANY TIME TO BE PLAYING WITH DOLLS?!
KEIICHI'S IN DANGER!
HEH...IT'S NOT LIKE SHE CAN ATTACK ME IN MEGUMI'S BODY... EVEN IF SHE BELIEVES HIM...

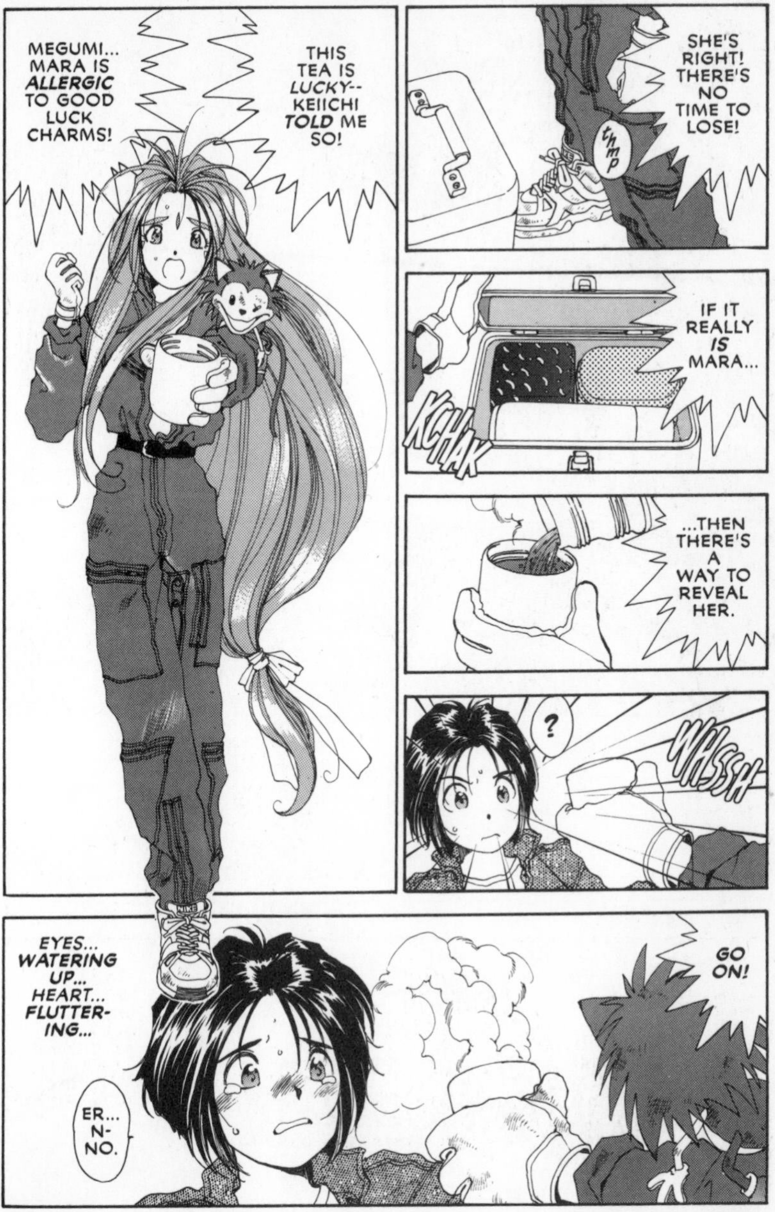
SHE'S RIGHT! THERE'S NO TIME TO LOSE!
thmp
IF IT REALLY IS MARA...
KCHAK
...THEN THERE'S A WAY TO REVEAL HER.
?
WHSSH
THIS TEA IS LUCKY-- KEIICHI TOLD ME SO!
MEGUMI... MARA IS ALLERGIC TO GOOD LUCK CHARMS!
GO ON!
EYES... WATERING UP... HEART... FLUTTERING...
ER... N-NO.

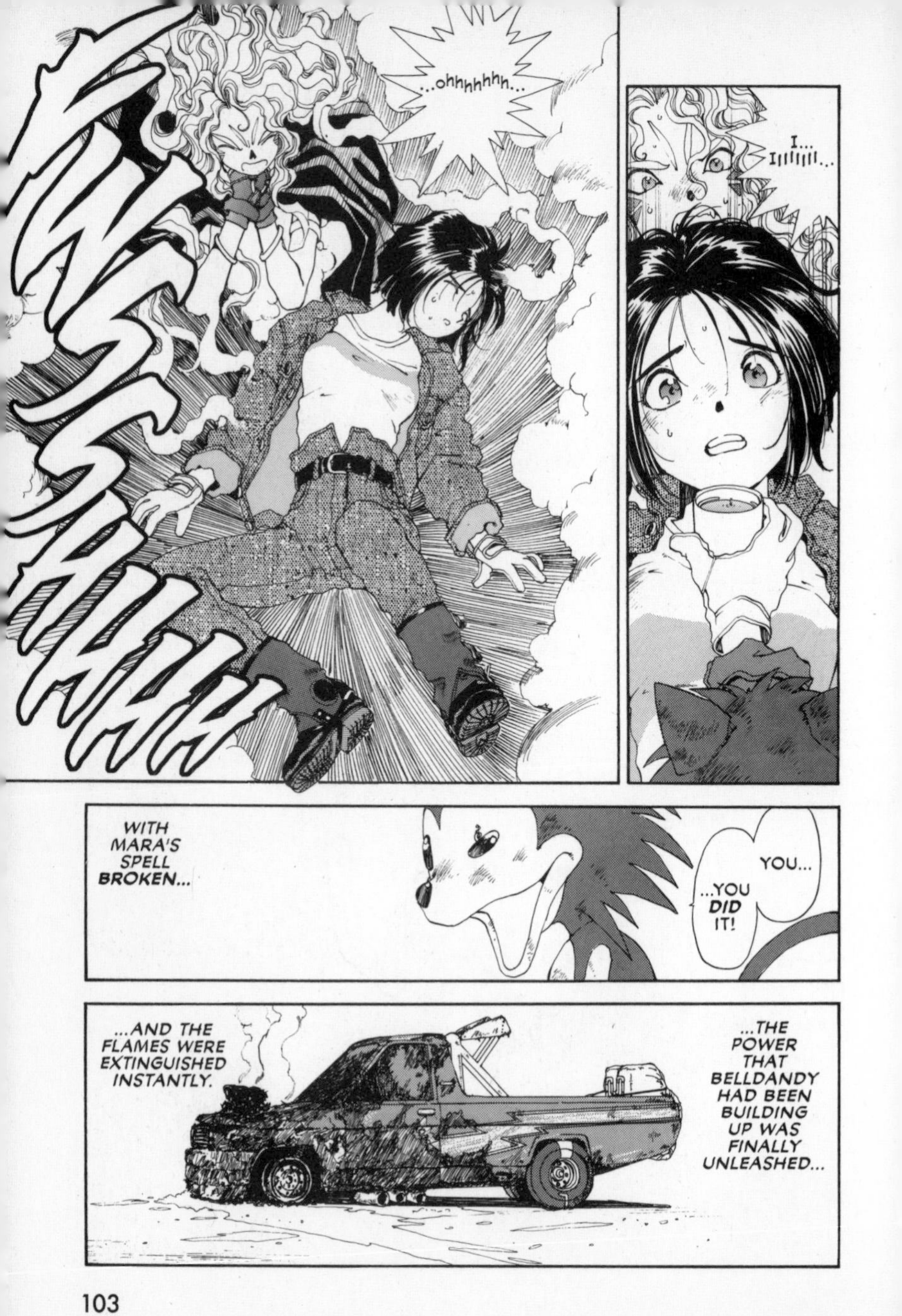
I... Illllll...
...ohhhhhhh...
YOU... ...YOU DID IT!
WITH MARA'S SPELL BROKEN...
...THE POWER THAT BELLDANDY HAD BEEN BUILDING UP WAS FINALLY UNLEASHED...
...AND THE FLAMES WERE EXTINGUISHED INSTANTLY.

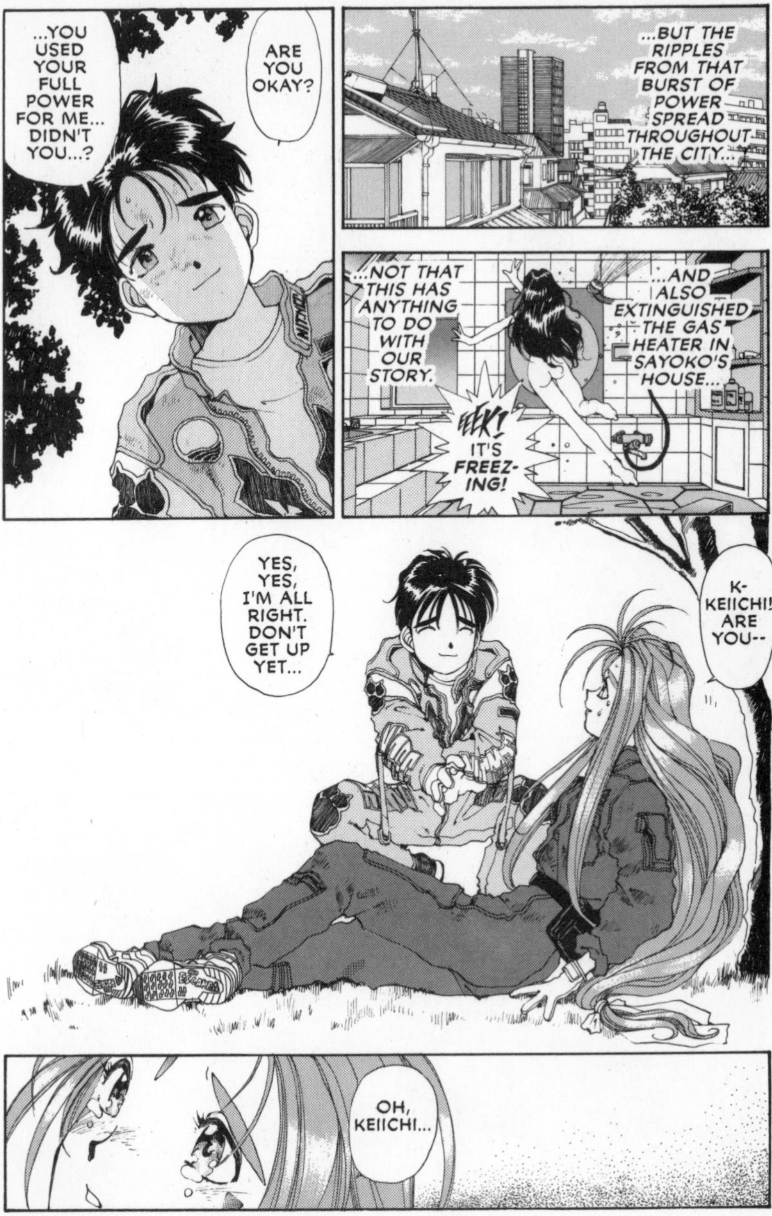
...BUT THE RIPPLES FROM THAT BURST OF POWER SPREAD THROUGHOUT THE CITY...
...AND ALSO EXTINGUISHED THE GAS HEATER IN SAYOKO'S HOUSE...
...NOT THAT THIS HAS ANYTHING TO DO WITH OUR STORY.
EEEK! IT'S FREEZ-ING!
ARE YOU OKAY?
...YOU USED YOUR FULL POWER FOR ME... DIDN'T YOU...?
K-KEIICHI! ARE YOU--
YES, YES, I'M ALL RIGHT. DON'T GET UP YET...
OH, KEIICHI...

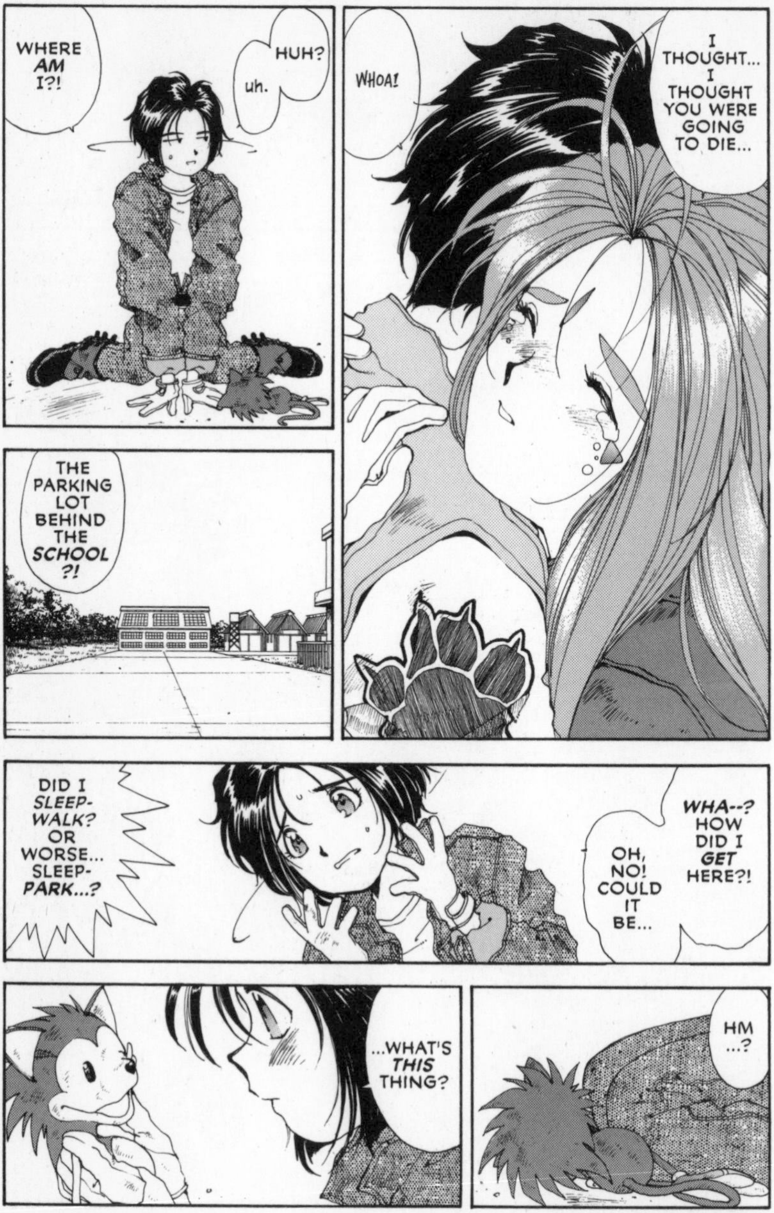
I THOUGHT... I THOUGHT YOU WERE GOING TO DIE...
WHOA!
HUH?
uh.
WHERE AM I?!
THE PARKING LOT BEHIND THE SCHOOL?!
WHA--? HOW DID I GET HERE?!
OH, NO! COULD IT BE...
DID I SLEEP-WALK? OR WORSE... SLEEP-PARK...?
HM ...?
...WHAT'S THIS THING?

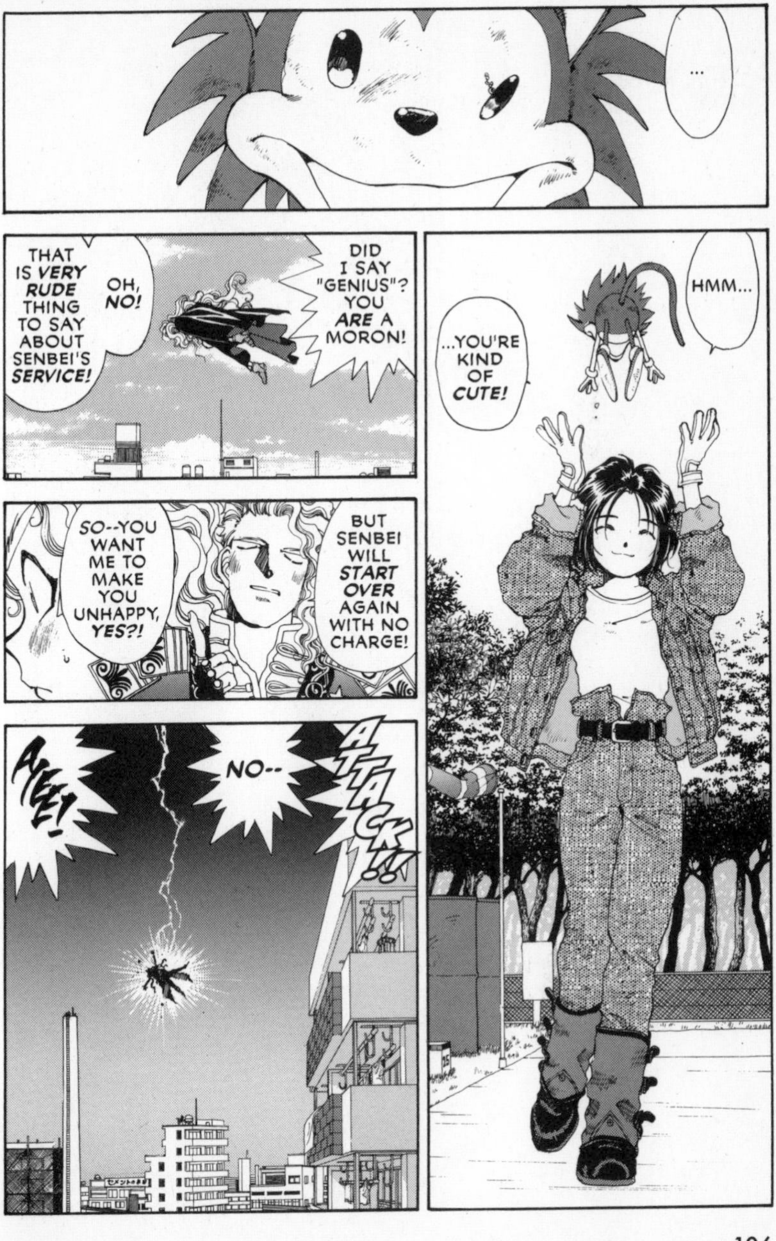
...
HMM...
...YOU'RE KIND OF CUTE!
DID I SAY "GENIUS"? YOU ARE A MORON!
OH, NO!
THAT IS VERY RUDE THING TO SAY ABOUT SENBEI'S SERVICE!
BUT SENBEI WILL START OVER AGAIN WITH NO CHARGE!
SO--YOU WANT ME TO MAKE YOU UNHAPPY, YES?!
ATTACK!!
NO--
AIEE!

CHAPTER 46

Thank You

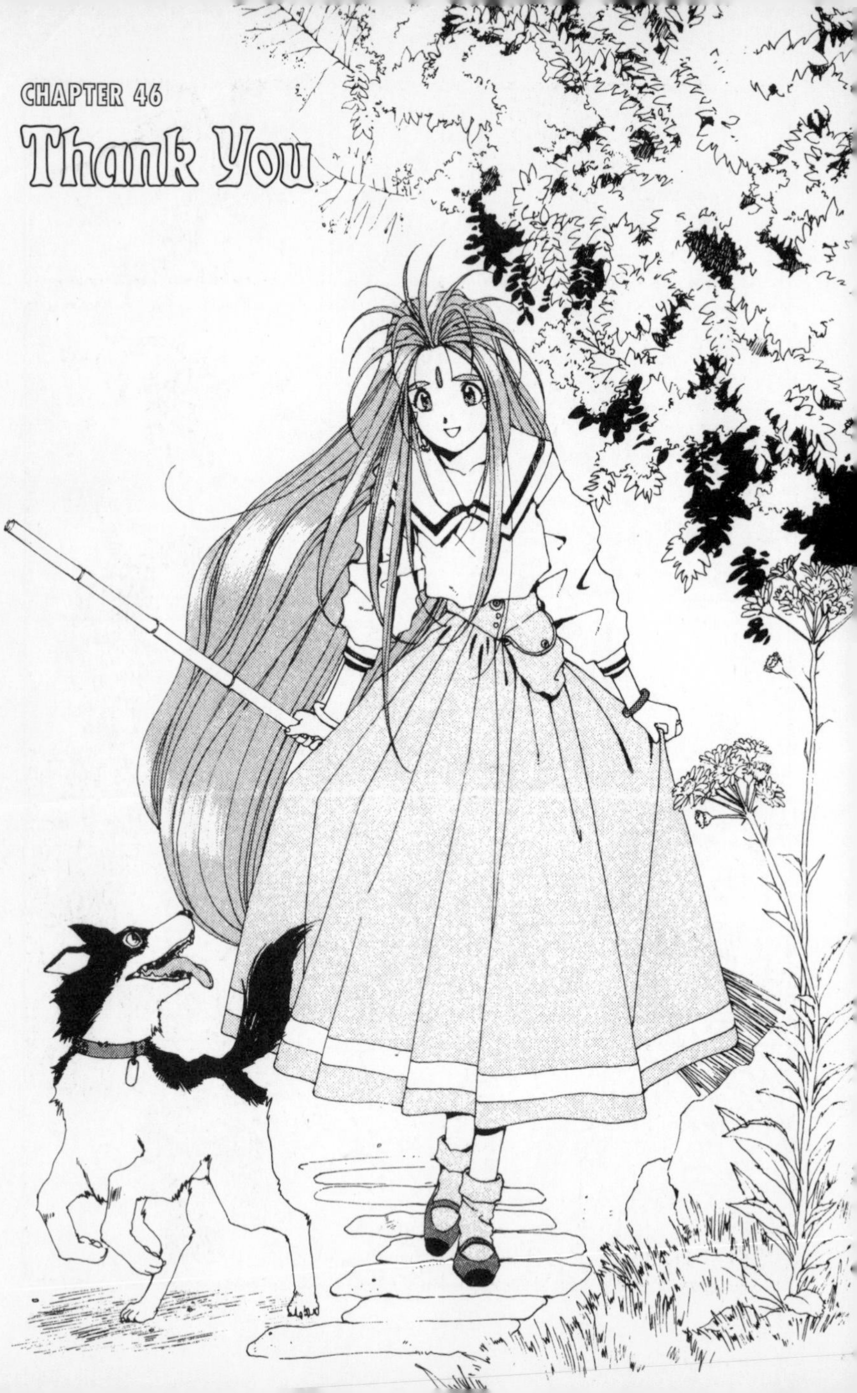

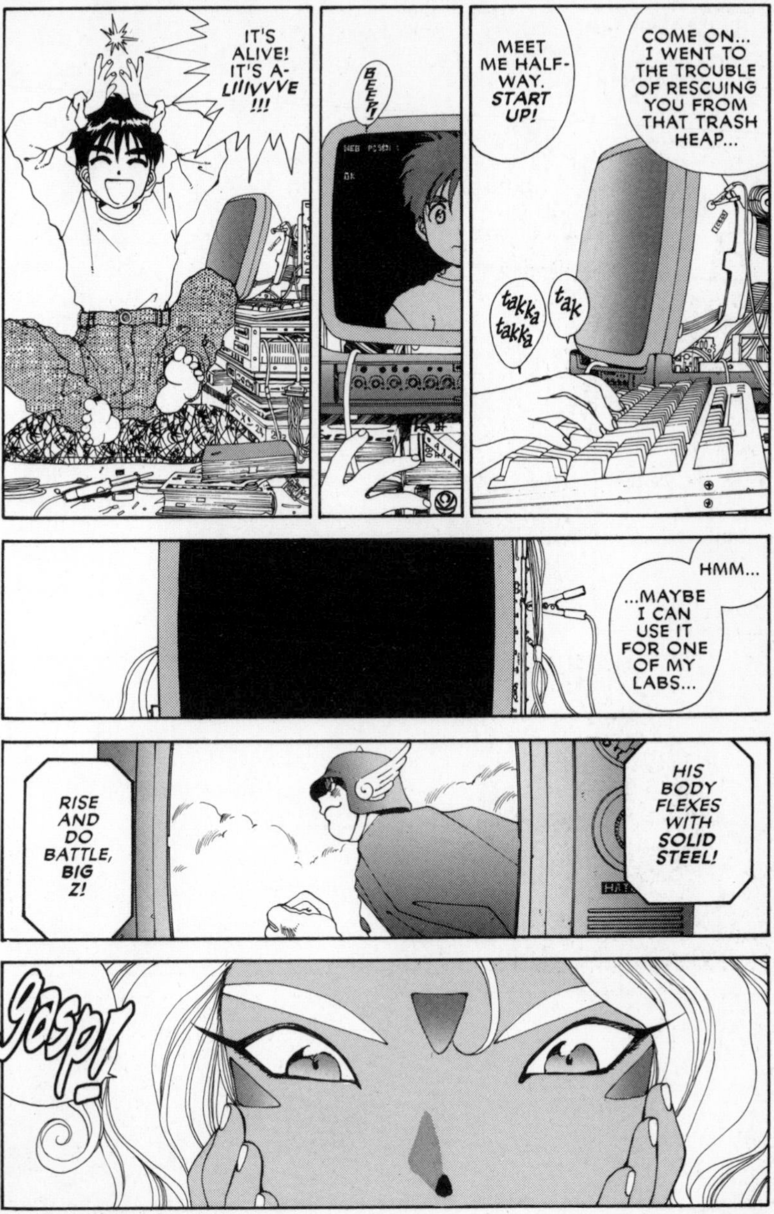
COME ON... I WENT TO THE TROUBLE OF RESCUING YOU FROM THAT TRASH HEAP...
MEET ME HALF-WAY. START UP!
tak
takka takka
BEEP!
IT'S ALIVE! IT'S A-LIIIVVVE !!!
HMM...
...MAYBE I CAN USE IT FOR ONE OF MY LABS...
HIS BODY FLEXES WITH SOLID STEEL!
RISE AND DO BATTLE, BIG Z!
gasp!

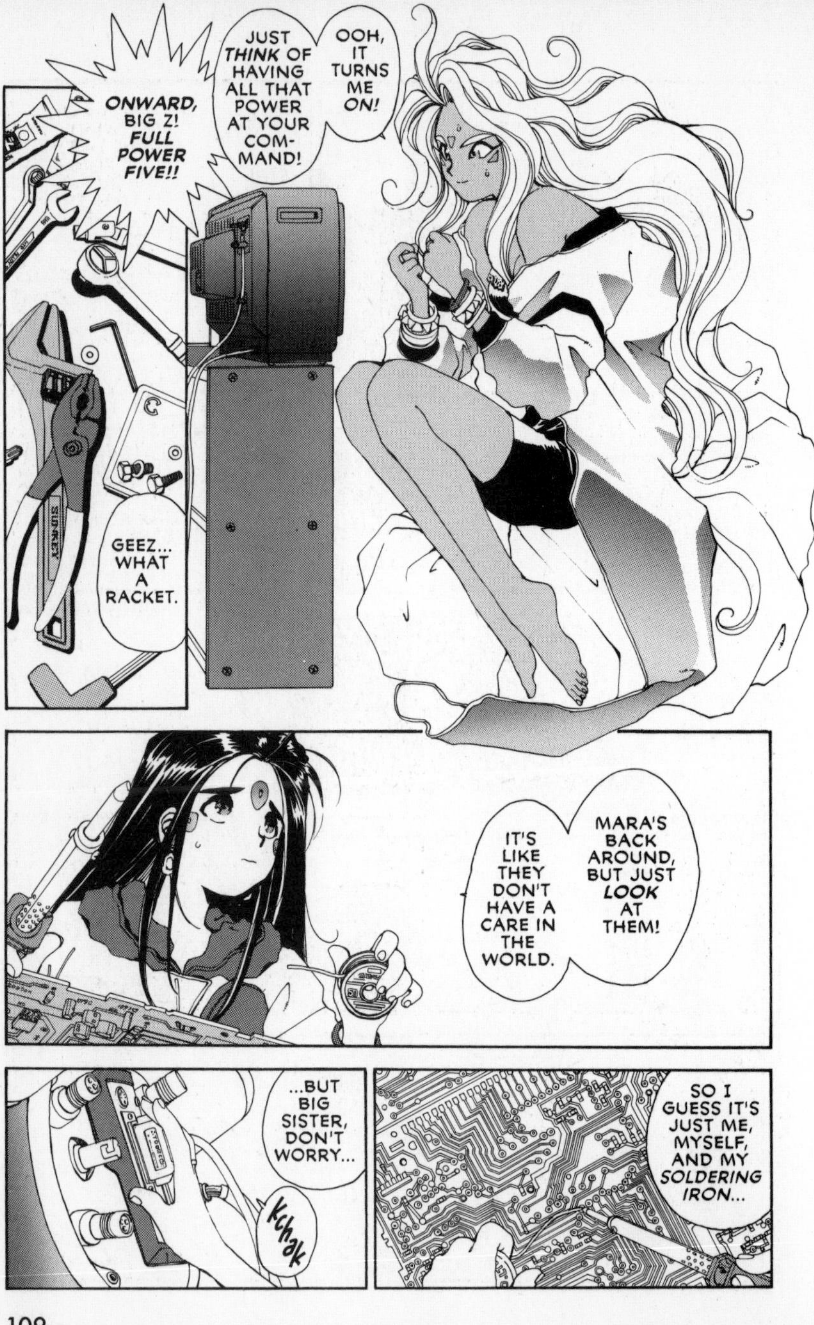
OOH, IT TURNS ME ON!
JUST THINK OF HAVING ALL THAT POWER AT YOUR COM-MAND!
ONWARD, BIG Z! FULL POWER FIVE!!
GEEZ... WHAT A RACKET.
MARA'S BACK AROUND, BUT JUST LOOK AT THEM!
IT'S LIKE THEY DON'T HAVE A CARE IN THE WORLD.
SO I GUESS IT'S JUST ME, MYSELF, AND MY SOLDERING IRON...
...BUT BIG SISTER, DON'T WORRY...
Kchak

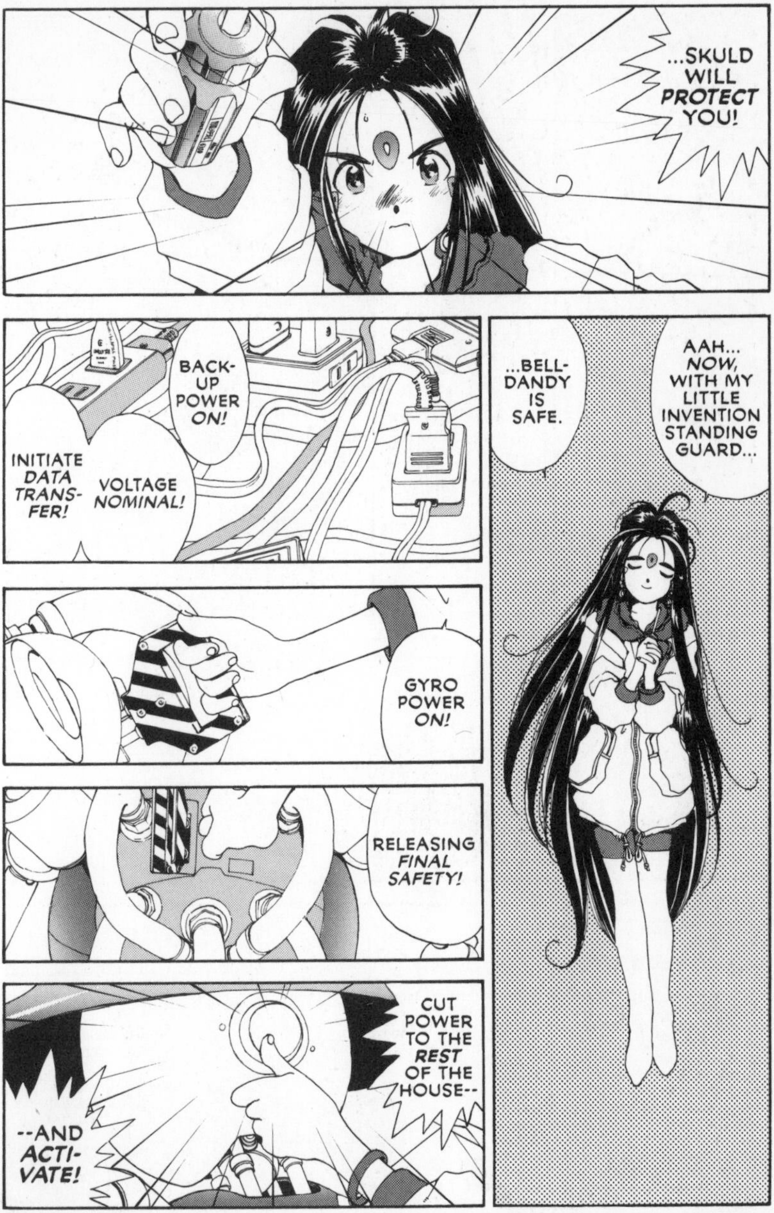
...SKULD WILL *PROTECT* YOU!
AAH... *NOW*, WITH MY LITTLE INVENTION STANDING GUARD...
...BELL-DANDY IS SAFE.
BACK-UP POWER *ON!*
VOLTAGE *NOMINAL!*
INITIATE *DATA TRANSFER!*
GYRO POWER *ON!*
RELEASING *FINAL SAFETY!*
CUT POWER TO THE *REST* OF THE HOUSE--
--AND *ACTIVATE!*

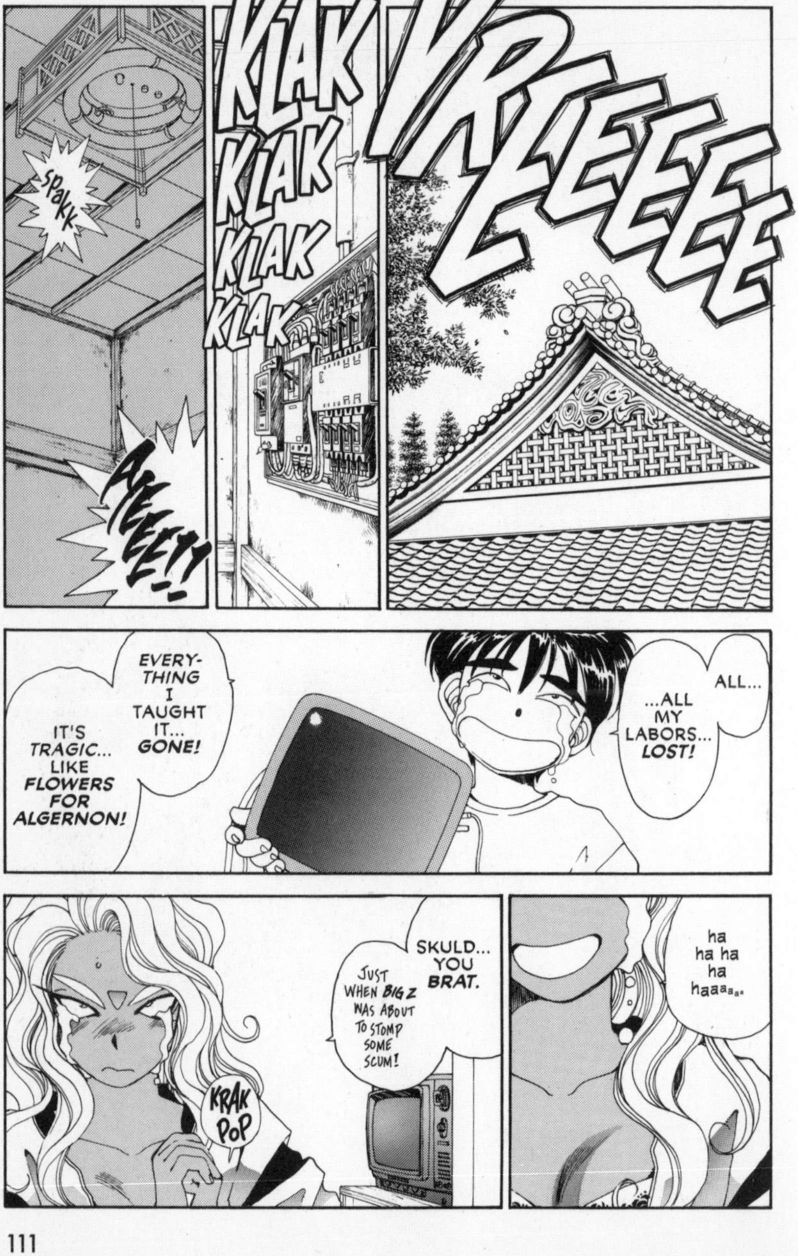

VRIEEEEEE
KLAK
KLAK
KLAK
KLAK
spakk
AIEEEE!!
ALL...
...ALL MY LABORS... LOST!
EVERYTHING I TAUGHT IT... GONE!
IT'S TRAGIC... LIKE FLOWERS FOR ALGERNON!
ha ha ha ha haaaaa
SKULD... YOU BRAT.
JUST WHEN BIG Z WAS ABOUT TO STOMP SOME SCUM!
KRAK POP

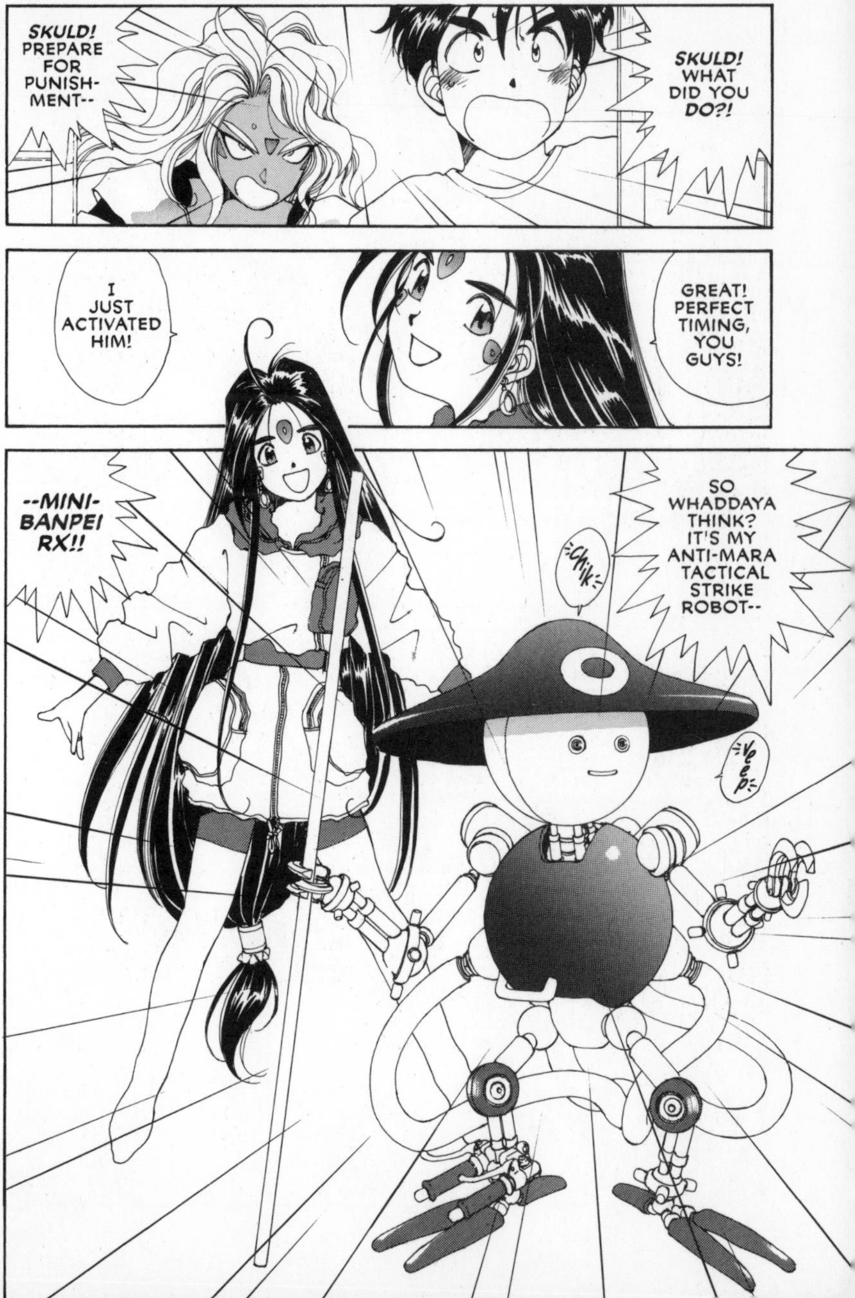
SKULD! WHAT DID YOU DO?!
SKULD! PREPARE FOR PUNISHMENT--
GREAT! PERFECT TIMING, YOU GUYS!
I JUST ACTIVATED HIM!
SO WHADDAYA THINK? IT'S MY ANTI-MARA TACTICAL STRIKE ROBOT--
Veep
Chik
--MINI-BANPEI RX!!

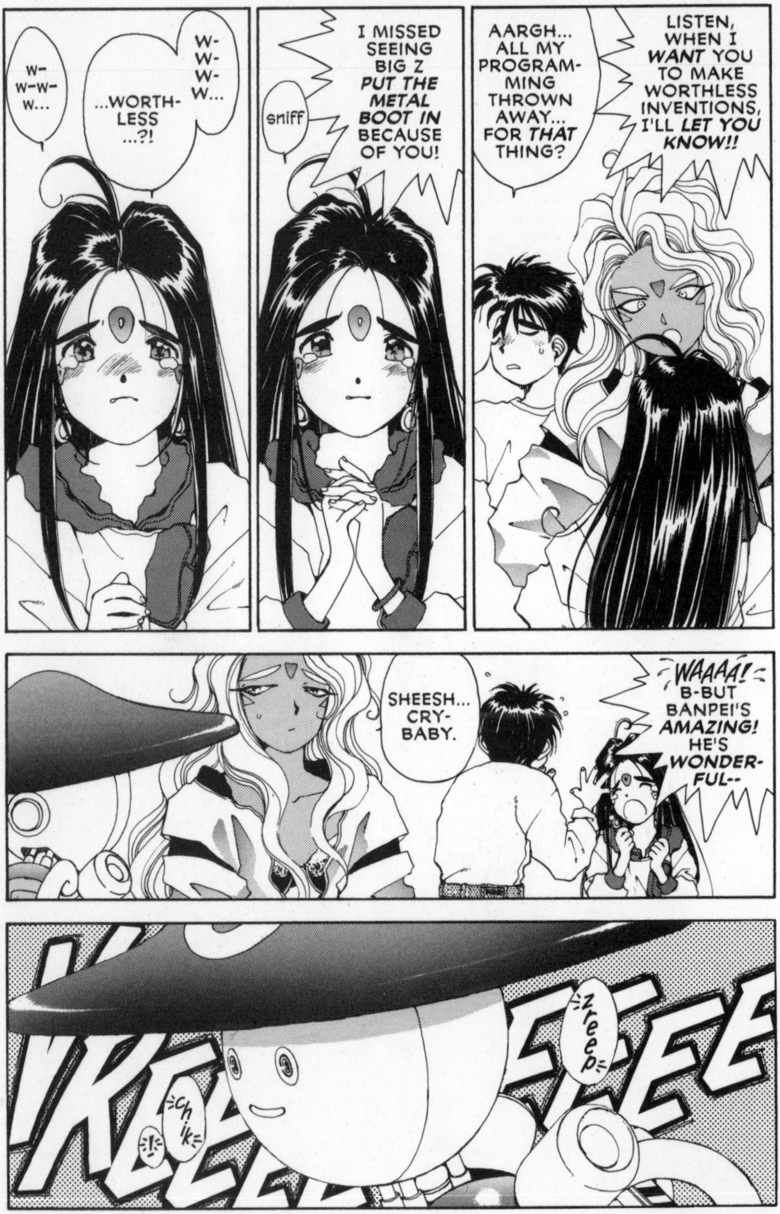
LISTEN, WHEN I *WANT* YOU TO MAKE WORTHLESS INVENTIONS, I'LL *LET YOU KNOW!!*
AARGH... ALL MY PROGRAM-MING THROWN AWAY... FOR *THAT* THING?
I MISSED SEEING BIG Z *PUT THE METAL BOOT IN* BECAUSE OF YOU!
sniff
W- W- W- W- W...
...WORTH-LESS ...?!
W- W-W-W- W...
WAAAA! B-BUT BANPEI'S *AMAZING!* HE'S *WONDER-FUL--*
SHEESH... CRY-BABY.
zreep
chik
!

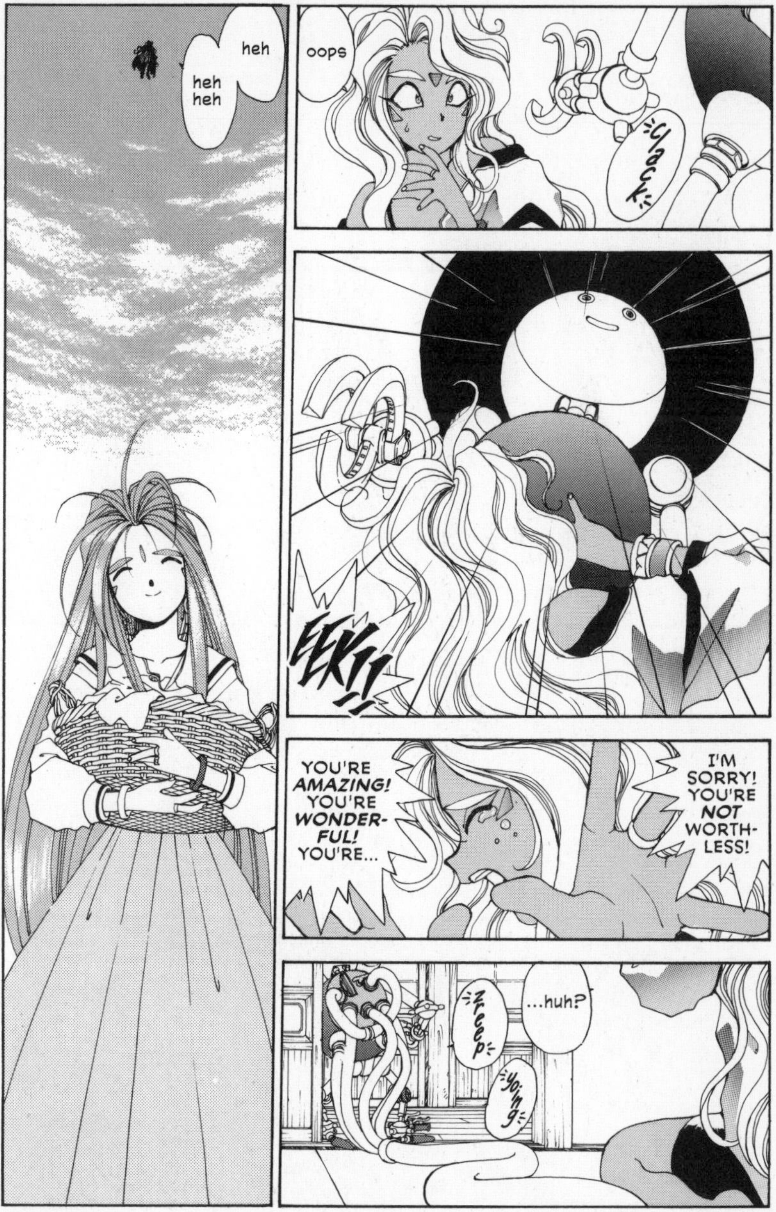
oops
clack
EEK!!
I'M SORRY! YOU'RE NOT WORTHLESS!
YOU'RE AMAZING! YOU'RE WONDERFUL! YOU'RE...
...huh?
zreep
yoing
heh
heh heh

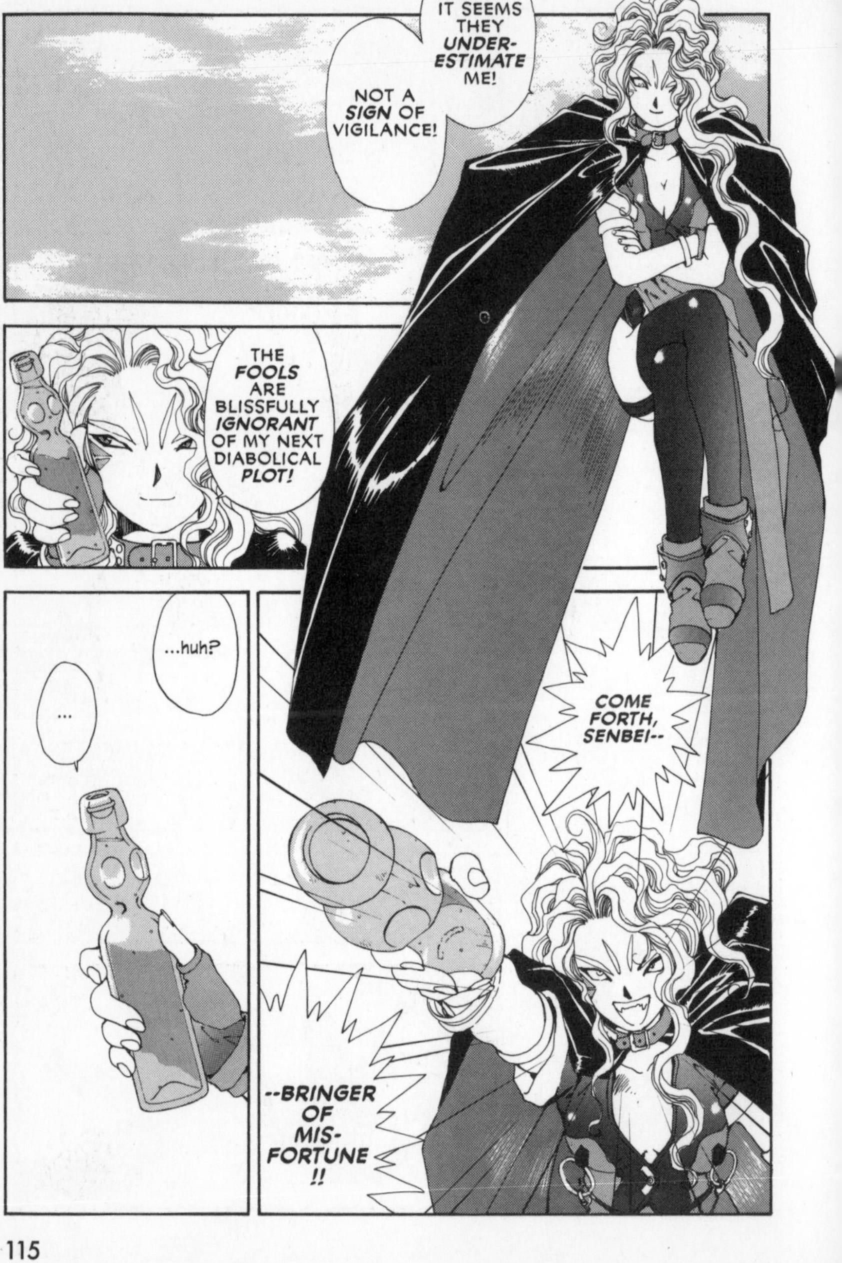
HMPH... IT SEEMS THEY UNDER-ESTIMATE ME!
NOT A SIGN OF VIGILANCE!
THE FOOLS ARE BLISSFULLY IGNORANT OF MY NEXT DIABOLICAL PLOT!
COME FORTH, SENBEI--
--BRINGER OF MIS-FORTUNE!!
...huh?
...

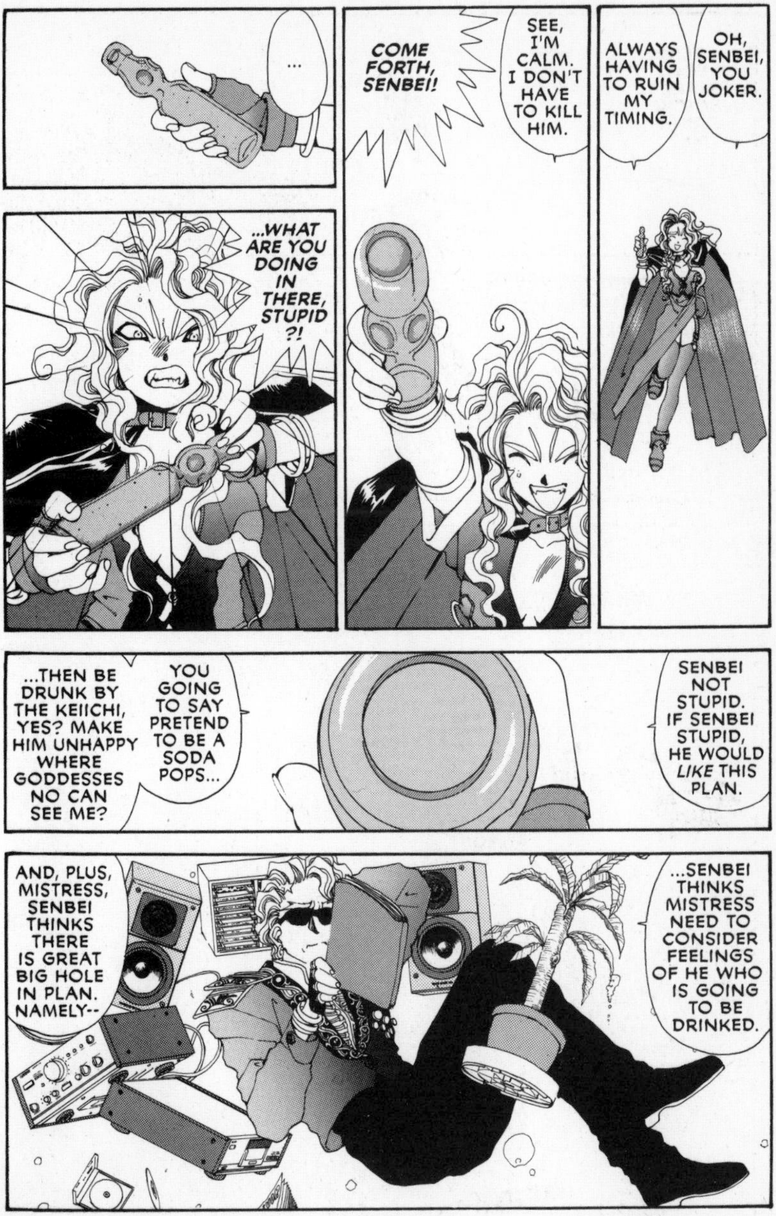

OH, SENBEI, YOU JOKER.
ALWAYS HAVING TO RUIN MY TIMING.
SEE, I'M CALM. I DON'T HAVE TO KILL HIM.
COME FORTH, SENBEI!
...
...WHAT ARE YOU DOING IN THERE, STUPID?!
SENBEI NOT STUPID. IF SENBEI STUPID, HE WOULD *LIKE* THIS PLAN.
YOU GOING TO SAY PRETEND TO BE A SODA POPS...
...THEN BE DRUNK BY THE KEIICHI, YES? MAKE HIM UNHAPPY WHERE GODDESSES NO CAN SEE ME?
...SENBEI THINKS MISTRESS NEED TO CONSIDER FEELINGS OF HE WHO IS GOING TO BE DRINKED.
AND, PLUS, MISTRESS, SENBEI THINKS THERE IS GREAT BIG HOLE IN PLAN. NAMELY--

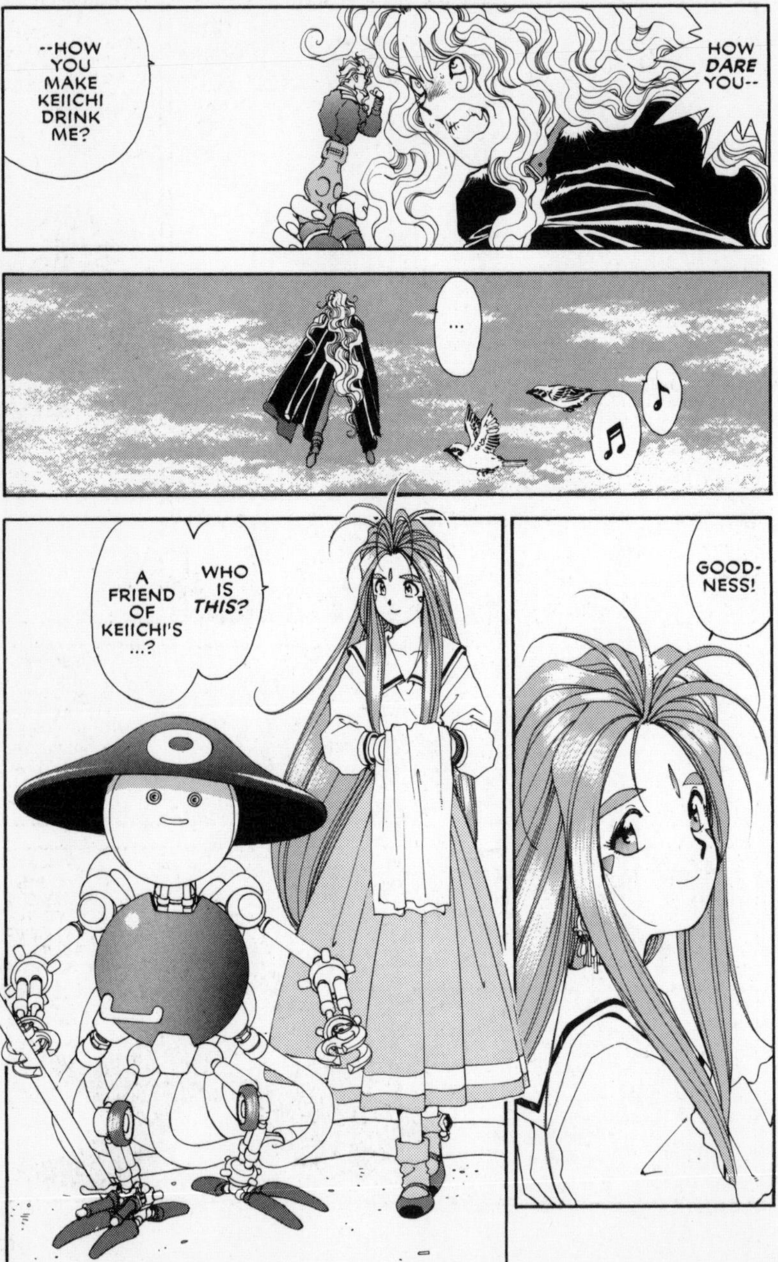
HOW *DARE* YOU--
--HOW YOU MAKE KEIICHI DRINK ME?
...
GOOD-NESS!
WHO IS *THIS?*
A FRIEND OF KEIICHI'S ...?

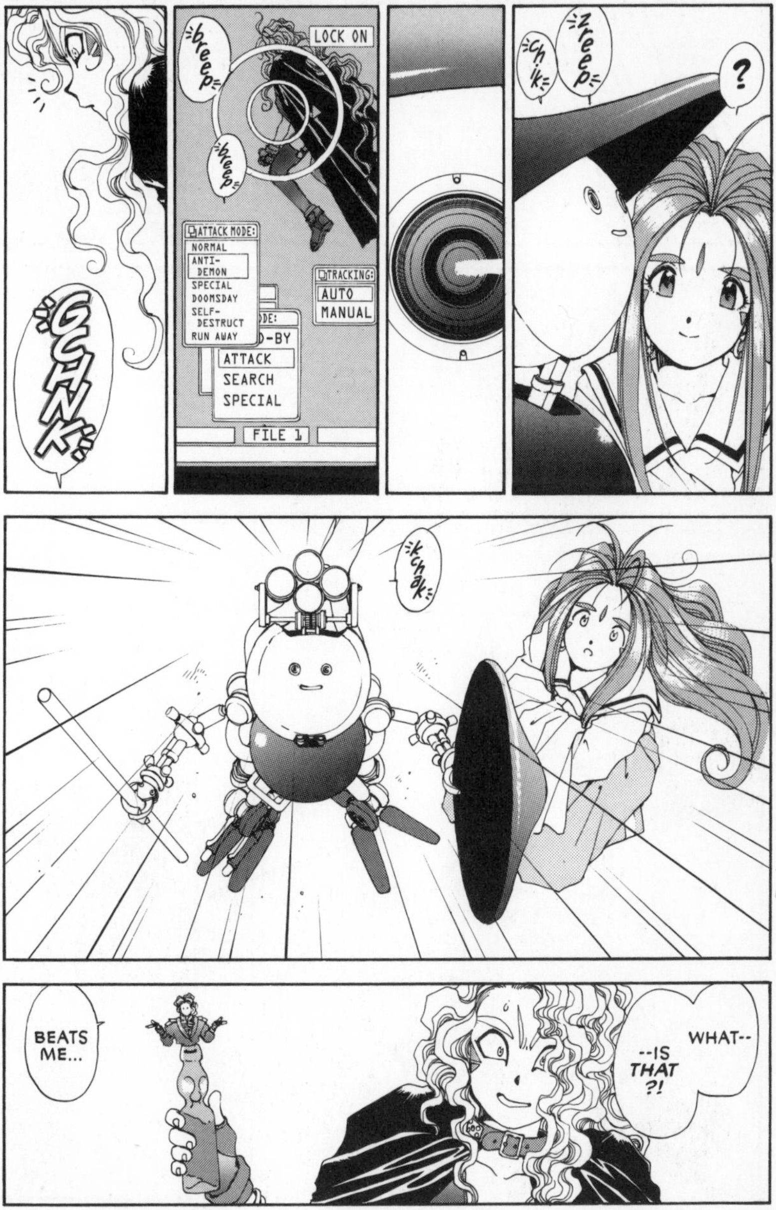
zreep
chik
?
LOCK ON
breep
breep
ATTACK MODE:
NORMAL
ANTI-DEMON
SPECIAL
DOOMSDAY
SELF-DESTRUCT
RUN AWAY
TRACKING:
AUTO
MANUAL
ATTACK
SEARCH
SPECIAL
FILE 1
GCHNK
kchak
WHAT-- --IS THAT?!
BEATS ME...

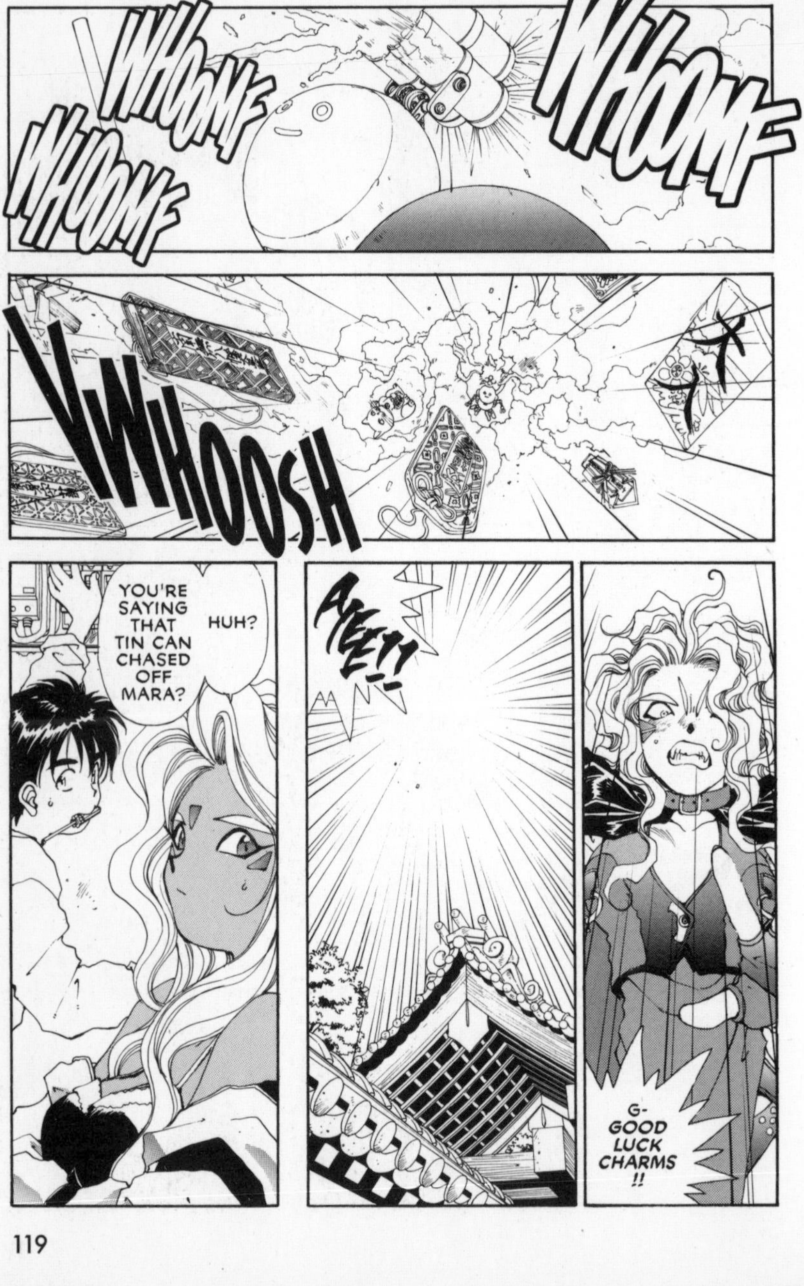
WHOOMF
WHOOMF
WHOOMF
VWHOOSH
G-GOOD LUCK CHARMS!!
AIEE!!
HUH?
YOU'RE SAYING THAT TIN CAN CHASED OFF MARA?

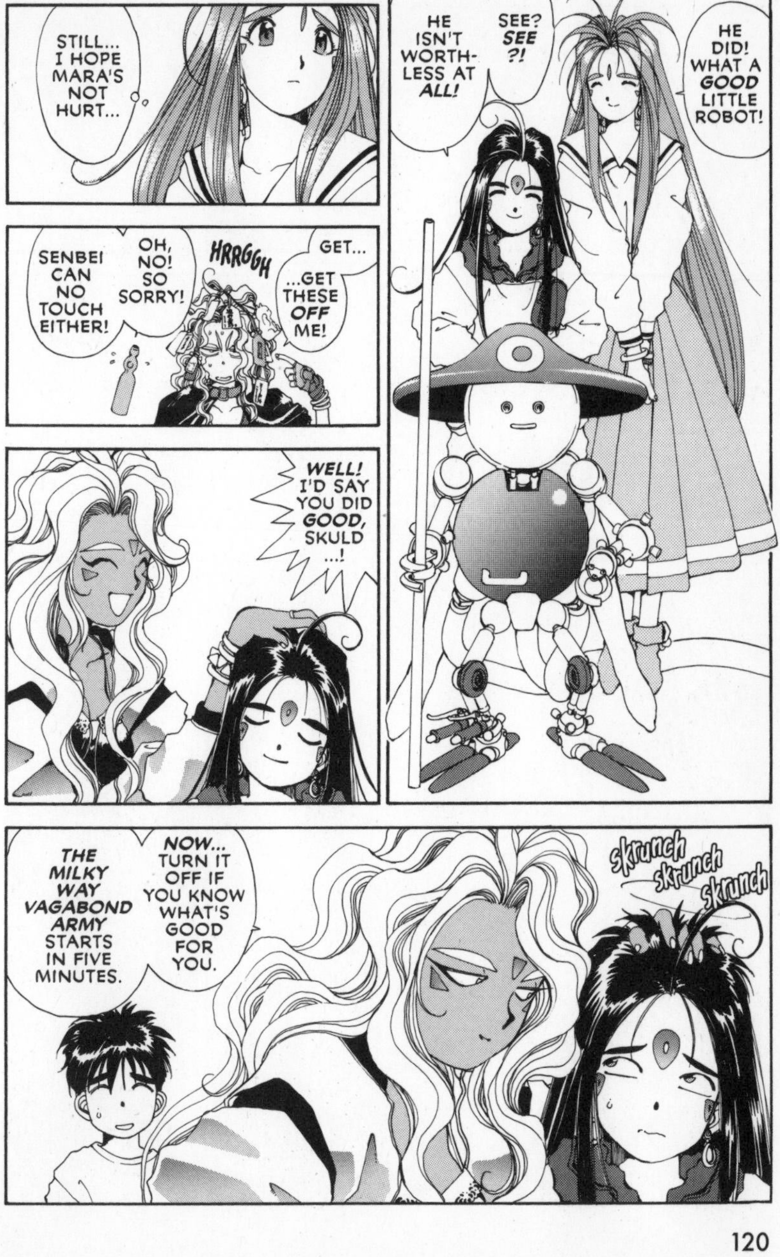
HE DID! WHAT A GOOD LITTLE ROBOT!
SEE? SEE?!
HE ISN'T WORTH-LESS AT ALL!
STILL... I HOPE MARA'S NOT HURT...
GET...
...GET THESE OFF ME!
HRRGGH
OH, NO! SO SORRY!
SENBEI CAN NO TOUCH EITHER!
WELL! I'D SAY YOU DID GOOD, SKULD ...!
skrunch skrunch skrunch
NOW... TURN IT OFF IF YOU KNOW WHAT'S GOOD FOR YOU.
THE MILKY WAY VAGABOND ARMY STARTS IN FIVE MINUTES.

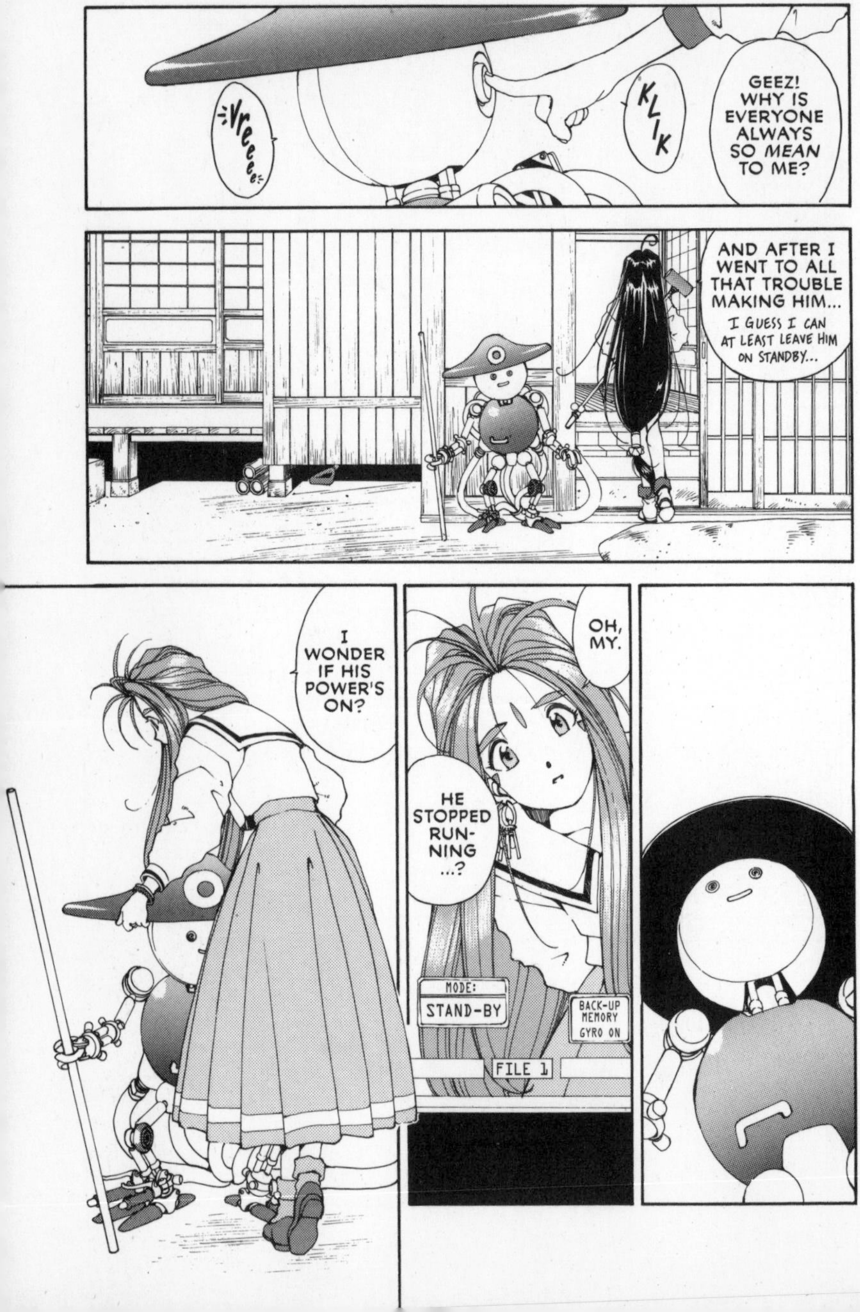
GEEZ! WHY IS EVERYONE ALWAYS SO *MEAN* TO ME?
KLIK
Vreeeee
AND AFTER I WENT TO ALL THAT TROUBLE MAKING HIM...
I GUESS I CAN AT LEAST LEAVE HIM ON STANDBY...
OH, MY.
HE STOPPED RUN-NING ...?
MODE: STAND-BY
BACK-UP MEMORY GYRO ON
FILE 1
I WONDER IF HIS POWER'S ON?

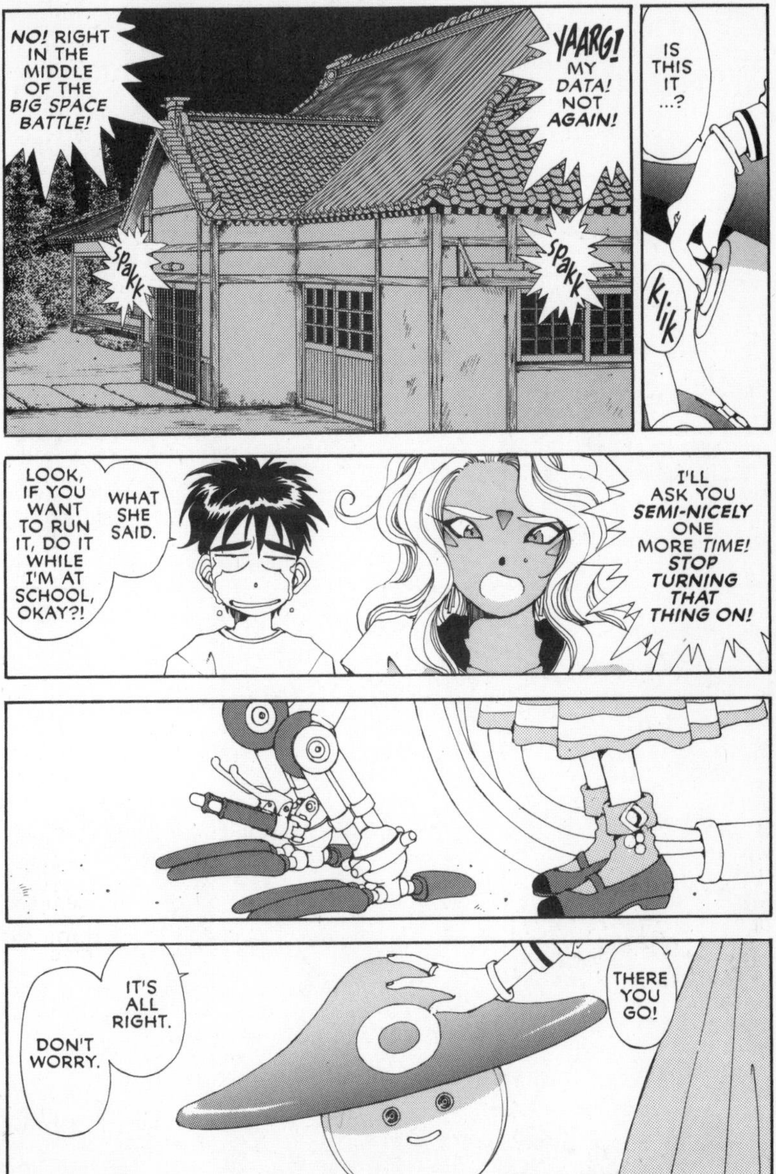
IS THIS IT ...?
klik
YAARG! MY DATA! NOT AGAIN!
spakk
NO! RIGHT IN THE MIDDLE OF THE BIG SPACE BATTLE!
spakk
I'LL ASK YOU SEMI-NICELY ONE MORE TIME! STOP TURNING THAT THING ON!
WHAT SHE SAID.
LOOK, IF YOU WANT TO RUN IT, DO IT WHILE I'M AT SCHOOL, OKAY?!
THERE YOU GO!
IT'S ALL RIGHT.
DON'T WORRY.

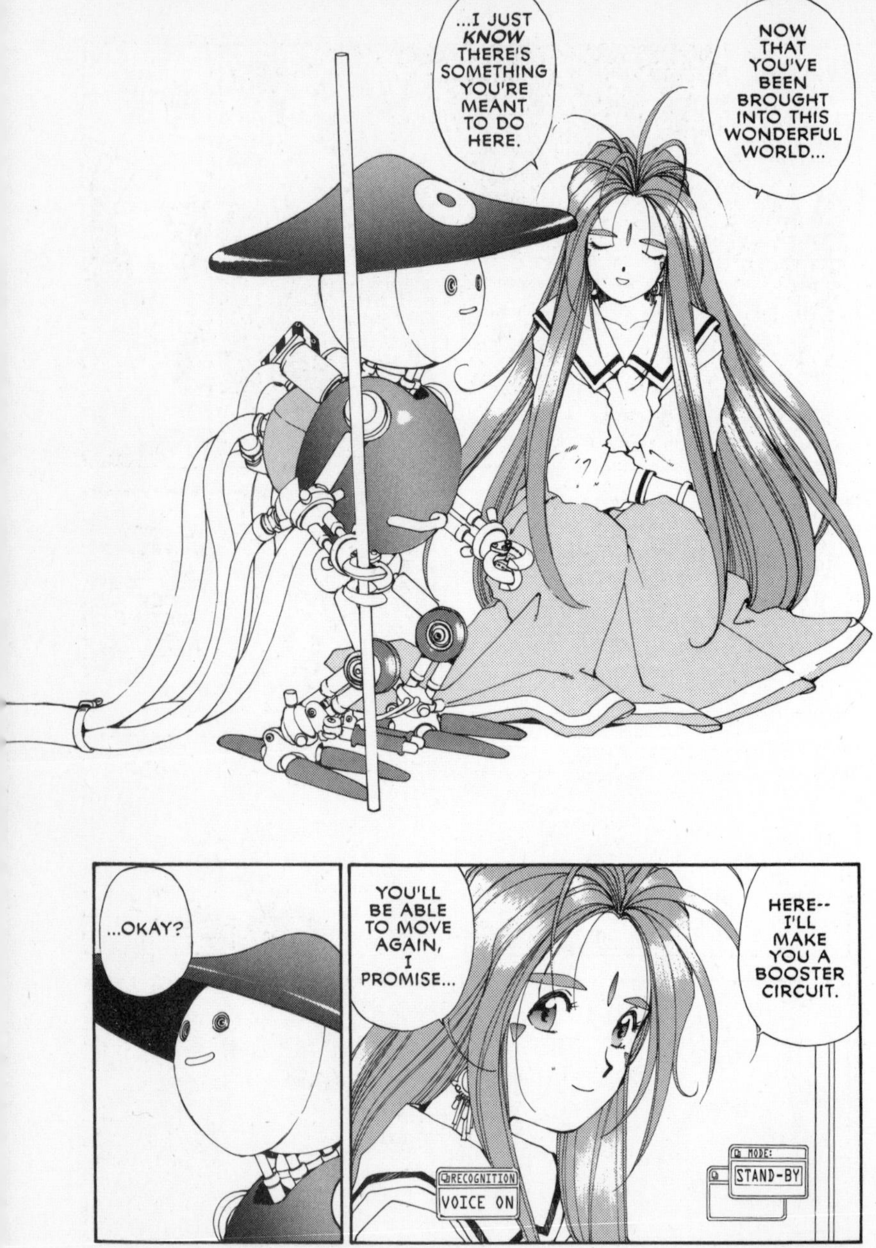
NOW THAT YOU'VE BEEN BROUGHT INTO THIS WONDERFUL WORLD...
...I JUST *KNOW* THERE'S SOMETHING YOU'RE MEANT TO DO HERE.
HERE-- I'LL MAKE YOU A BOOSTER CIRCUIT.
YOU'LL BE ABLE TO MOVE AGAIN, I PROMISE...
MODE:
STAND-BY
RECOGNITION
VOICE ON
...OKAY?

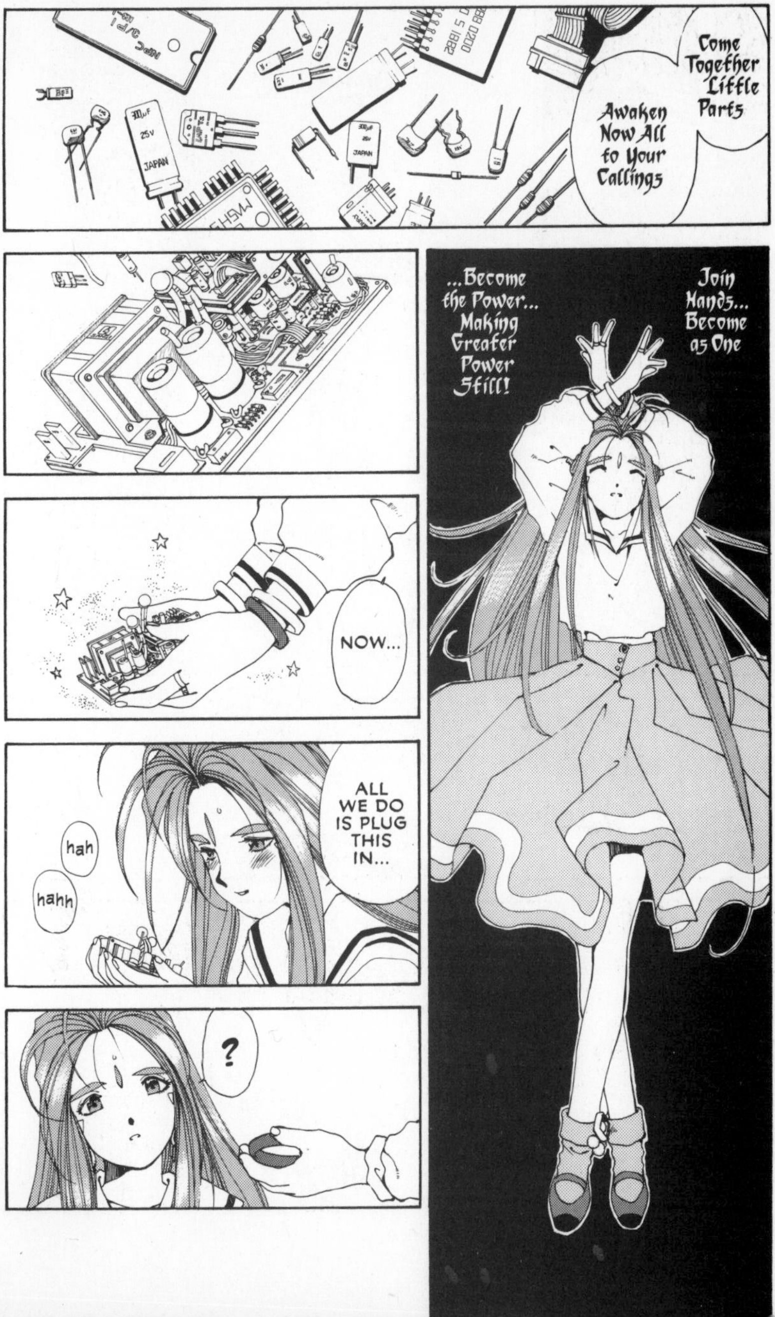
Come Together Little Parts
Awaken Now All to Your Callings
Join Hands... Become as One
...Become the Power... Making Greater Power Still!
NOW...
ALL WE DO IS PLUG THIS IN...
hah
hahh
?

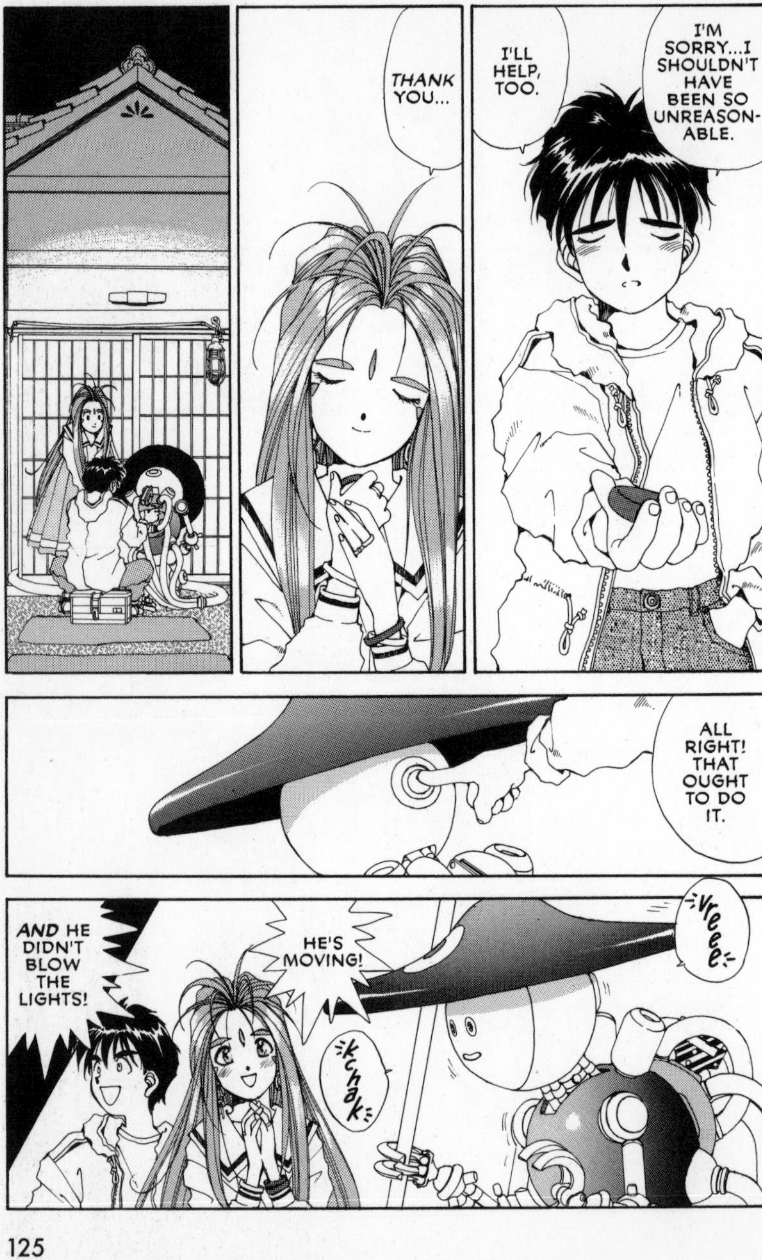

I'M SORRY...I SHOULDN'T HAVE BEEN SO UNREASON-ABLE.
I'LL HELP, TOO.
THANK YOU...
ALL RIGHT! THAT OUGHT TO DO IT.
Vreee
HE'S MOVING!
AND HE DIDN'T BLOW THE LIGHTS!
Kchak

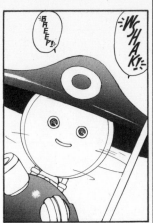

:BREEP!:
:WSHAK!:

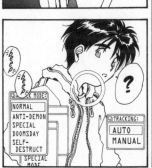

:beep: :beep: :beep:

?

ATTACK MODE:
NORMAL
ANTI-DEMON
SPECIAL
DOOMSDAY
SELF-
DESTRUCT
SPECIAL
MODE

TRACKING:
AUTO
MANUAL

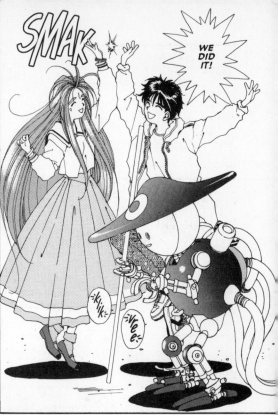

SMAK

WE
DID
IT!

:KLIK:
:VLEE:

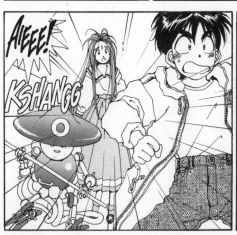

AIEEE!

KSHANGG

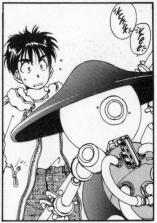

:KLIK: :VLEE:

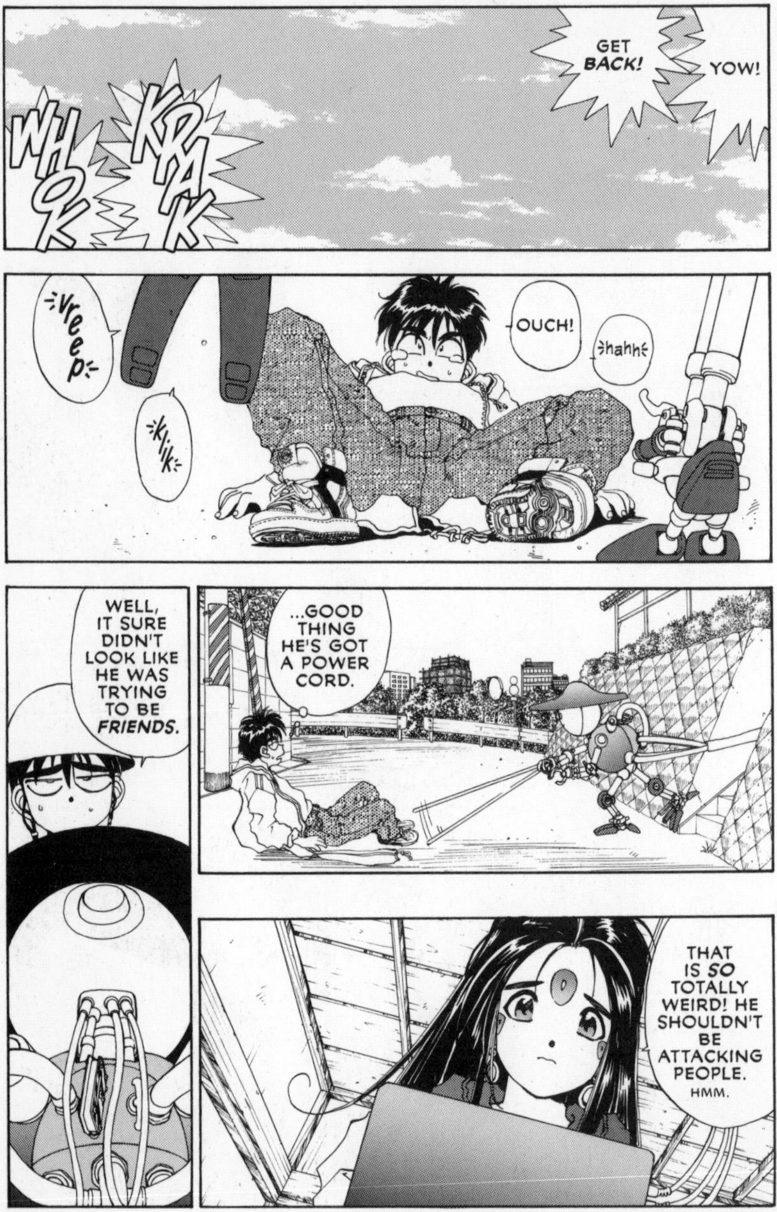
YOW!
GET BACK!
KRAK
WHOK
hahh
OUCH!
vreep
klik
...GOOD THING HE'S GOT A POWER CORD.
THAT IS *SO* TOTALLY WEIRD! HE SHOULDN'T BE ATTACKING PEOPLE.
HMM.
WELL, IT SURE DIDN'T LOOK LIKE HE WAS TRYING TO BE *FRIENDS*.

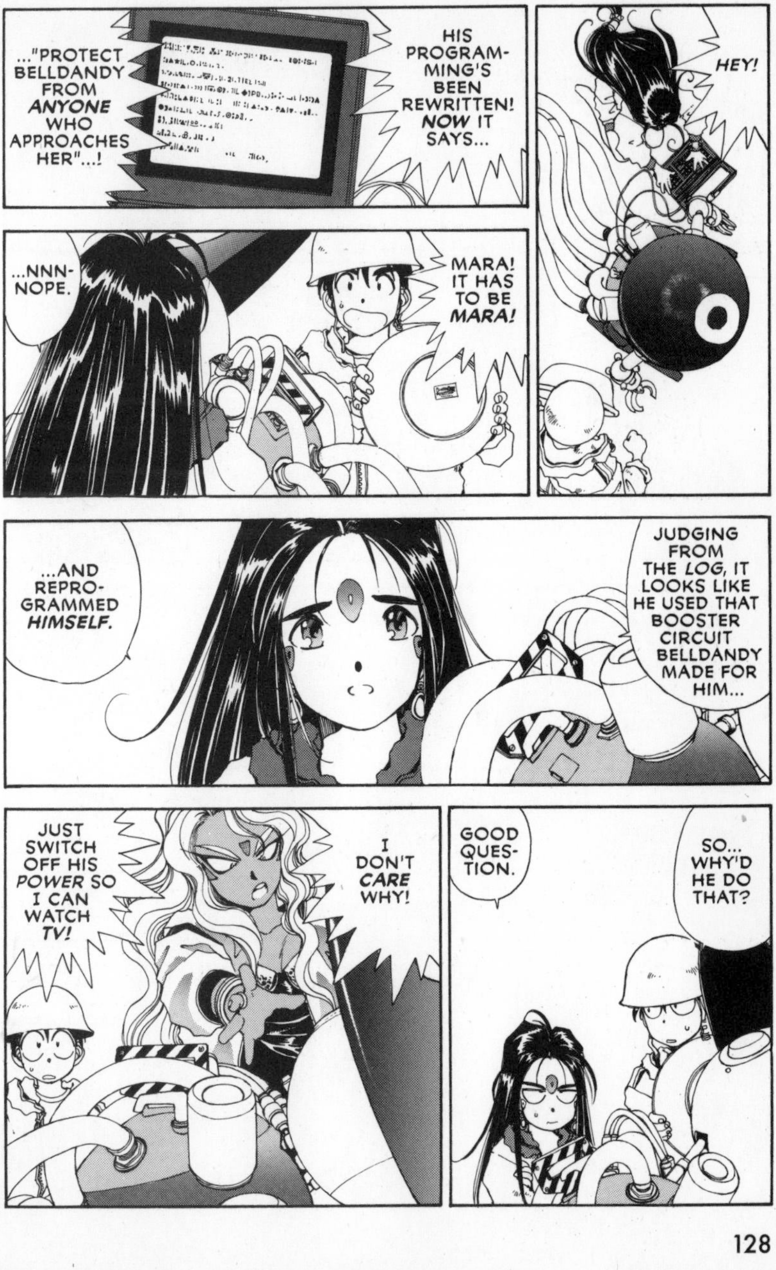
HEY!
HIS PROGRAMMING'S BEEN REWRITTEN! *NOW* IT SAYS...
..."PROTECT BELLDANDY FROM *ANYONE* WHO APPROACHES HER"...!
MARA! IT HAS TO BE *MARA!*
...NNN-NOPE.
JUDGING FROM THE *LOG*, IT LOOKS LIKE HE USED THAT BOOSTER CIRCUIT BELLDANDY MADE FOR HIM...
...AND REPROGRAMMED *HIMSELF*.
SO... WHY'D HE DO THAT?
GOOD QUESTION.
I DON'T *CARE* WHY!
JUST SWITCH OFF HIS *POWER* SO I CAN WATCH *TV!*

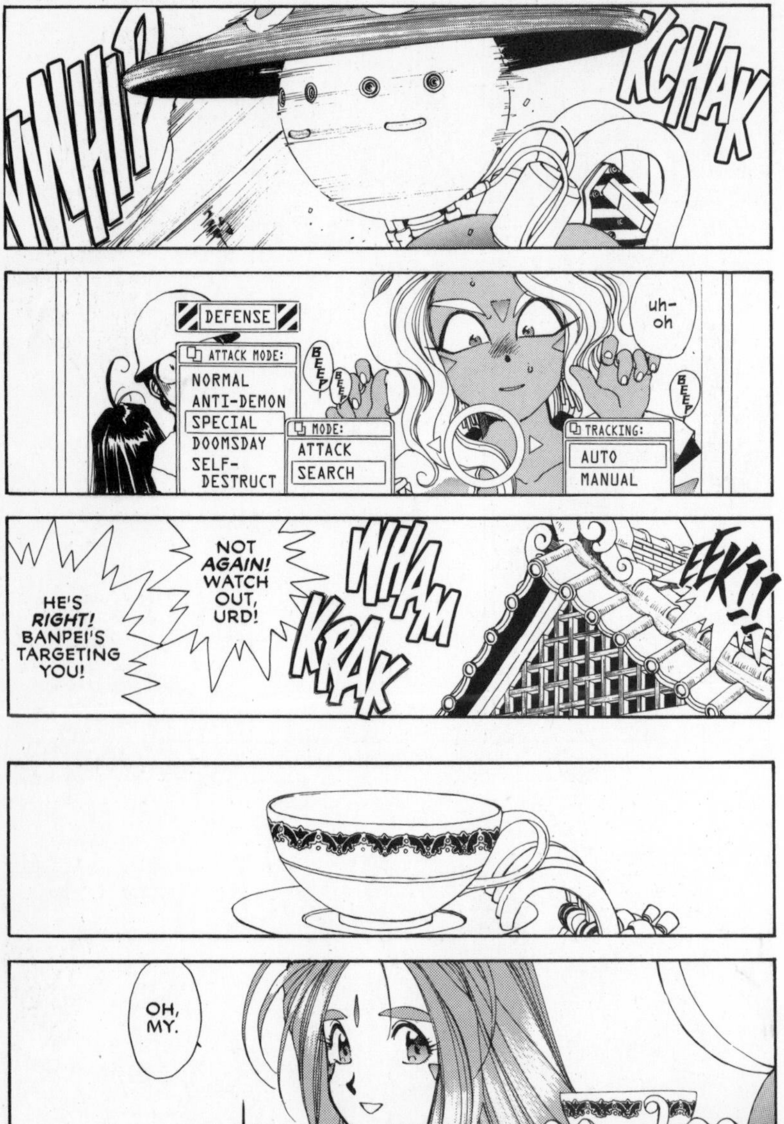
KCHAK
VWHIP
uh-oh
BEEP
TRACKING:
AUTO
MANUAL
MODE:
ATTACK
SEARCH
BEEP
BEEP
ATTACK MODE:
NORMAL
ANTI-DEMON
SPECIAL
DOOMSDAY
SELF-DESTRUCT
DEFENSE
EEK!!!
WHAM
KRAK
NOT *AGAIN!* WATCH OUT, URD!
HE'S *RIGHT!* BANPEI'S TARGETING YOU!
OH, MY.

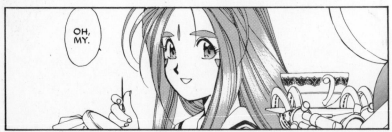

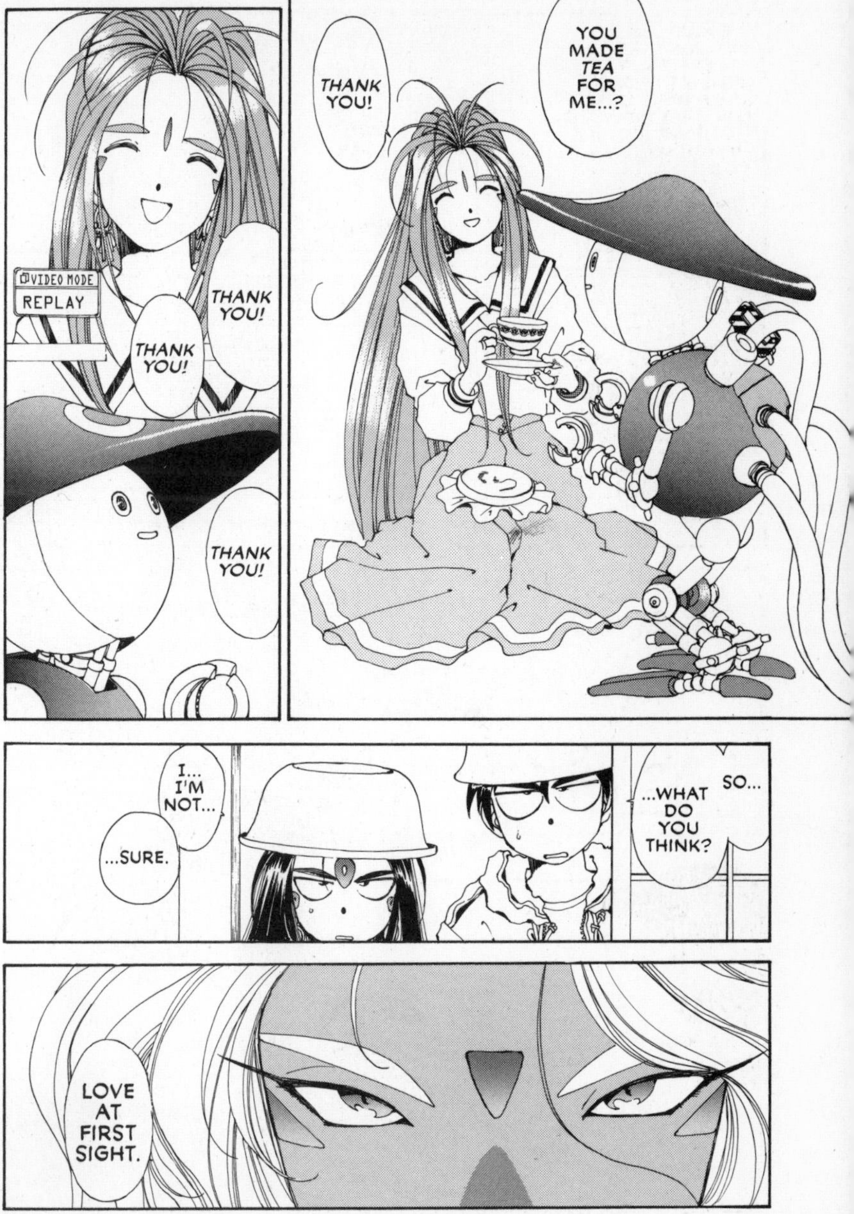
YOU MADE TEA FOR ME...?
THANK YOU!
VIDEO MODE
REPLAY
THANK YOU!
THANK YOU!
THANK YOU!
SO...
...WHAT DO YOU THINK?
I... I'M NOT...
...SURE.
LOVE AT FIRST SIGHT.

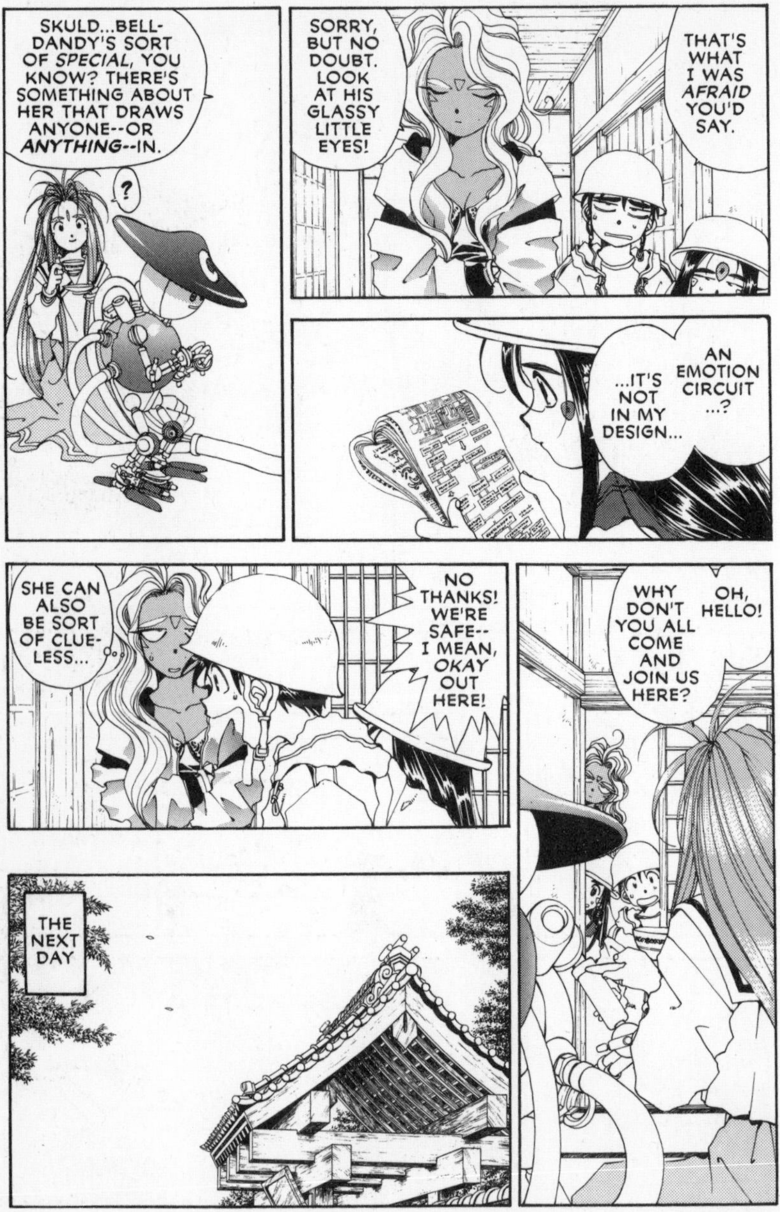
THAT'S WHAT I WAS *AFRAID* YOU'D SAY.
SORRY, BUT NO DOUBT. LOOK AT HIS GLASSY LITTLE EYES!
AN EMOTION CIRCUIT ...?
...IT'S NOT IN MY DESIGN...
SKULD...BELL-DANDY'S SORT OF *SPECIAL*, YOU KNOW? THERE'S SOMETHING ABOUT HER THAT DRAWS ANYONE--OR ***ANYTHING***--IN.
?
OH, HELLO!
WHY DON'T YOU ALL COME AND JOIN US HERE?
NO THANKS! WE'RE SAFE-- I MEAN, *OKAY* OUT HERE!
SHE CAN ALSO BE SORT OF CLUE-LESS...
THE NEXT DAY

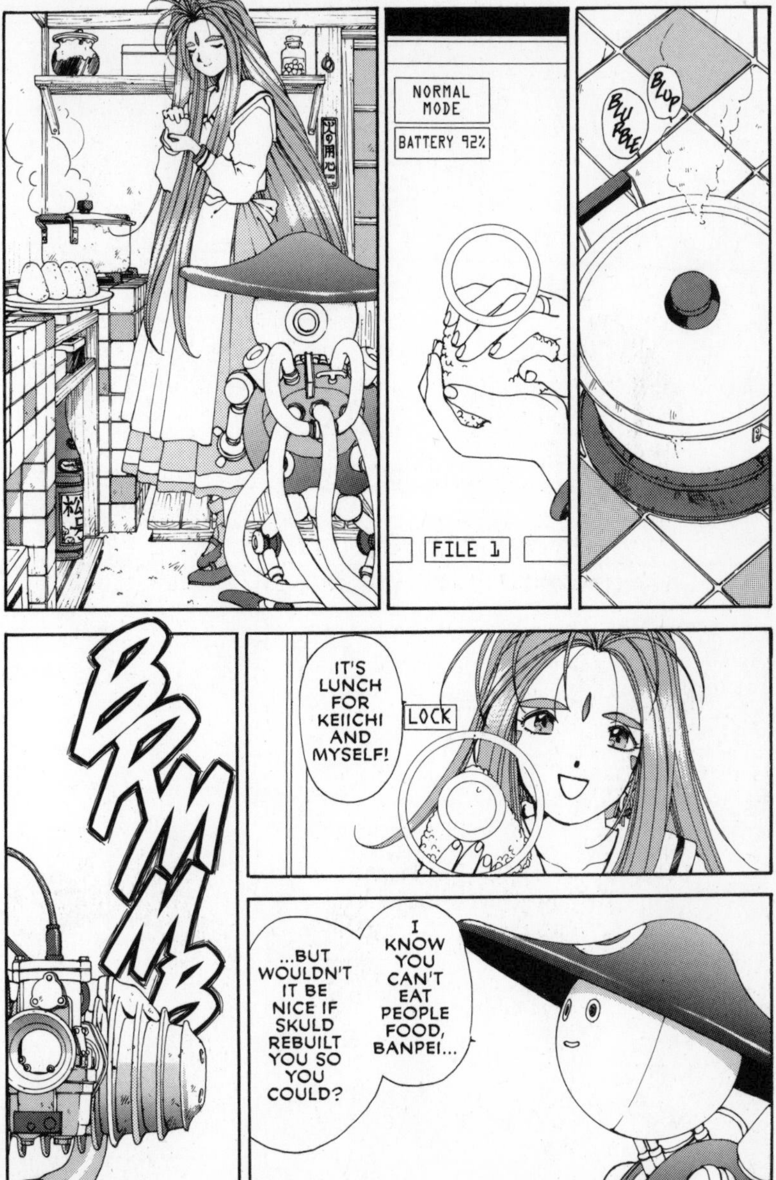

BLUP
BLURBLE
NORMAL MODE
BATTERY 92%
FILE 1
IT'S LUNCH FOR KEIICHI AND MYSELF!
LOCK
I KNOW YOU CAN'T EAT PEOPLE FOOD, BANPEI...
...BUT WOULDN'T IT BE NICE IF SKULD REBUILT YOU SO YOU COULD?
BRMMB

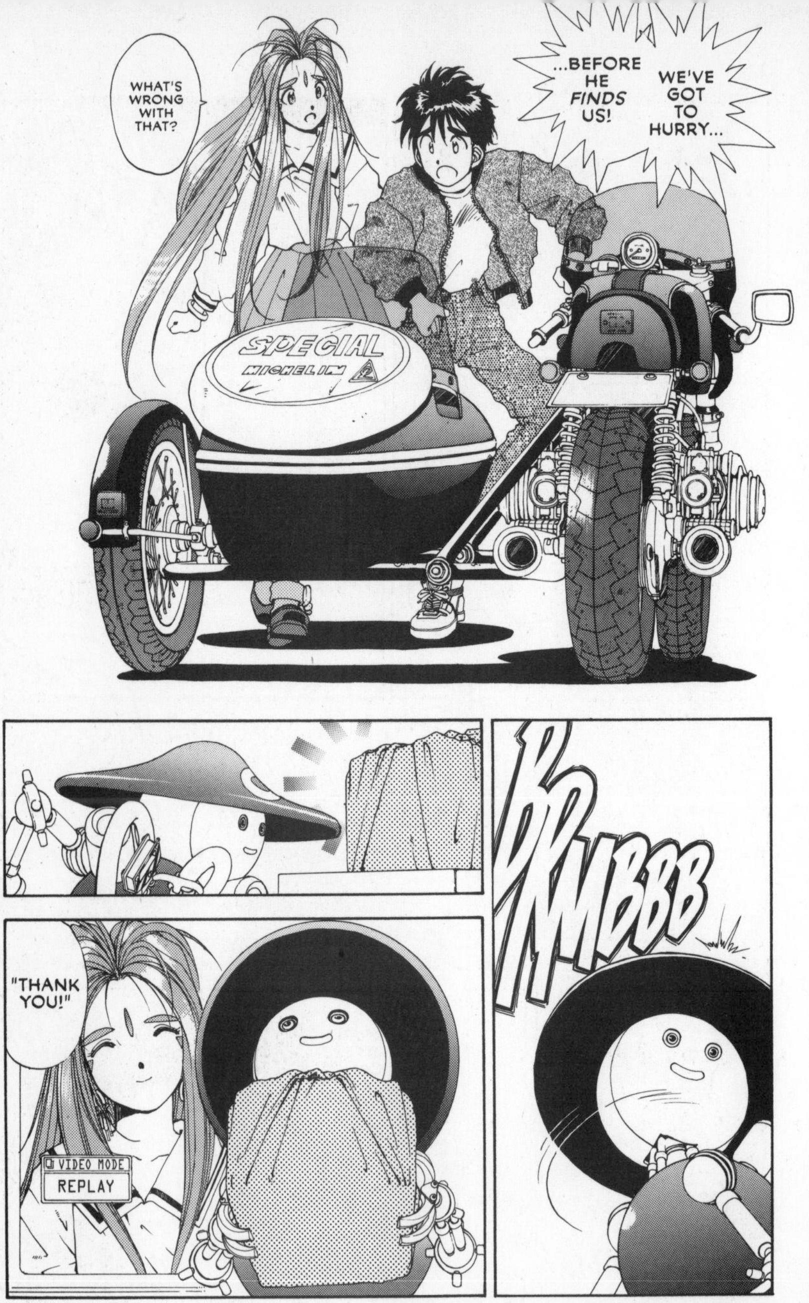
WE'VE GOT TO HURRY...
...BEFORE HE FINDS US!
WHAT'S WRONG WITH THAT?
BRMBBB
VIDEO MODE
REPLAY
"THANK YOU!"

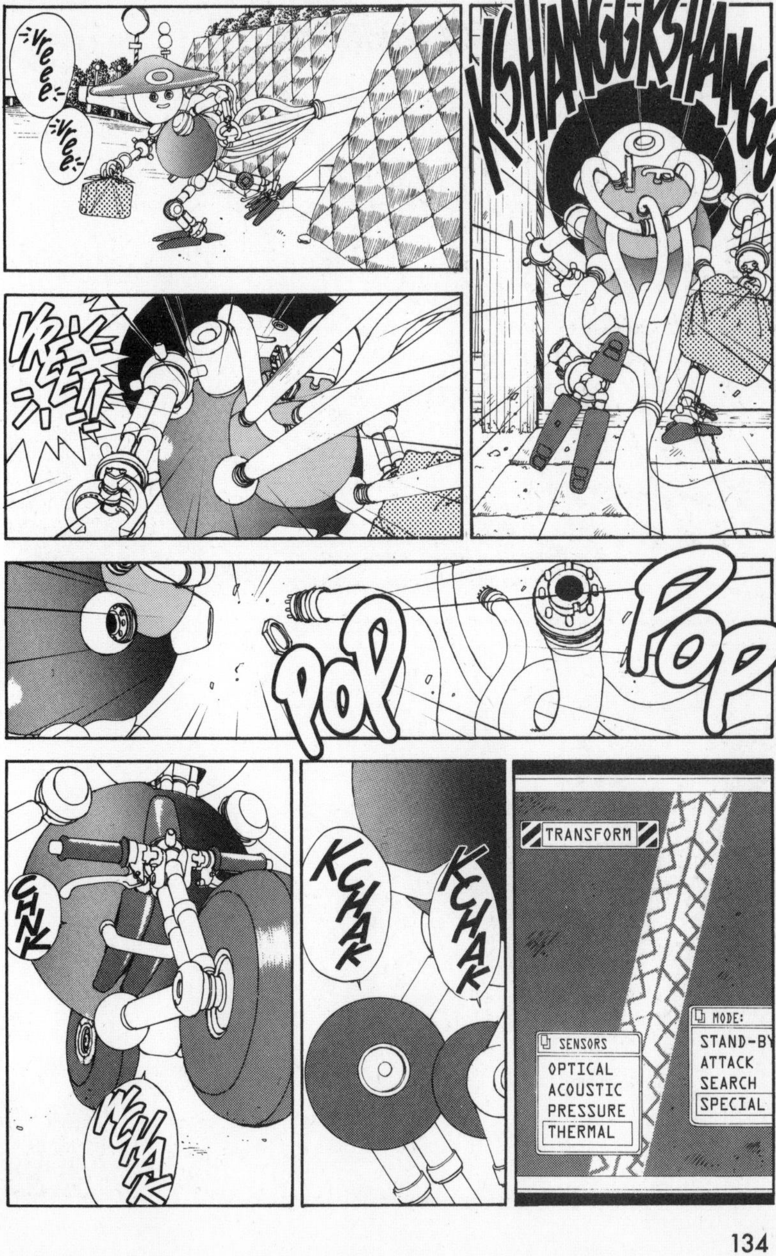
KSHANGGKSHANGG
vreee
vree
VREEE!!
POP
POP
TRANSFORM
SENSORS
OPTICAL
ACOUSTIC
PRESSURE
THERMAL
MODE:
STAND-BY
ATTACK
SEARCH
SPECIAL
KCHAK
KCHAK
CHNK
WCHAK

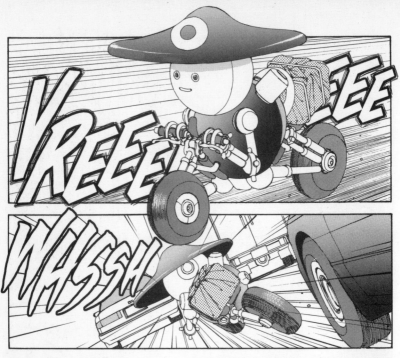

VREEEEEEE
WASSH
NEKOMI TECH
??
BANPEI IS IN LOVE WITH ME?
THAT'S RIGHT.
THAT'S WHY I HAVEN'T BEEN ABLE TO GET NEAR YOU.

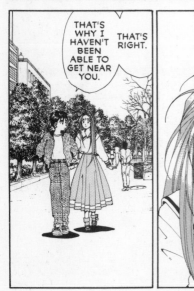

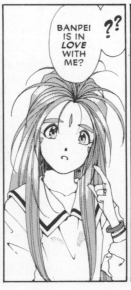

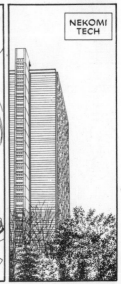

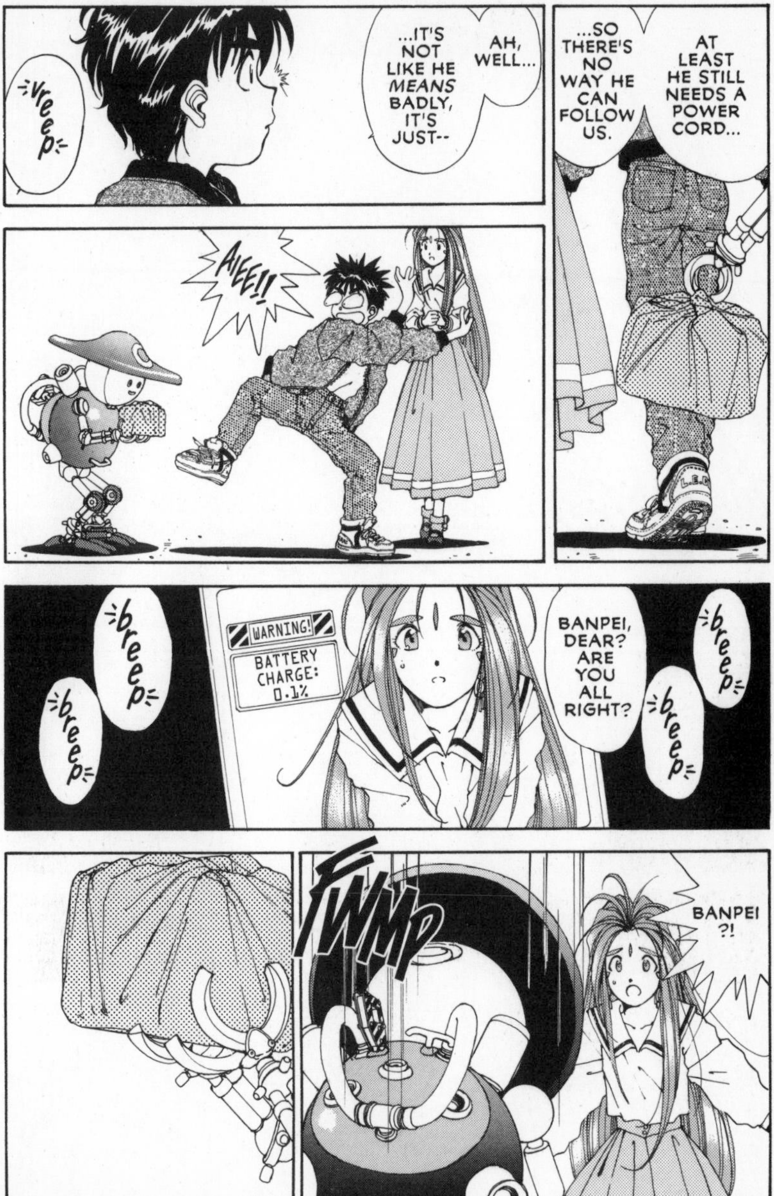
AT LEAST HE STILL NEEDS A POWER CORD...
...SO THERE'S NO WAY HE CAN FOLLOW US.
AH, WELL...
...IT'S NOT LIKE HE *MEANS* BADLY, IT'S JUST--
vreep
AIEE!!
breep
breep
BANPEI, DEAR? ARE YOU ALL RIGHT?
WARNING!
BATTERY CHARGE: 0.1%
breep
breep
BANPEI ?!
FWMP

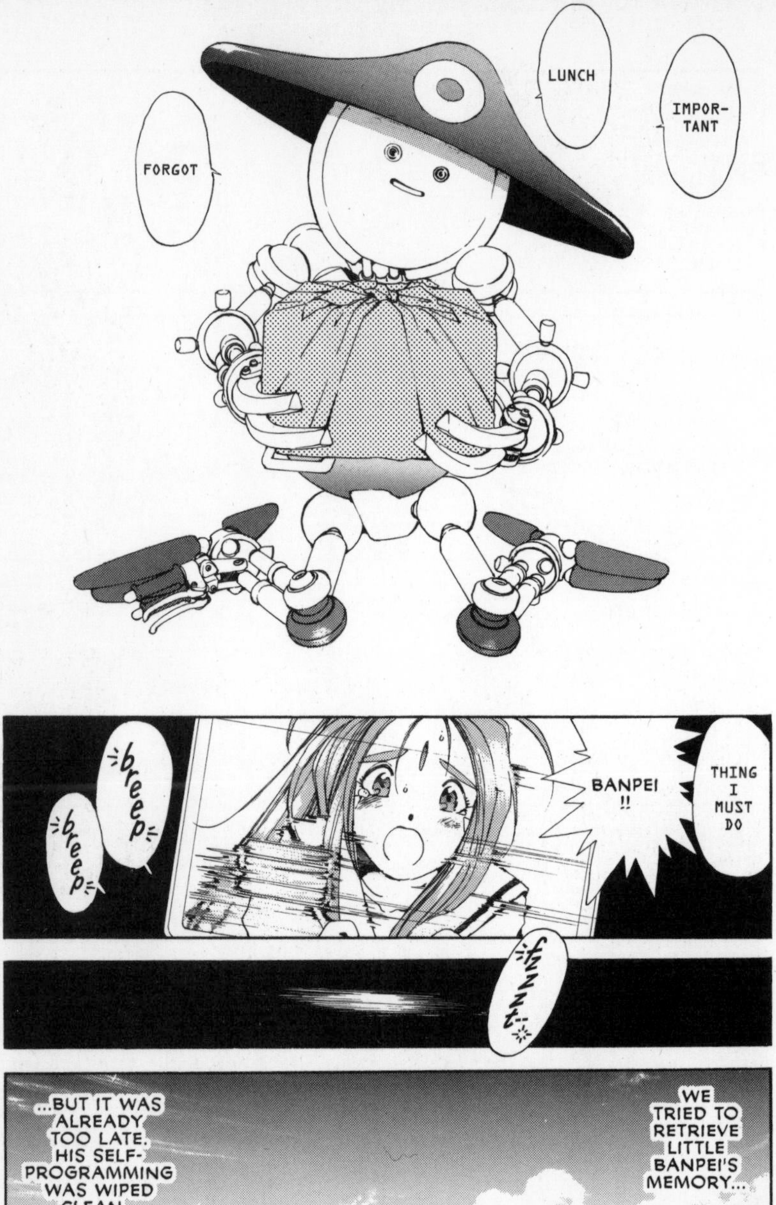
IMPOR-TANT
LUNCH
FORGOT
THING I MUST DO
BANPEI!!
breep
breep
fnzzt
WE TRIED TO RETRIEVE LITTLE BANPEI'S MEMORY...
...BUT IT WAS ALREADY TOO LATE. HIS SELF-PROGRAMMING WAS WIPED CLEAN...

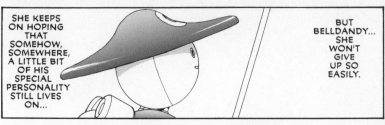

BUT BELLDANDY... SHE WON'T GIVE UP SO EASILY.
SHE KEEPS ON HOPING THAT SOMEHOW, SOMEWHERE, A LITTLE BIT OF HIS SPECIAL PERSONALITY STILL LIVES ON...
SEE YOU LATER, BANPEI!
Vreeee
COME BACK SOON.

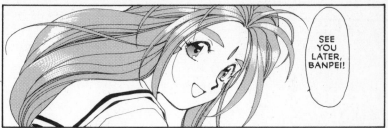

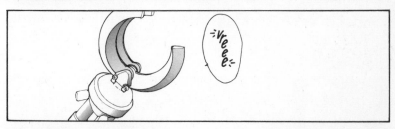

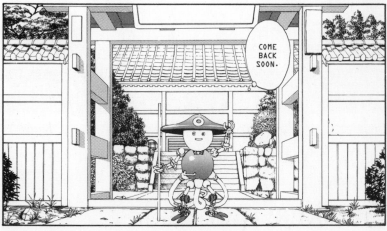

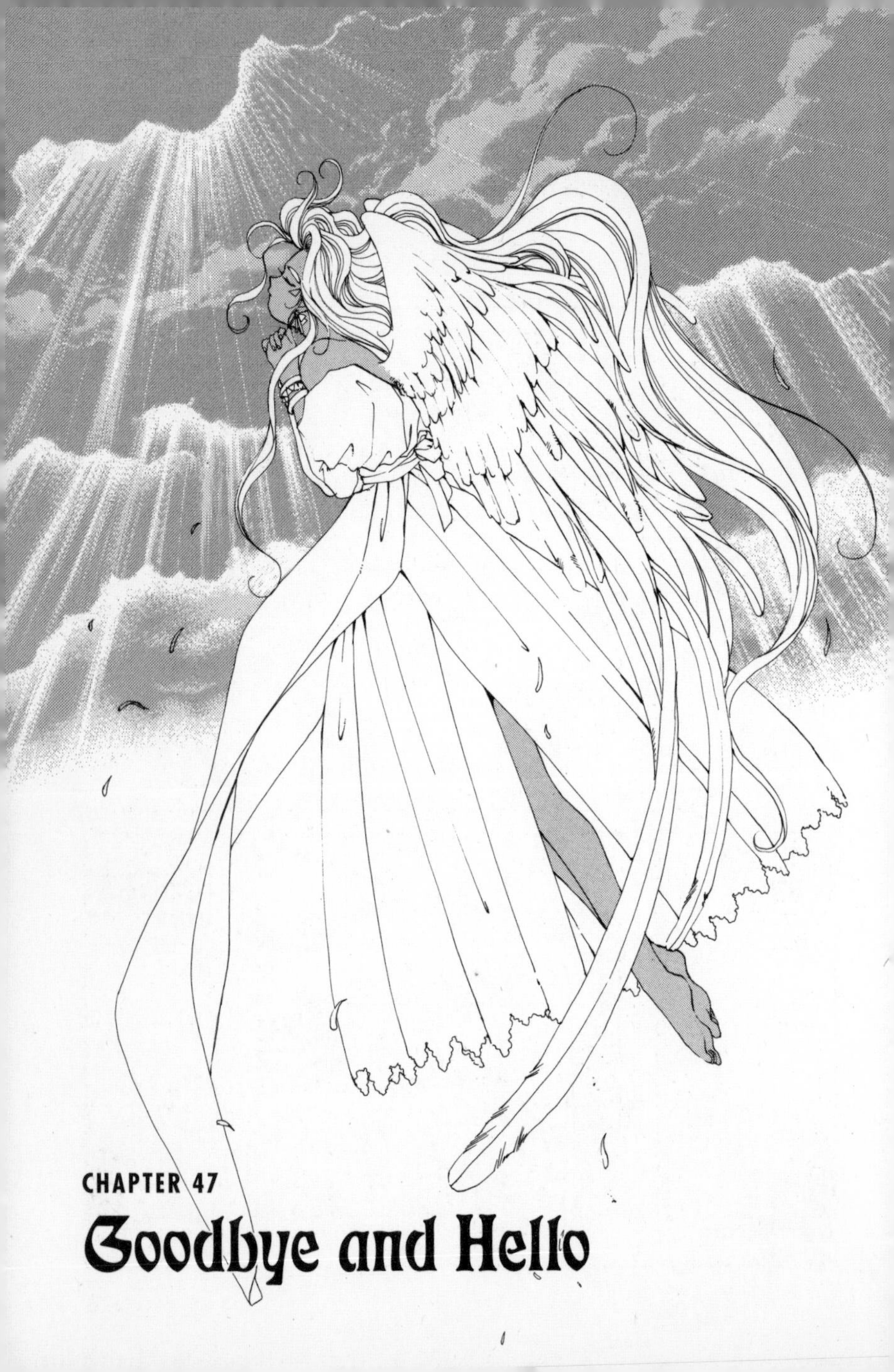

CHAPTER 47

Goodbye and Hello

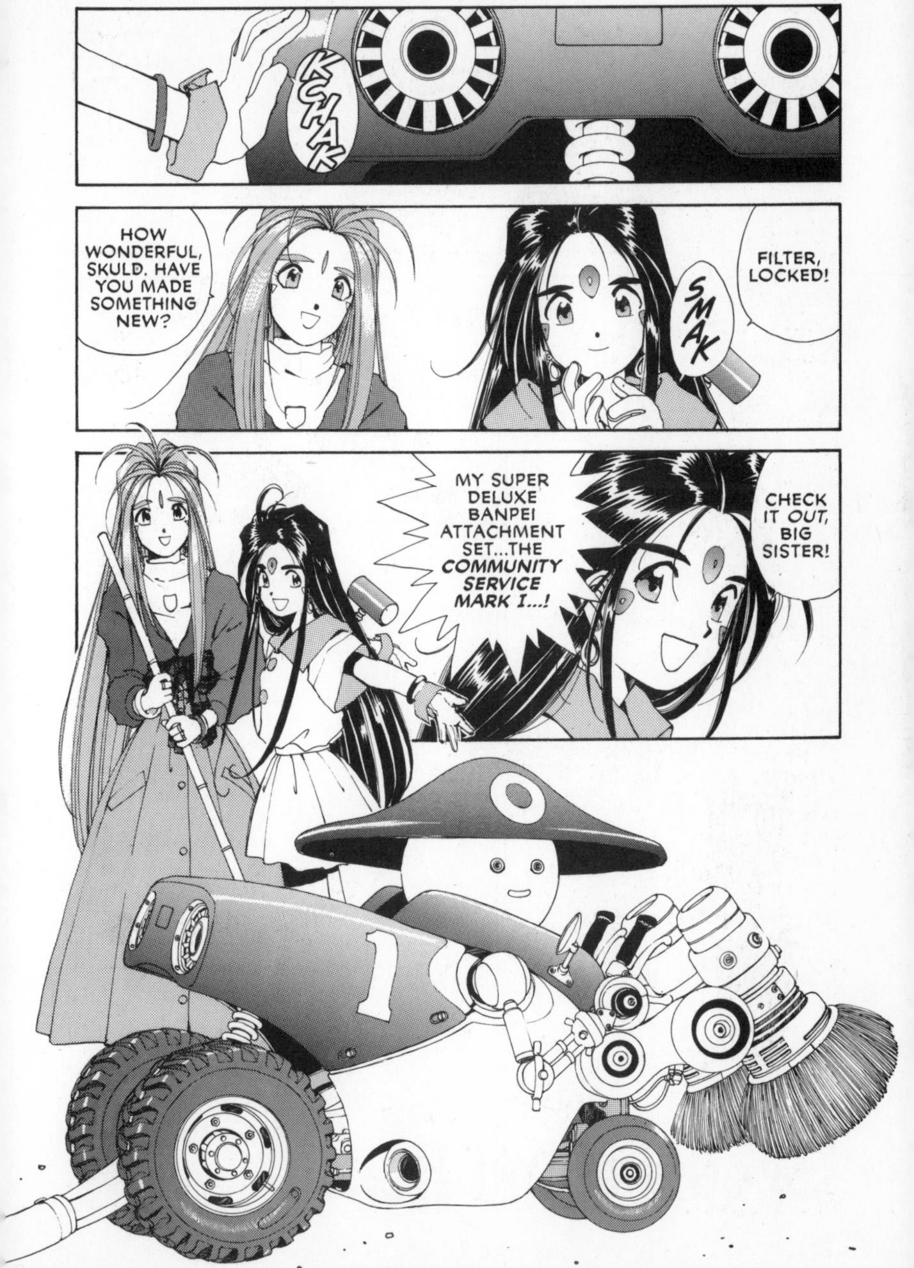
KCHAK
FILTER, LOCKED!
SMAK
HOW WONDERFUL, SKULD. HAVE YOU MADE SOMETHING NEW?
CHECK IT OUT, BIG SISTER!
MY SUPER DELUXE BANPEI ATTACHMENT SET...THE COMMUNITY SERVICE MARK I...!

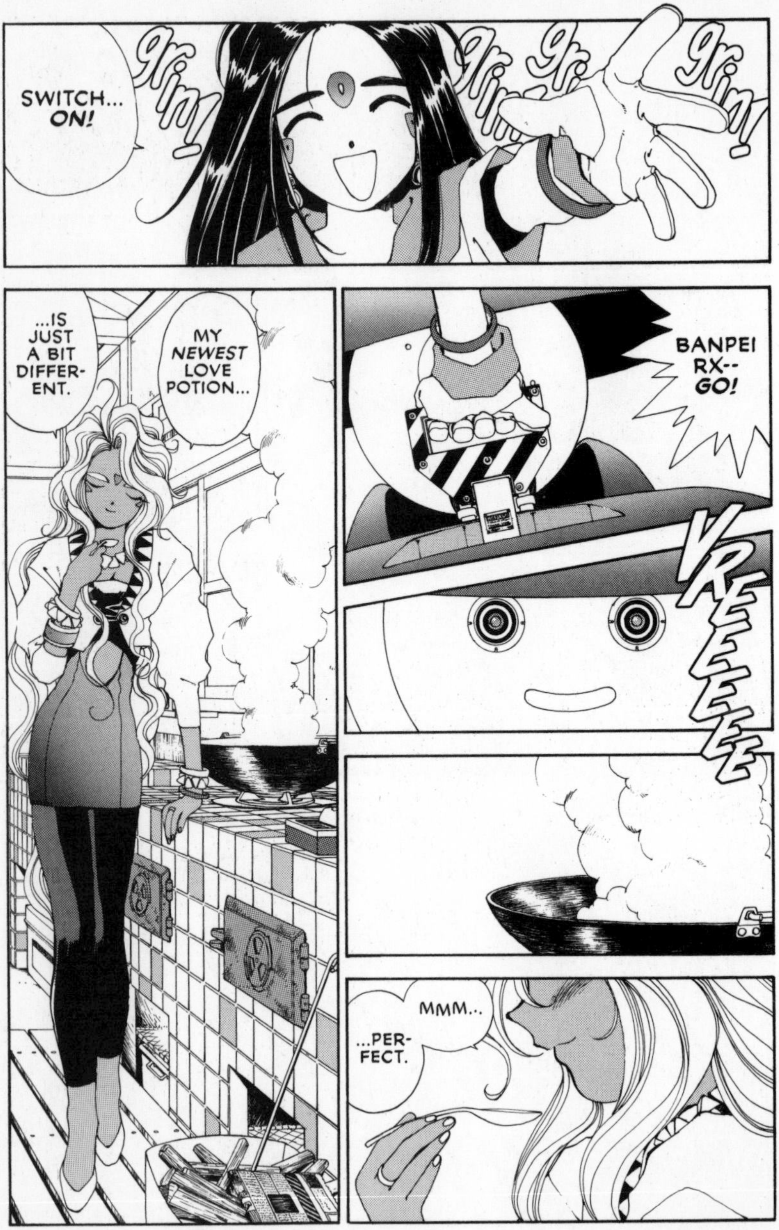
grin!
grin!
SWITCH... ON!
BANPEI RX--GO!
VREEEEE
MMM...
...PER-FECT.
MY NEWEST LOVE POTION...
...IS JUST A BIT DIFFER-ENT.

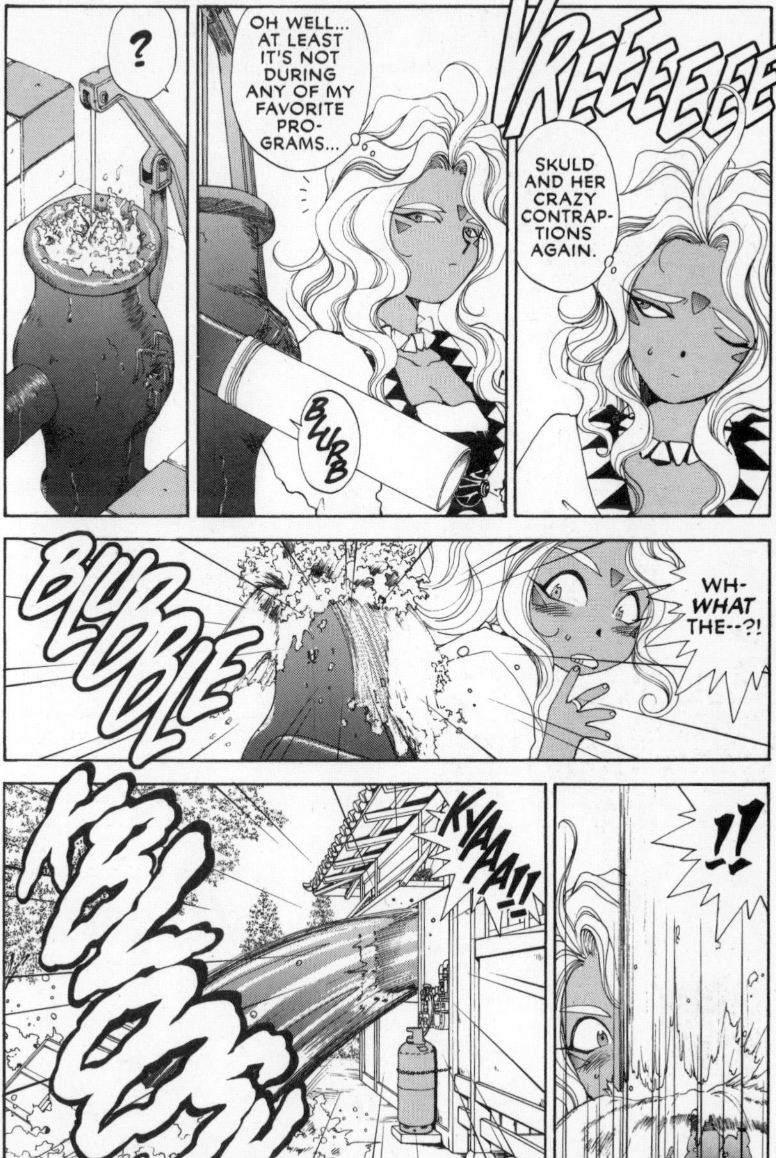
VREEEEEE
SKULD AND HER CRAZY CONTRAP-TIONS AGAIN.
OH WELL... AT LEAST IT'S NOT DURING ANY OF MY FAVORITE PRO-GRAMS...
BLURB
?
WH- WHAT THE--?!
BLUBBLE
!!
KYAAAA!!

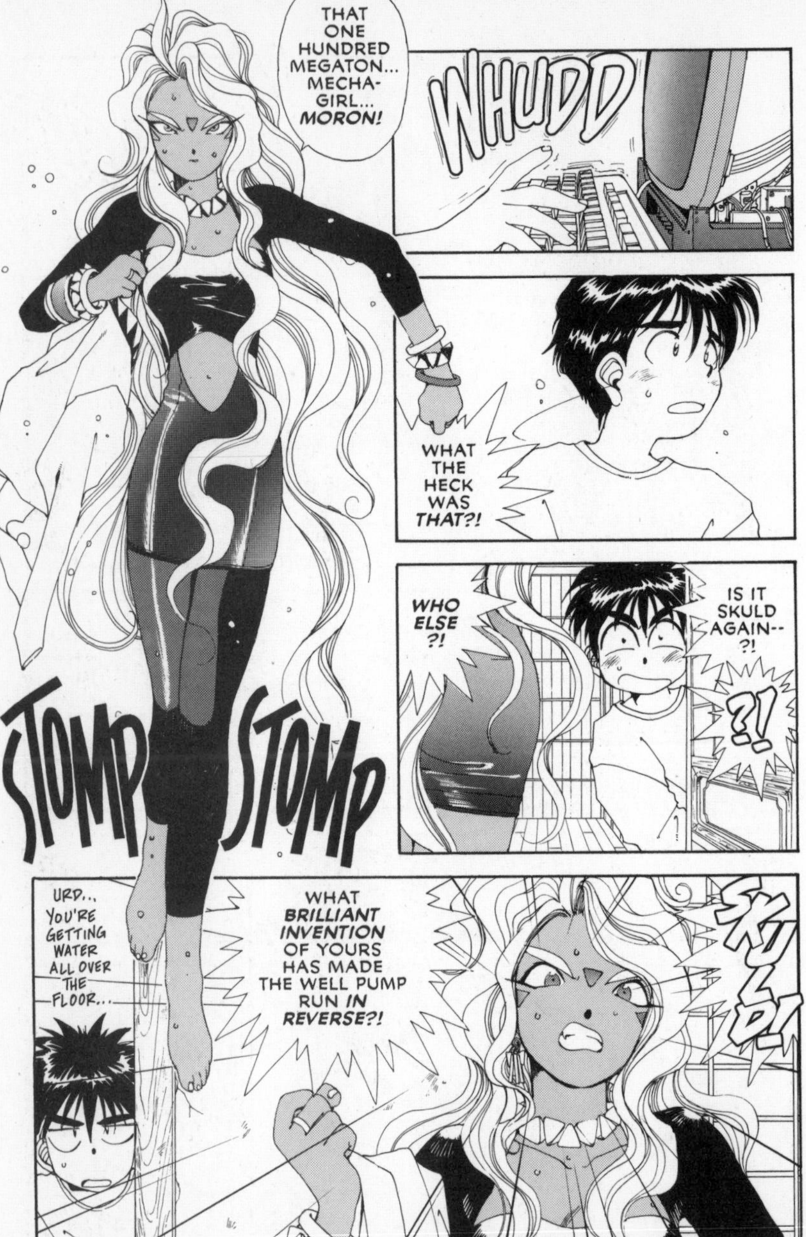

WHUDD
WHAT THE HECK WAS *THAT?!*
IS IT SKULD AGAIN--?!
?!
WHO ELSE?!
THAT ONE HUNDRED MEGATON... MECHA-GIRL... ***MORON!***
STOMP STOMP
SKULD!
WHAT **BRILLIANT INVENTION** OF YOURS HAS MADE THE WELL PUMP RUN ***IN REVERSE?!***
URD... YOU'RE GETTING WATER ALL OVER THE FLOOR...

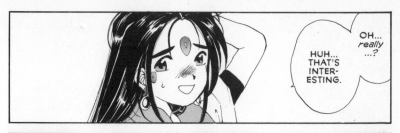

OH... *really* ...?
HUH... THAT'S INTER-ESTING.
UM...
WHAT HAPPENED WAS, I ACCIDEN-TALLY KINDA PUT HIM IN THE WRONG *GEAR*...
...HE SORTA DID EVERY-THING BACK-WARDS.
GOOD-NESS! WELL. I GUESS WE MUST BE ***EVER*** SO CAREFUL WITH NEW MACHINES, YES?
Sizzle
...I SEE.
YES. YES, OF COURSE, IT'S JUST AN UNFOR-TUNATE ACCIDENT. OF ***COURSE*** IT'S NOT YOUR FAUL--
--***SKULD!!***
REVENGE!
REVENGE !!

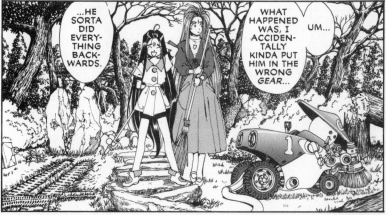

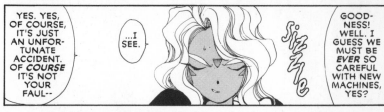

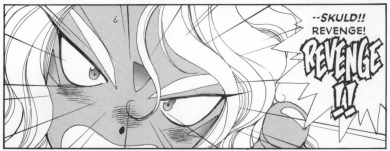

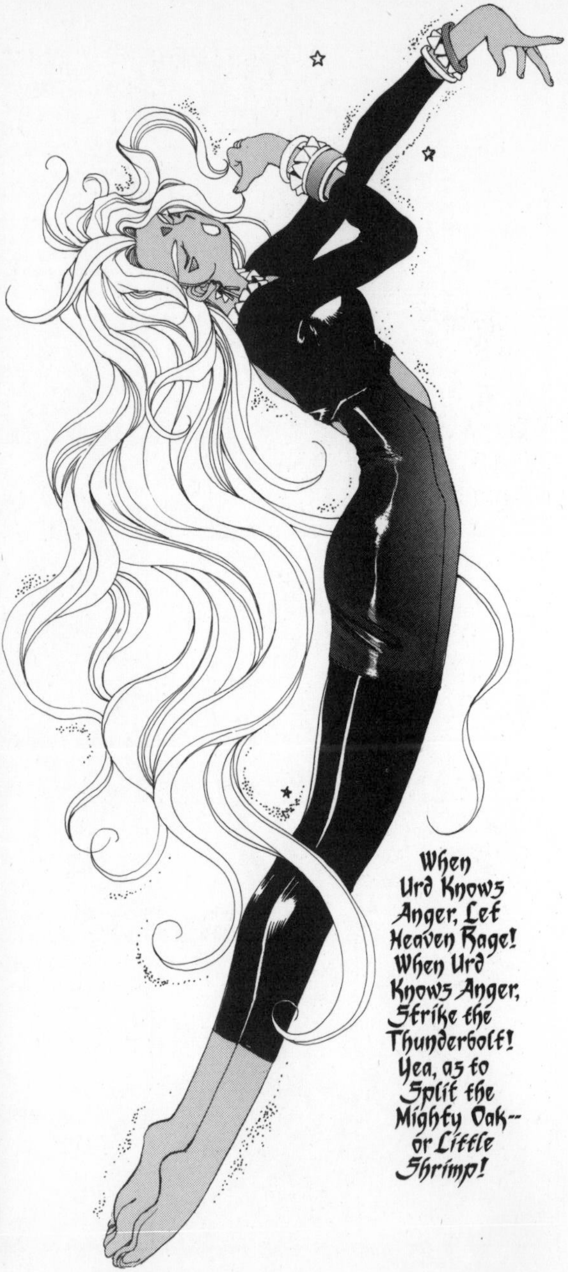
When Urd Knows Anger, Let Heaven Rage! When Urd Knows Anger, Strike the Thunderbolt! Yea, as to Split the Mighty Oak--or Little Shrimp!
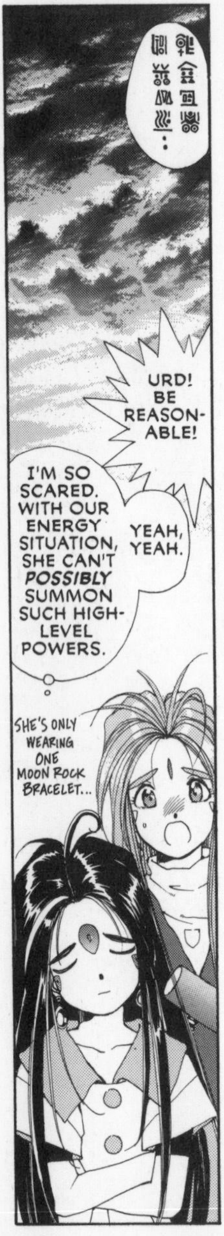
URD! BE REASON-ABLE!
YEAH, YEAH.
I'M SO SCARED. WITH OUR ENERGY SITUATION, SHE CAN'T *POSSIBLY* SUMMON SUCH HIGH-LEVEL POWERS.
SHE'S ONLY WEARING ONE MOON ROCK BRACELET...

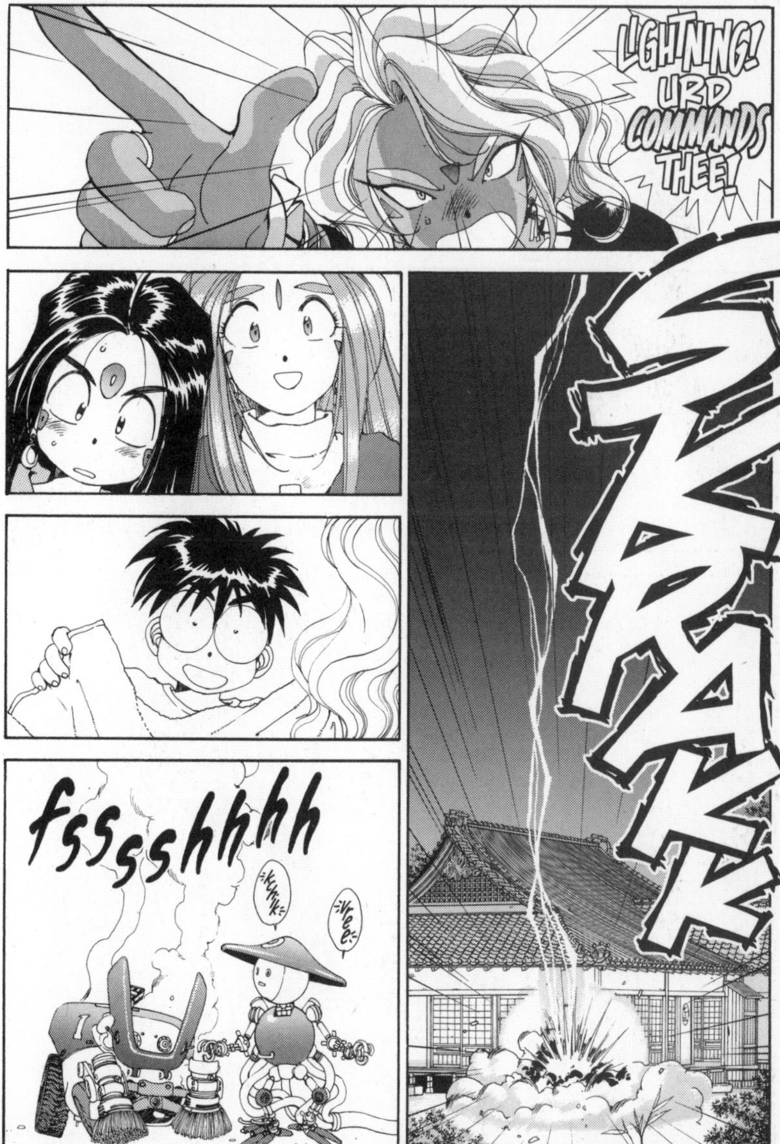
LIGHTNING! URD COMMANDS THEE!
fsssshhhh
vree

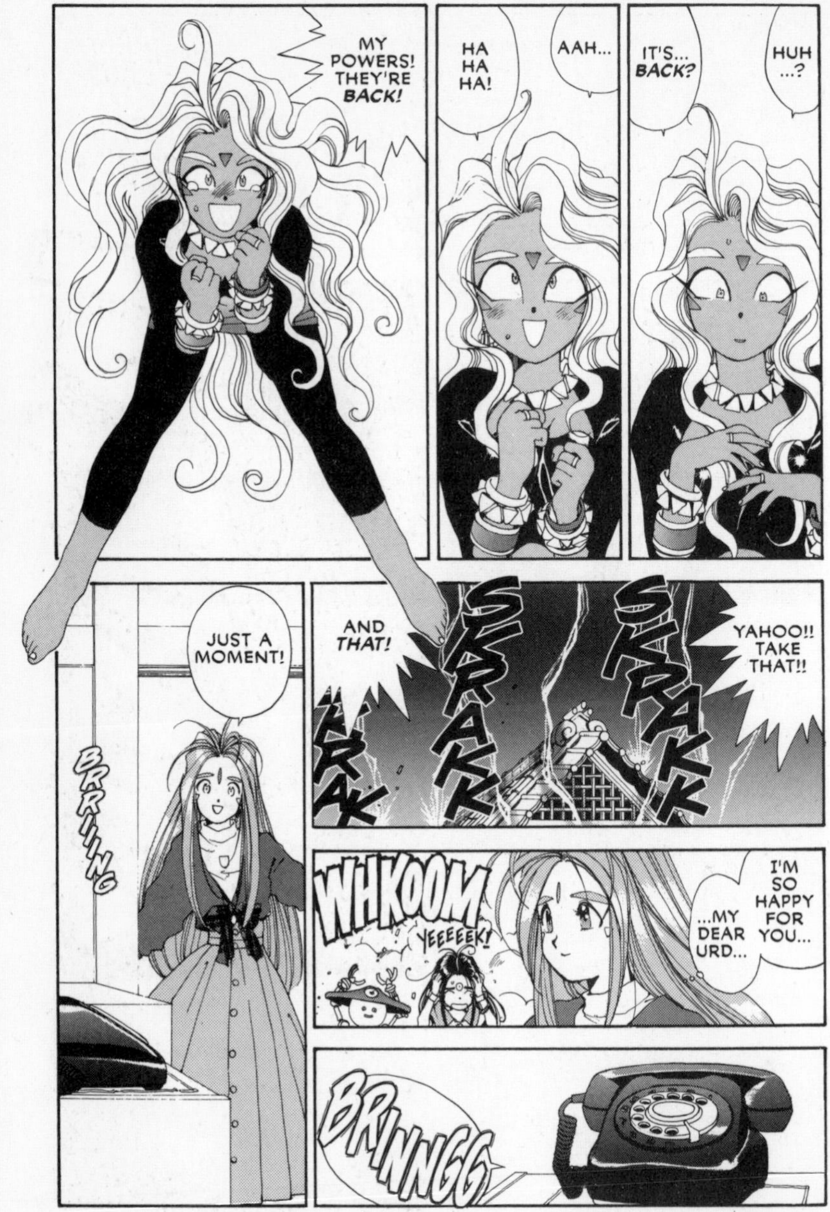
HUH ...?
IT'S... BACK?
AAH...
HA HA HA!
MY POWERS! THEY'RE BACK!
YAHOO!! TAKE THAT!!
SKRAKK
SKRAKK
AND THAT!
KRAK
I'M SO HAPPY FOR YOU...
...MY DEAR URD...
WHKOOM
YEEEEEK!
BRINNGG
JUST A MOMENT!
BRRIIING

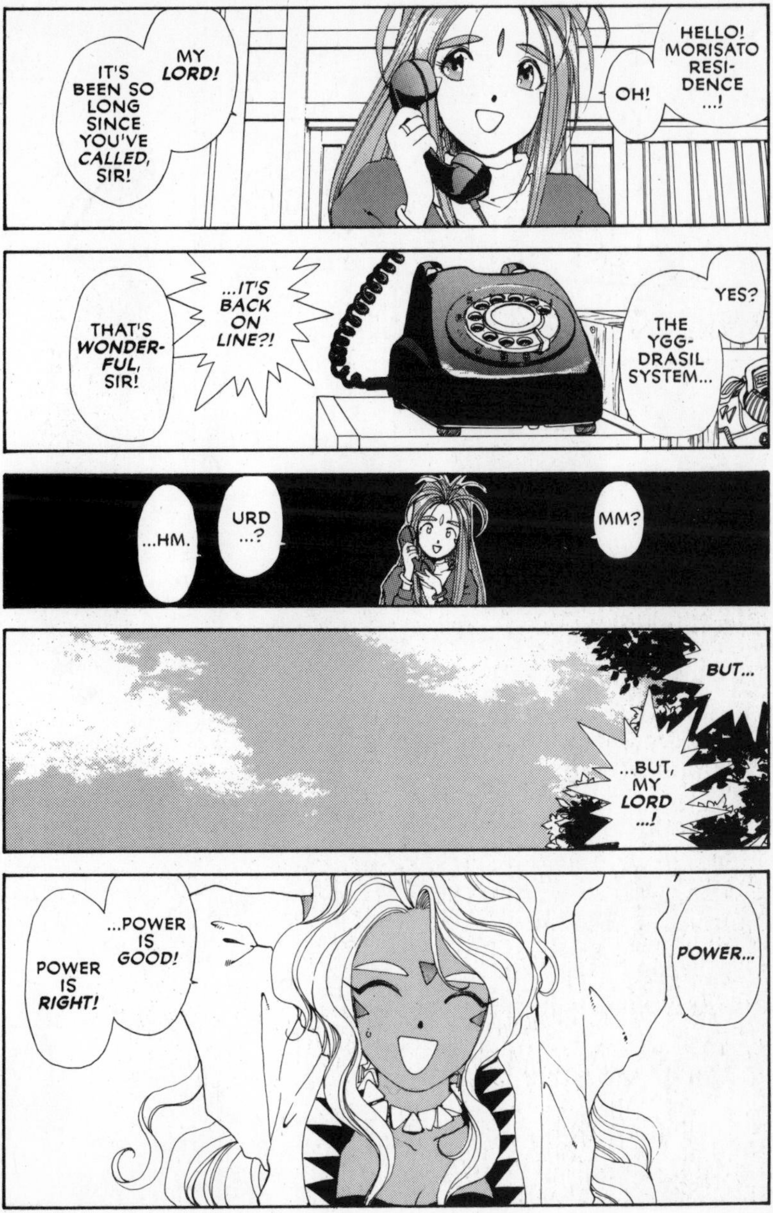
HELLO! MORISATO RESI-DENCE ...!
OH!
MY LORD! IT'S BEEN SO LONG SINCE YOU'VE CALLED, SIR!
YES? THE YGG-DRASIL SYSTEM...
...IT'S BACK ON LINE?!
THAT'S WONDER-FUL, SIR!
MM?
URD ...?
...HM.
BUT...
...BUT, MY LORD ...!
POWER...
...POWER IS GOOD!
POWER IS RIGHT!

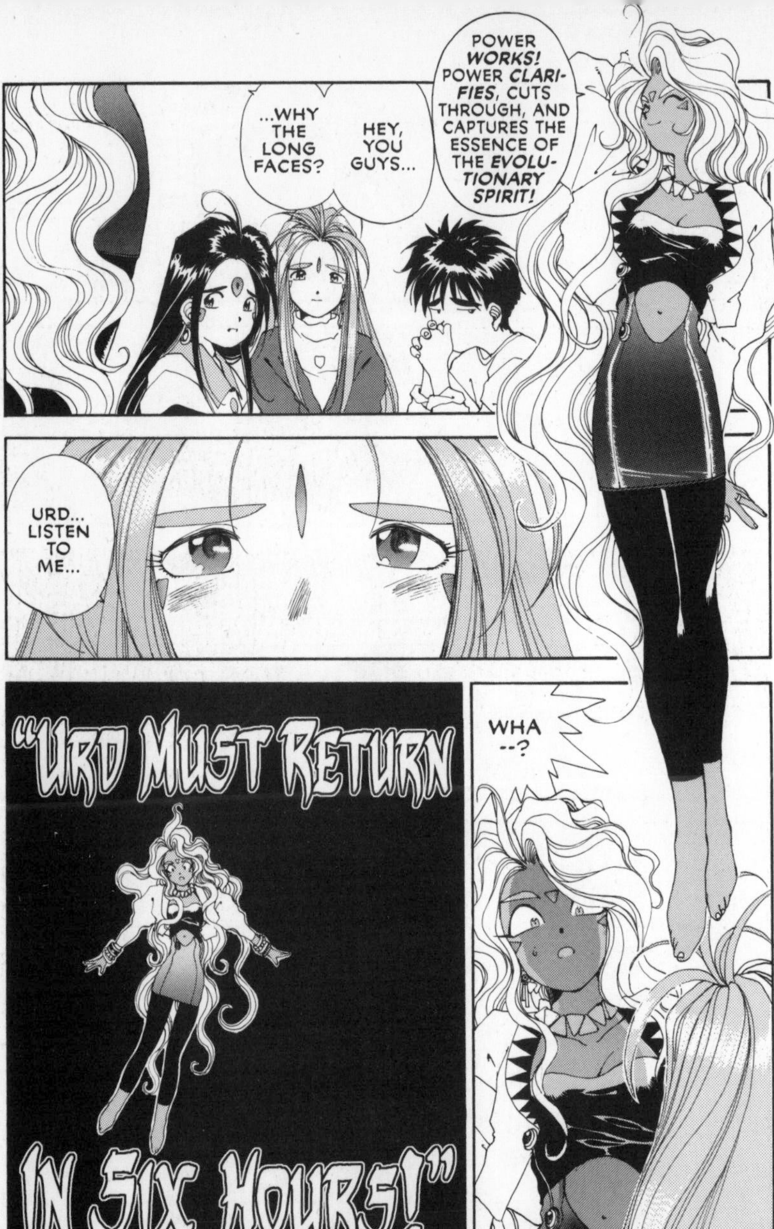
POWER WORKS! POWER CLARIFIES, CUTS THROUGH, AND CAPTURES THE ESSENCE OF THE EVOLUTIONARY SPIRIT!
HEY, YOU GUYS...
...WHY THE LONG FACES?
URD... LISTEN TO ME...
WHA --?
"URD MUST RETURN IN SIX HOURS!"

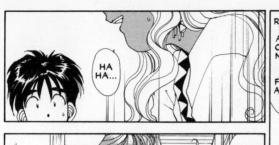

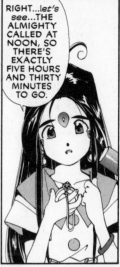

RIGHT...let's see...THE ALMIGHTY CALLED AT NOON, SO THERE'S EXACTLY FIVE HOURS AND THIRTY MINUTES TO GO.
HA HA...
HA HA HA HA...
...
STOMP
STOMP
heh heh heh!
SHE FELL!
THAT'S LIFE.
OH, DEAR!
WHAMM
OH, HOW AMUSING!
I'VE BEEN THROUGH A LOTTA GRIEF BECAUSE OF THAT BROAD.
THIS COULDN'T HAPPEN TO A LOUSIER GODDESS!

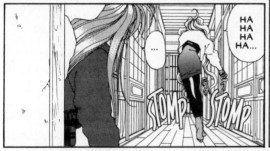

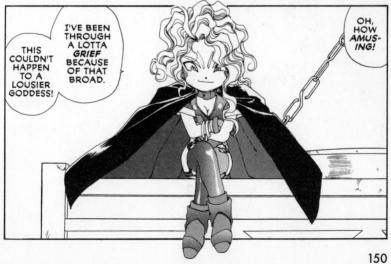

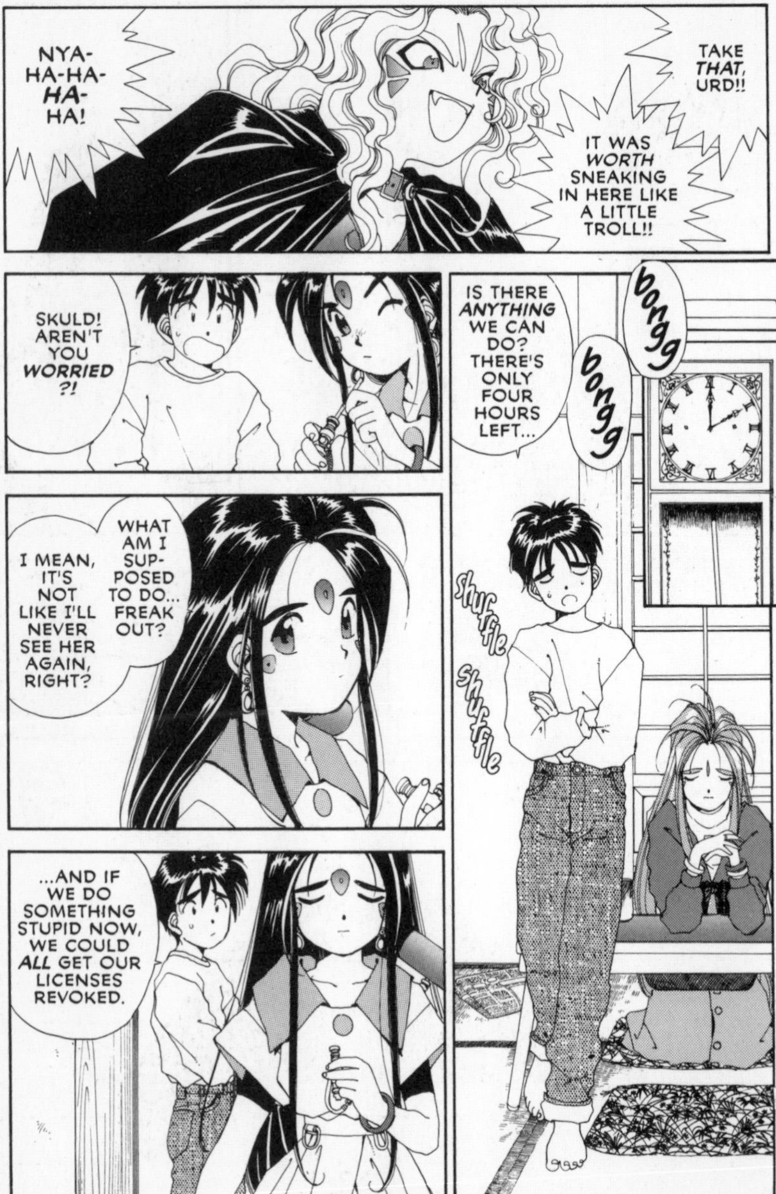
TAKE THAT, URD!!
IT WAS WORTH SNEAKING IN HERE LIKE A LITTLE TROLL!!
NYA-HA-HA-HA-HA!
bongg
bongg
IS THERE ANYTHING WE CAN DO? THERE'S ONLY FOUR HOURS LEFT...
shuffle
shuffle
SKULD! AREN'T YOU WORRIED?!
WHAT AM I SUP-POSED TO DO... FREAK OUT?
I MEAN, IT'S NOT LIKE I'LL NEVER SEE HER AGAIN, RIGHT?
...AND IF WE DO SOMETHING STUPID NOW, WE COULD ALL GET OUR LICENSES REVOKED.

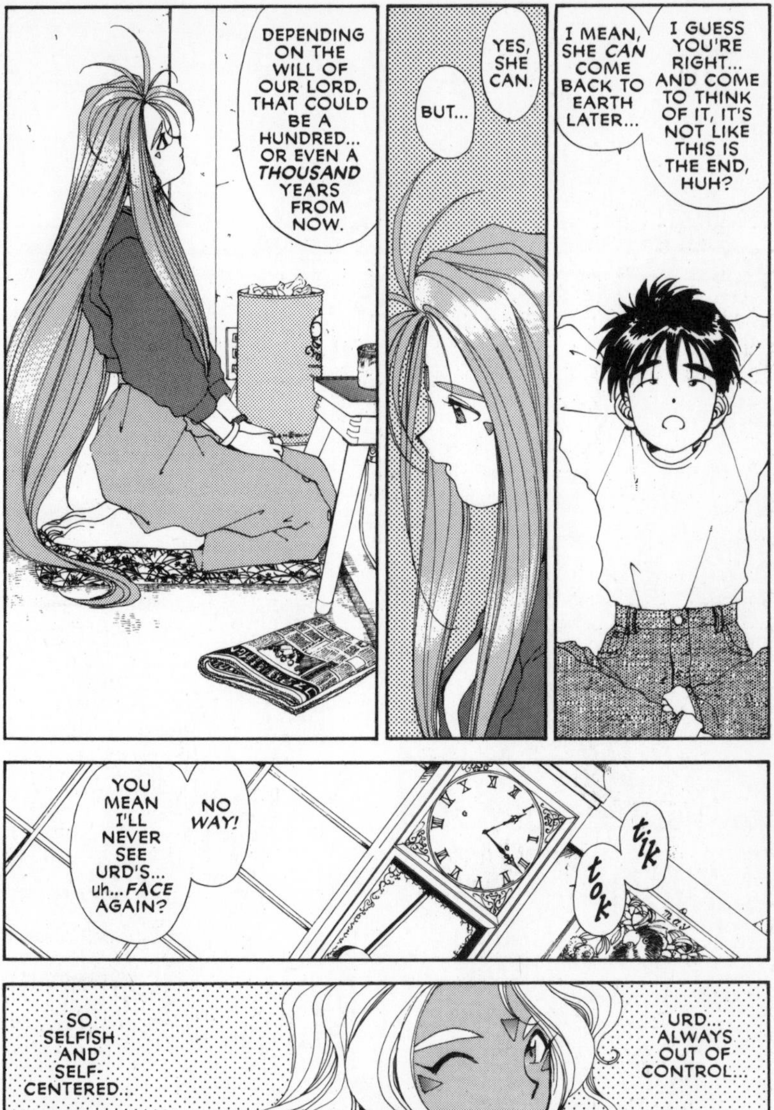
I GUESS YOU'RE RIGHT... AND COME TO THINK OF IT, IT'S NOT LIKE THIS IS THE END, HUH?
I MEAN, SHE *CAN* COME BACK TO EARTH LATER...
YES, SHE CAN.
BUT...
DEPENDING ON THE WILL OF OUR LORD, THAT COULD BE A HUNDRED... OR EVEN A *THOUSAND* YEARS FROM NOW.
tik
tok
NO *WAY!*
YOU MEAN I'LL NEVER SEE URD'S... uh...*FACE* AGAIN?
URD... ALWAYS OUT OF CONTROL...
SO SELFISH AND SELF-CENTERED...

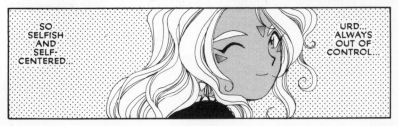

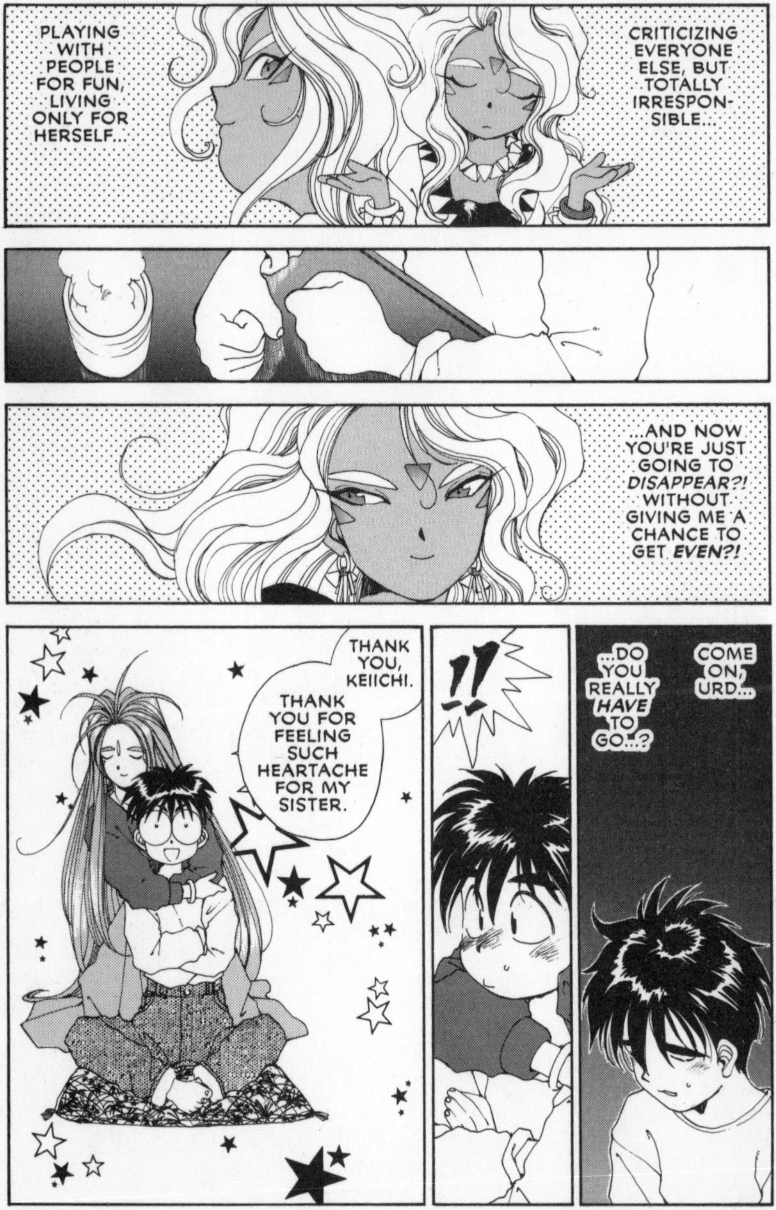

CRITICIZING EVERYONE ELSE, BUT TOTALLY IRRESPON-SIBLE...
PLAYING WITH PEOPLE FOR FUN, LIVING ONLY FOR HERSELF...
...AND NOW YOU'RE JUST GOING TO *DISAPPEAR?!* WITHOUT GIVING ME A CHANCE TO GET *EVEN?!*
COME ON, URD...
...DO YOU REALLY *HAVE* TO GO...?
!!
THANK YOU, KEIICHI.
THANK YOU FOR FEELING SUCH HEARTACHE FOR MY SISTER.

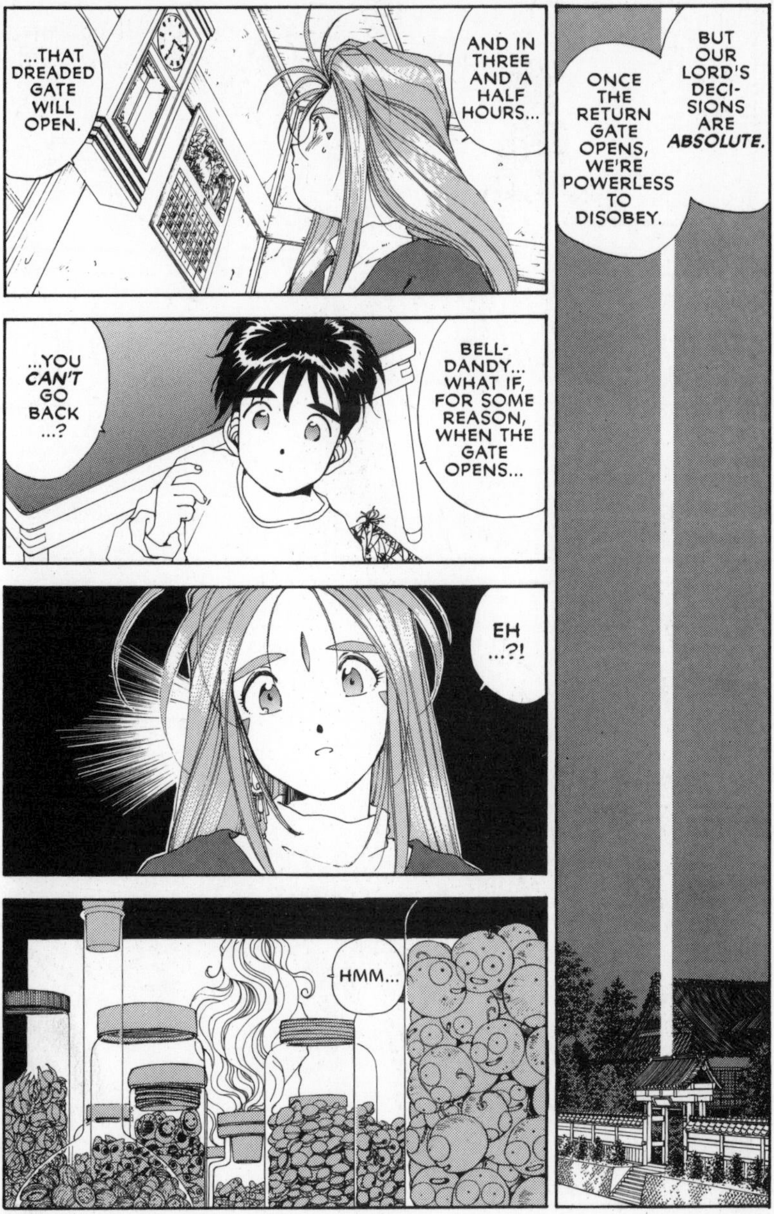
BUT OUR LORD'S DECISIONS ARE ABSOLUTE.
ONCE THE RETURN GATE OPENS, WE'RE POWERLESS TO DISOBEY.
AND IN THREE AND A HALF HOURS...
...THAT DREADED GATE WILL OPEN.
BELL-DANDY... WHAT IF, FOR SOME REASON, WHEN THE GATE OPENS...
...YOU CAN'T GO BACK ...?
EH ...?!
HMM...

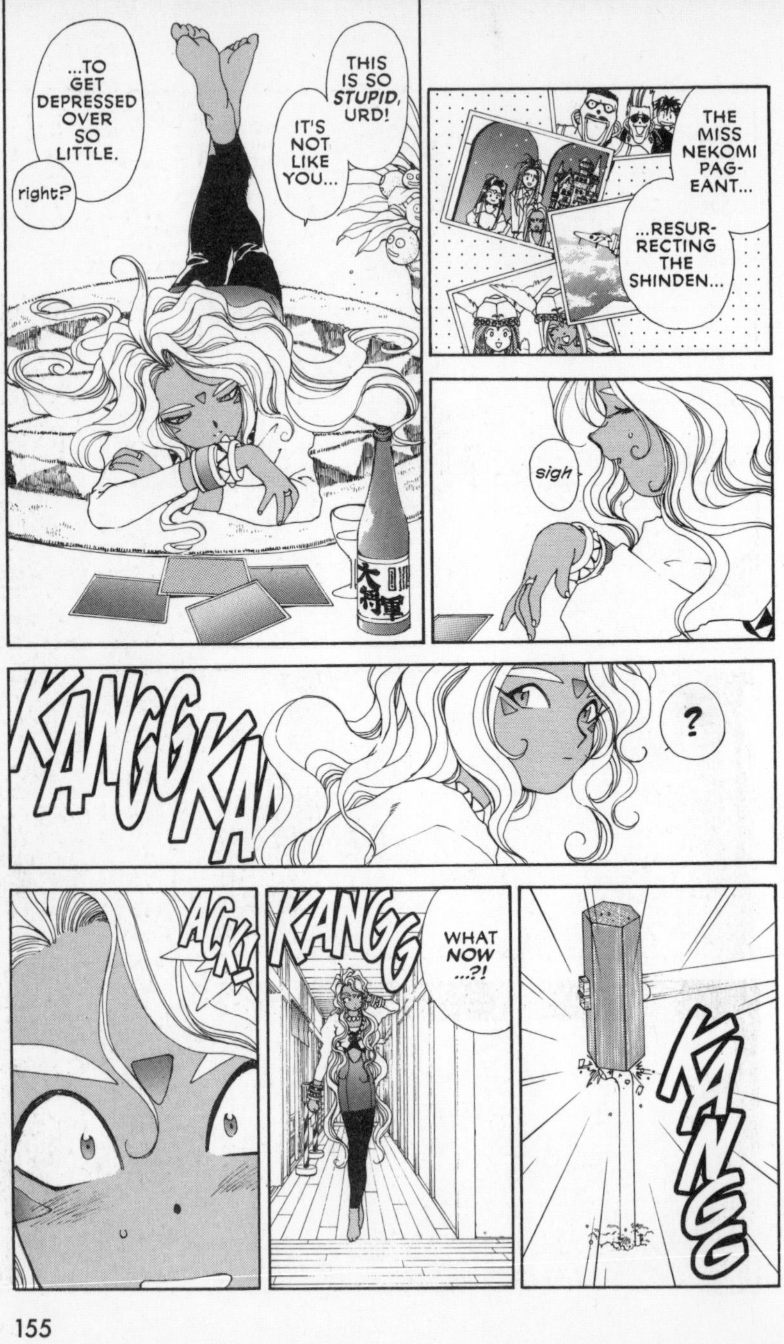
THE MISS NEKOMI PAGEANT...
...RESURRECTING THE SHINDEN...
sigh
THIS IS SO STUPID, URD!
IT'S NOT LIKE YOU...
...TO GET DEPRESSED OVER SO LITTLE.
right?
大将軍
?
KANGGKA
KANGG
WHAT NOW ...?!
KANGG
ACK!

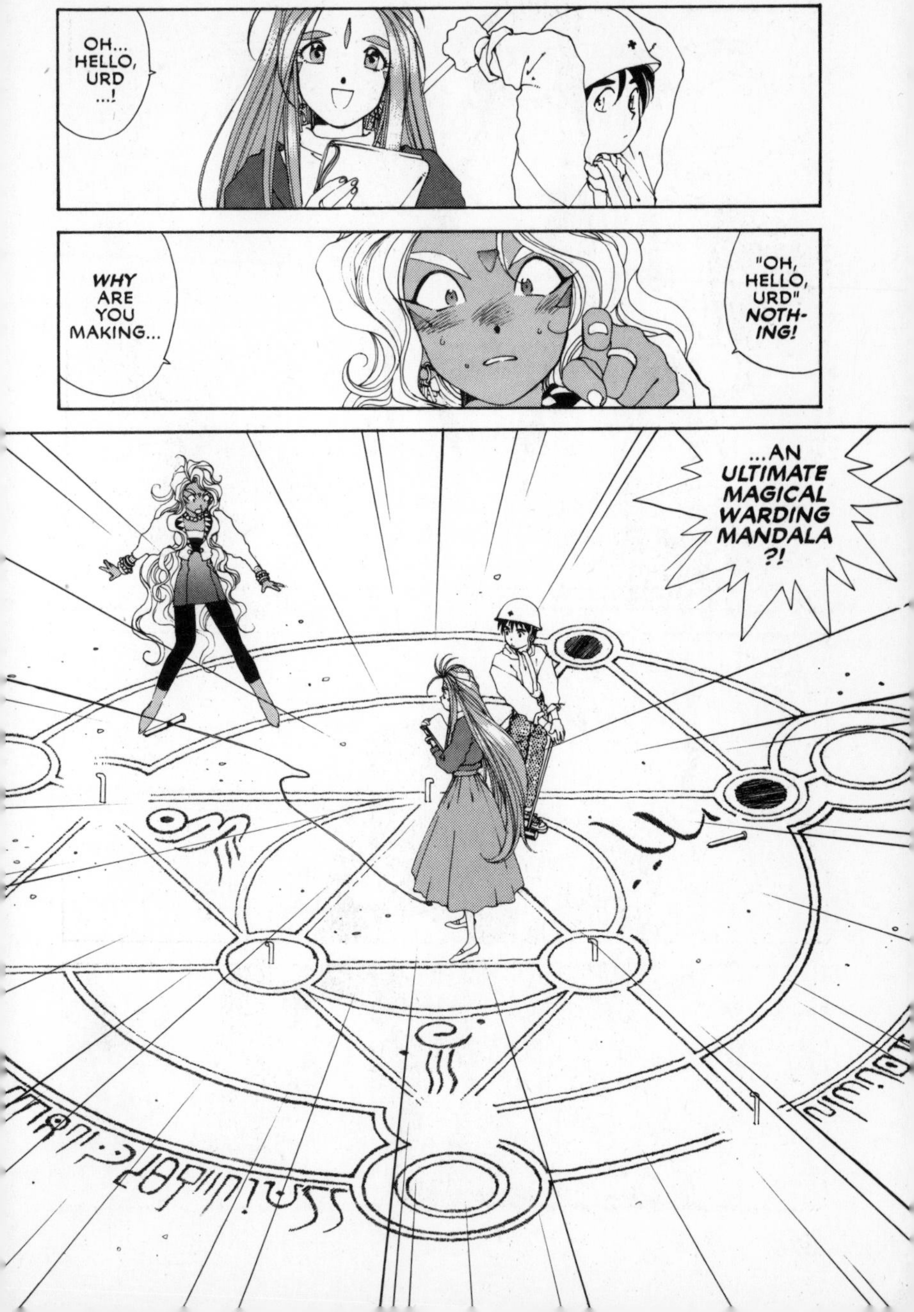
OH... HELLO, URD ...!
"OH, HELLO, URD" NOTHING!
WHY ARE YOU MAKING...
...AN ULTIMATE MAGICAL WARDING MANDALA?!

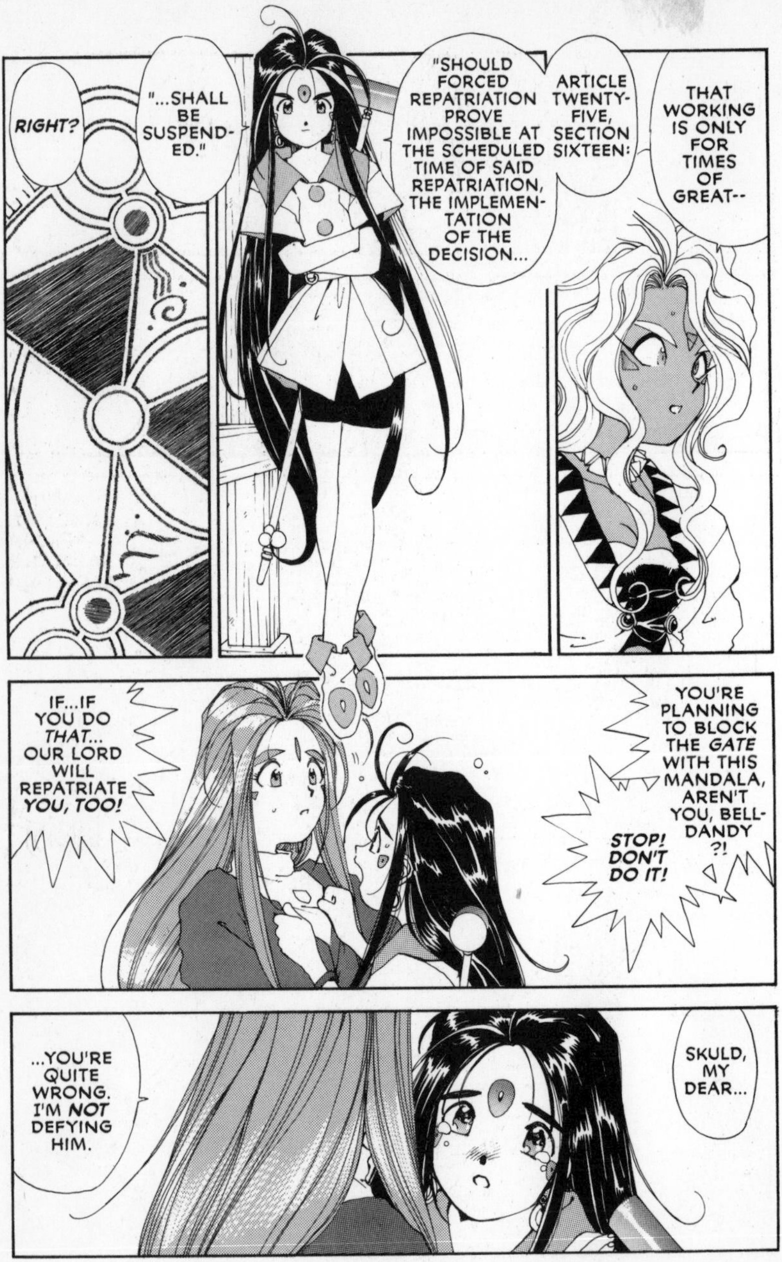
THAT WORKING IS ONLY FOR TIMES OF GREAT--
ARTICLE TWENTY-FIVE, SECTION SIXTEEN:
"SHOULD FORCED REPATRIATION PROVE IMPOSSIBLE AT THE SCHEDULED TIME OF SAID REPATRIATION, THE IMPLEMENTATION OF THE DECISION...
"...SHALL BE SUSPENDED."
RIGHT?
YOU'RE PLANNING TO BLOCK THE *GATE* WITH THIS MANDALA, AREN'T YOU, BELLDANDY?!
STOP! DON'T DO IT!
IF...IF YOU DO *THAT*... OUR LORD WILL REPATRIATE *YOU, TOO!*
SKULD, MY DEAR...
...YOU'RE QUITE WRONG. I'M ***NOT*** DEFYING HIM.

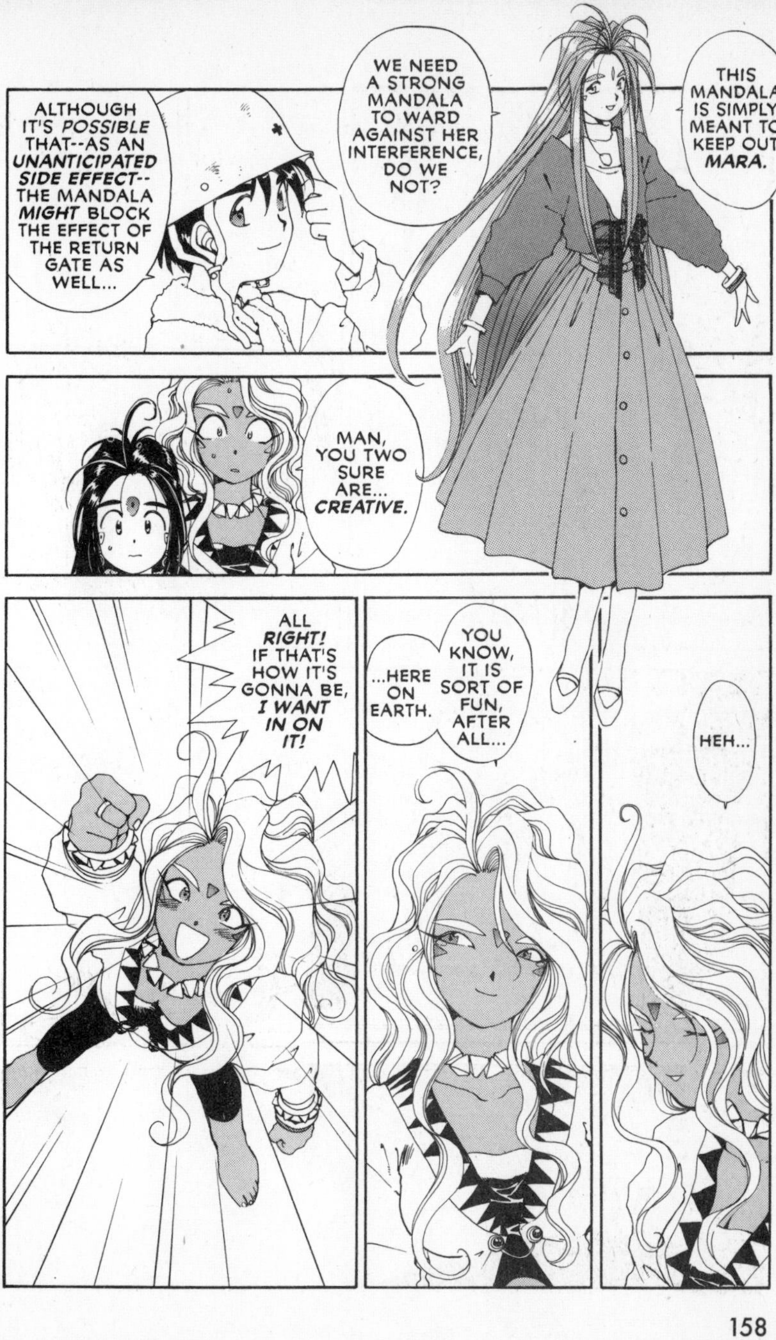
THIS MANDALA IS SIMPLY MEANT TO KEEP OUT *MARA.*
WE NEED A STRONG MANDALA TO WARD AGAINST HER INTERFERENCE, DO WE NOT?
ALTHOUGH IT'S *POSSIBLE* THAT--AS AN *UNANTICIPATED SIDE EFFECT*-- THE MANDALA *MIGHT* BLOCK THE EFFECT OF THE RETURN GATE AS WELL...
MAN, YOU TWO SURE ARE... *CREATIVE.*
HEH...
YOU KNOW, IT IS SORT OF FUN, AFTER ALL...
...HERE ON EARTH.
ALL *RIGHT!* IF THAT'S HOW IT'S GONNA BE, *I WANT IN ON IT!*

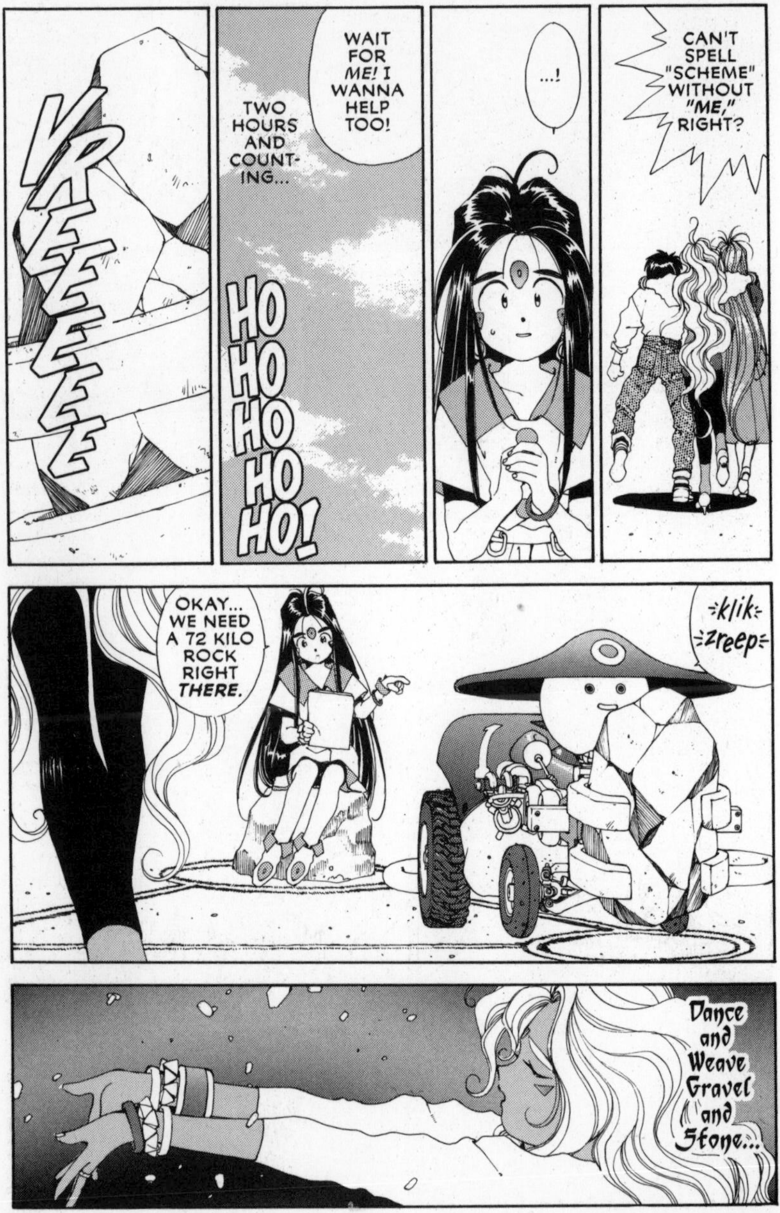

CAN'T SPELL "SCHEME" WITHOUT "ME," RIGHT?
...!
WAIT FOR ME! I WANNA HELP TOO!
TWO HOURS AND COUNT-ING...
HO HO HO HO HO HO!
VREEEEEE
klik zreep
OKAY... WE NEED A 72 KILO ROCK RIGHT THERE.
Dance and Weave Gravel and Stone...

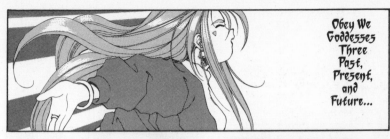

Obey We Goddesses Three Past, Present, and Future...

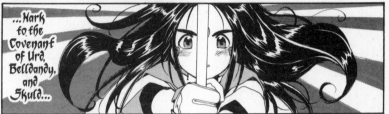

...Hark to the Covenant of Urd, Belldandy, and Skuld...

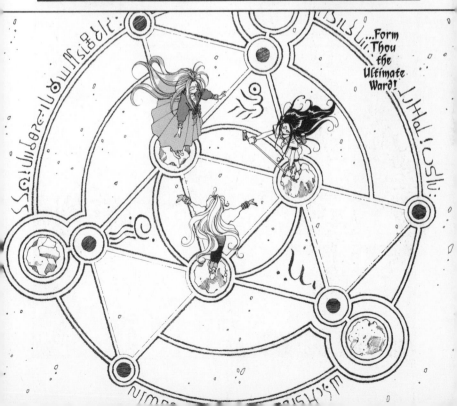

...Form Thou the Ultimate Ward!

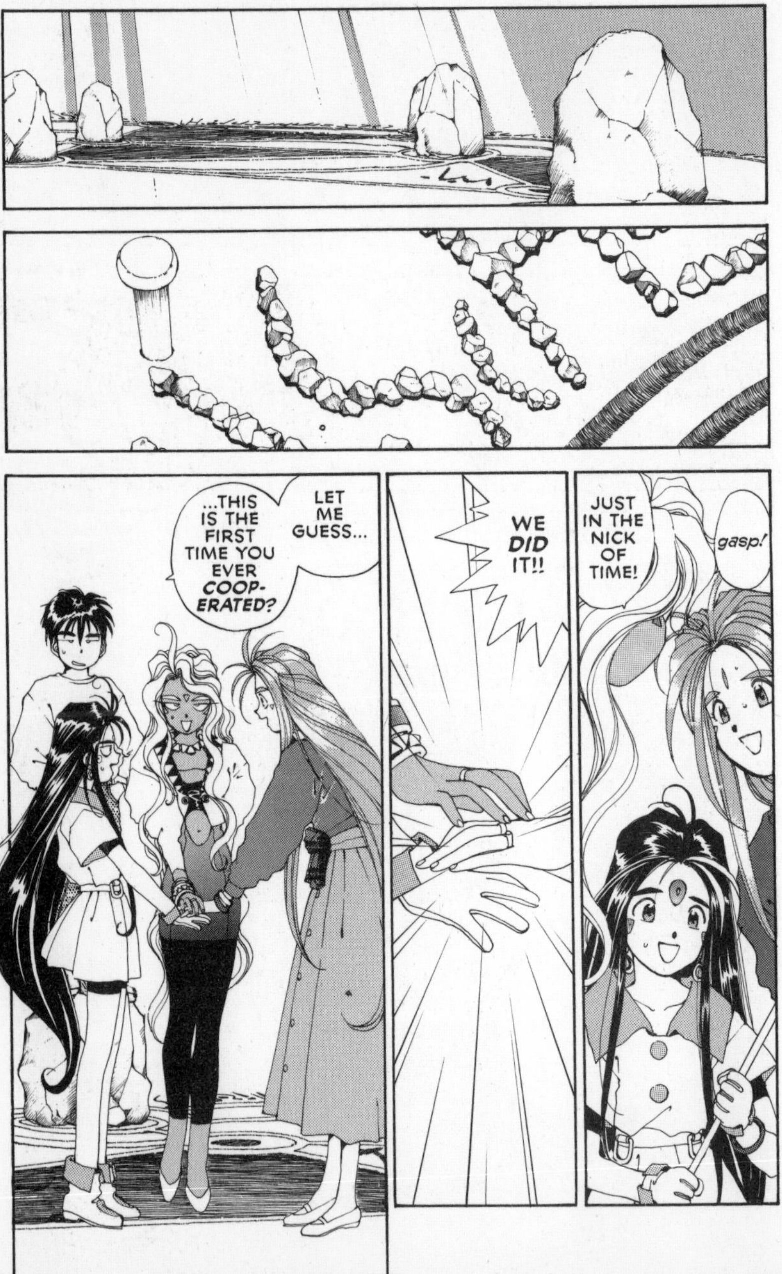
gasp!
JUST IN THE NICK OF TIME!
WE DID IT!!
LET ME GUESS...
...THIS IS THE FIRST TIME YOU EVER COOP-ERATED?

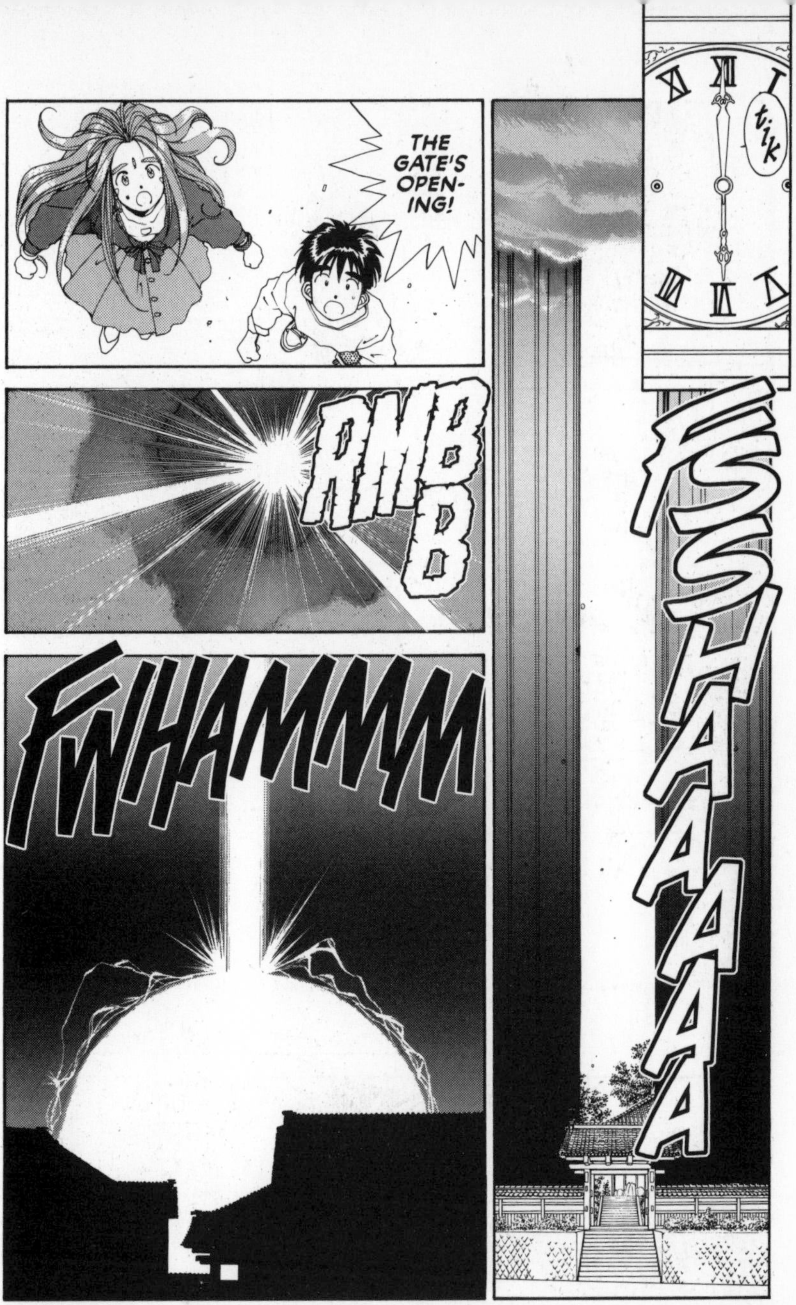
tik
FSHAAAAAA
THE GATE'S OPEN-ING!
RMBB
FWHAMMMM

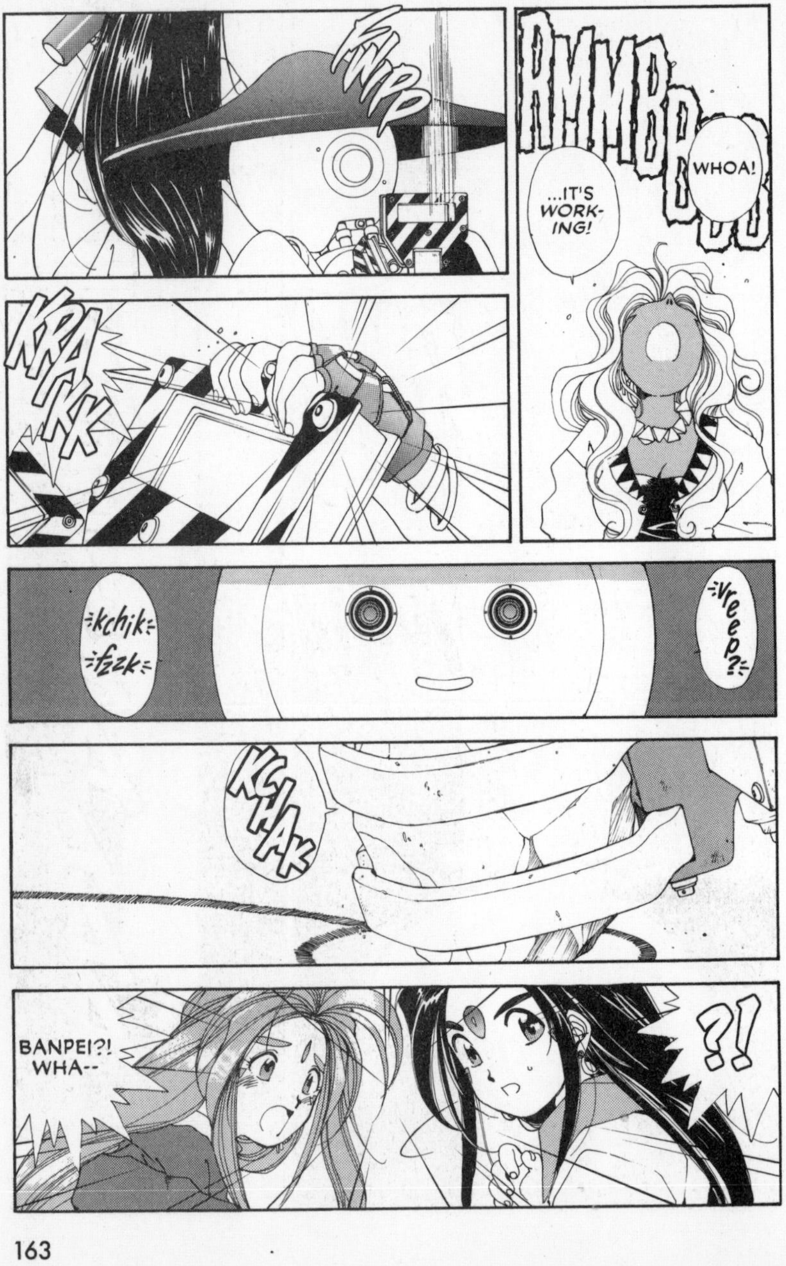
RMMBBOO
WHOA!
...IT'S WORKING!
FWIPP
KRAKKK
vreep?
kchik fzzk
KCHAK
?!
BANPEI?! WHA--

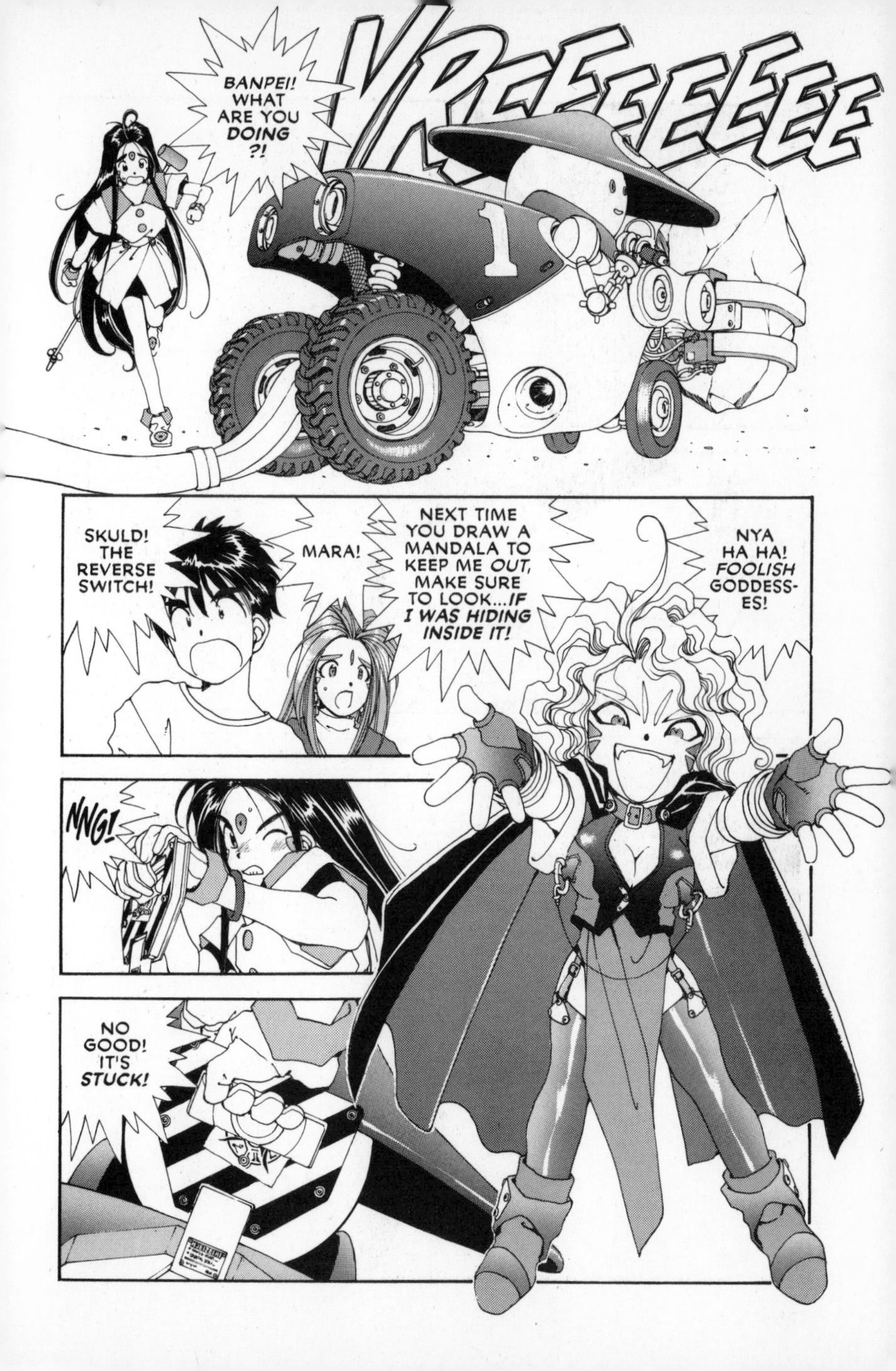
VREEEEEEEE
BANPEI! WHAT ARE YOU *DOING* ?!
NYA HA HA! *FOOLISH* GODDESS-ES!
NEXT TIME YOU DRAW A MANDALA TO KEEP ME *OUT*, MAKE SURE TO LOOK...*IF I WAS HIDING INSIDE IT!*
MARA!
SKULD! THE REVERSE SWITCH!
NNG!
NO GOOD! IT'S *STUCK!*

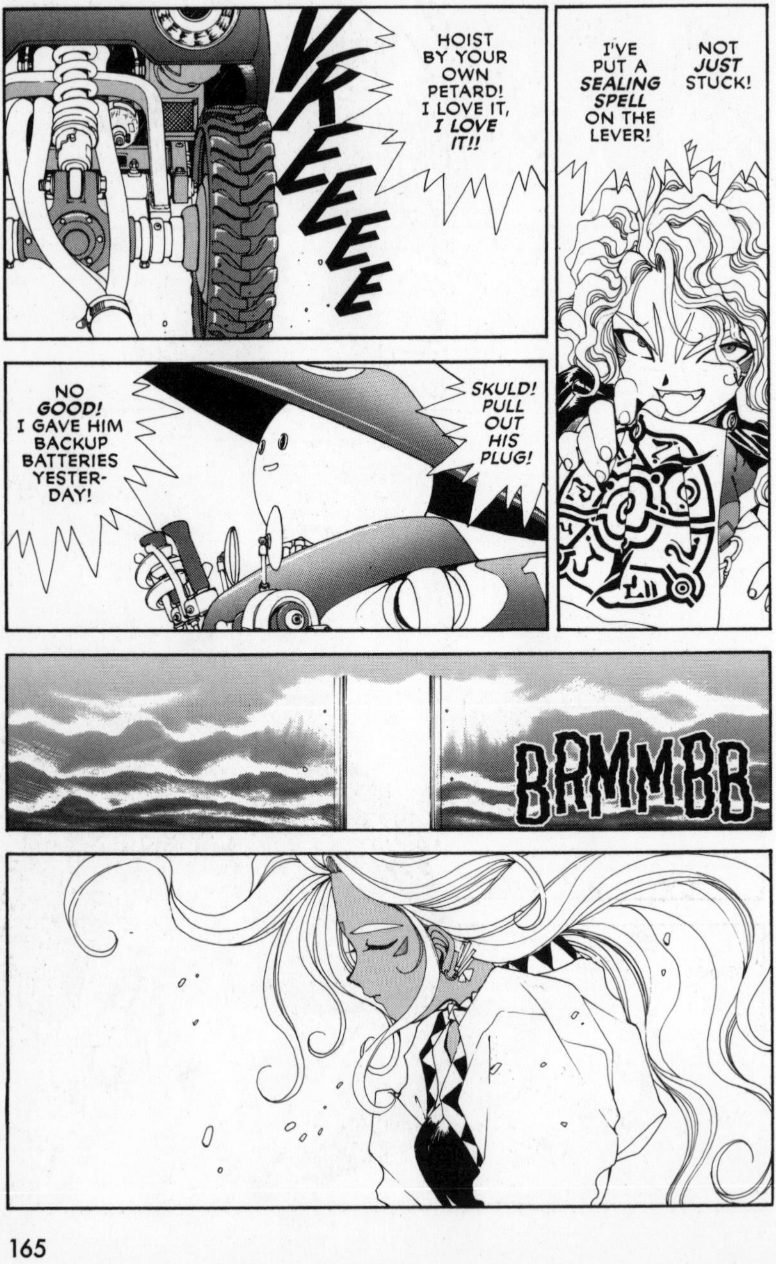
NOT JUST STUCK!
I'VE PUT A SEALING SPELL ON THE LEVER!
HOIST BY YOUR OWN PETARD! I LOVE IT, I LOVE IT!!
VKEEEEE
SKULD! PULL OUT HIS PLUG!
NO GOOD! I GAVE HIM BACKUP BATTERIES YESTER-DAY!
BRMMBB

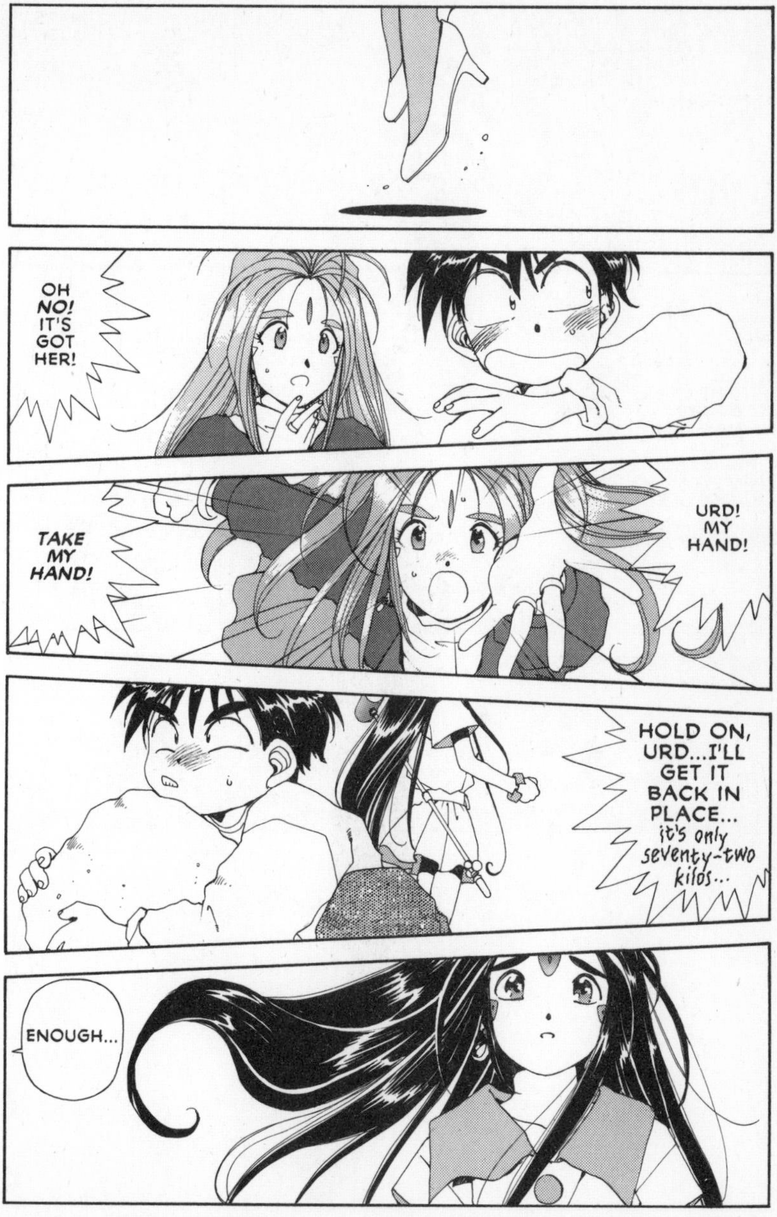
OH NO! IT'S GOT HER!
URD! MY HAND!
TAKE MY HAND!
HOLD ON, URD...I'LL GET IT BACK IN PLACE... it's only seventy-two kilos...
ENOUGH...

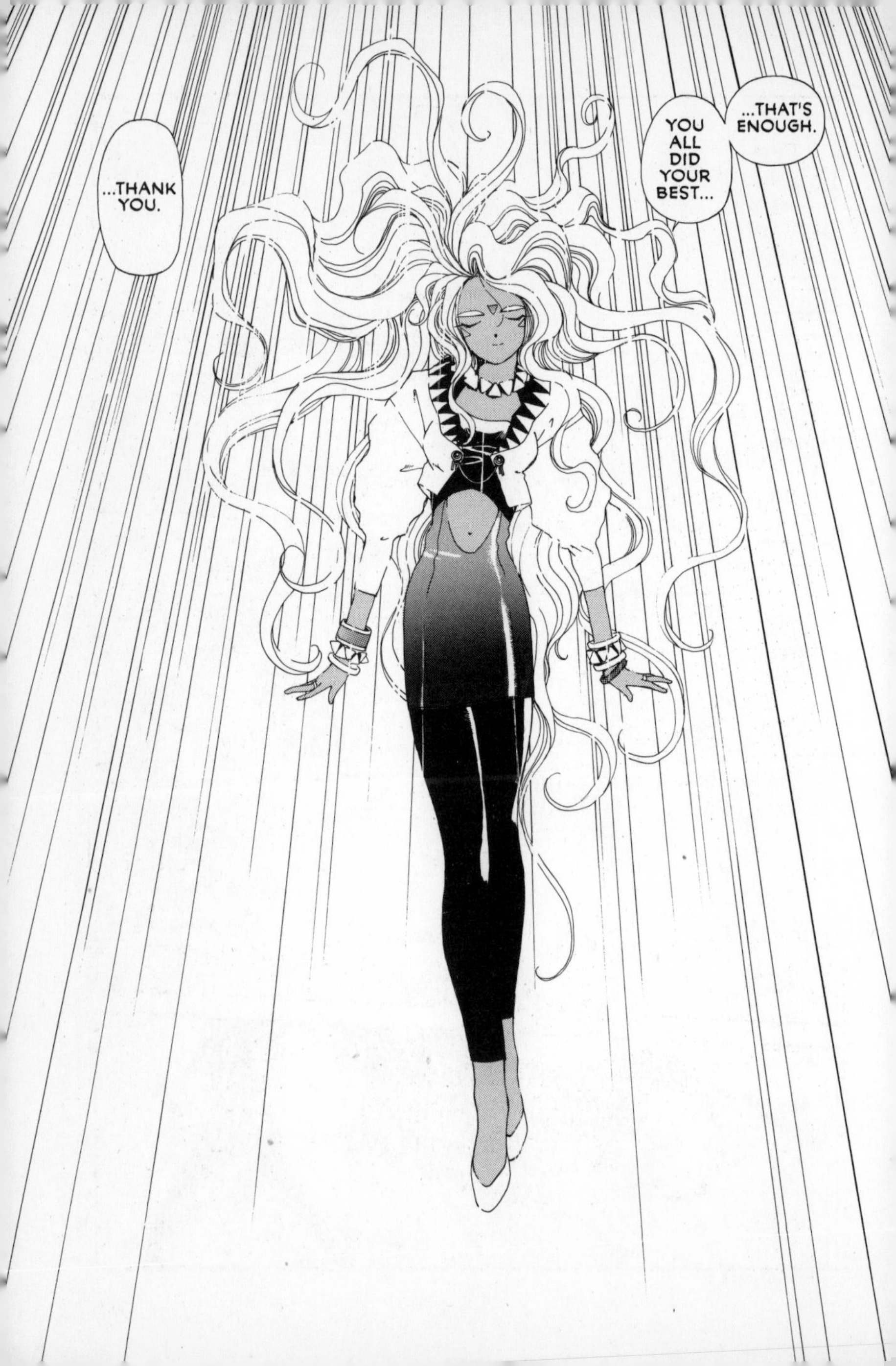
...THAT'S ENOUGH.
YOU ALL DID YOUR BEST...
...THANK YOU.

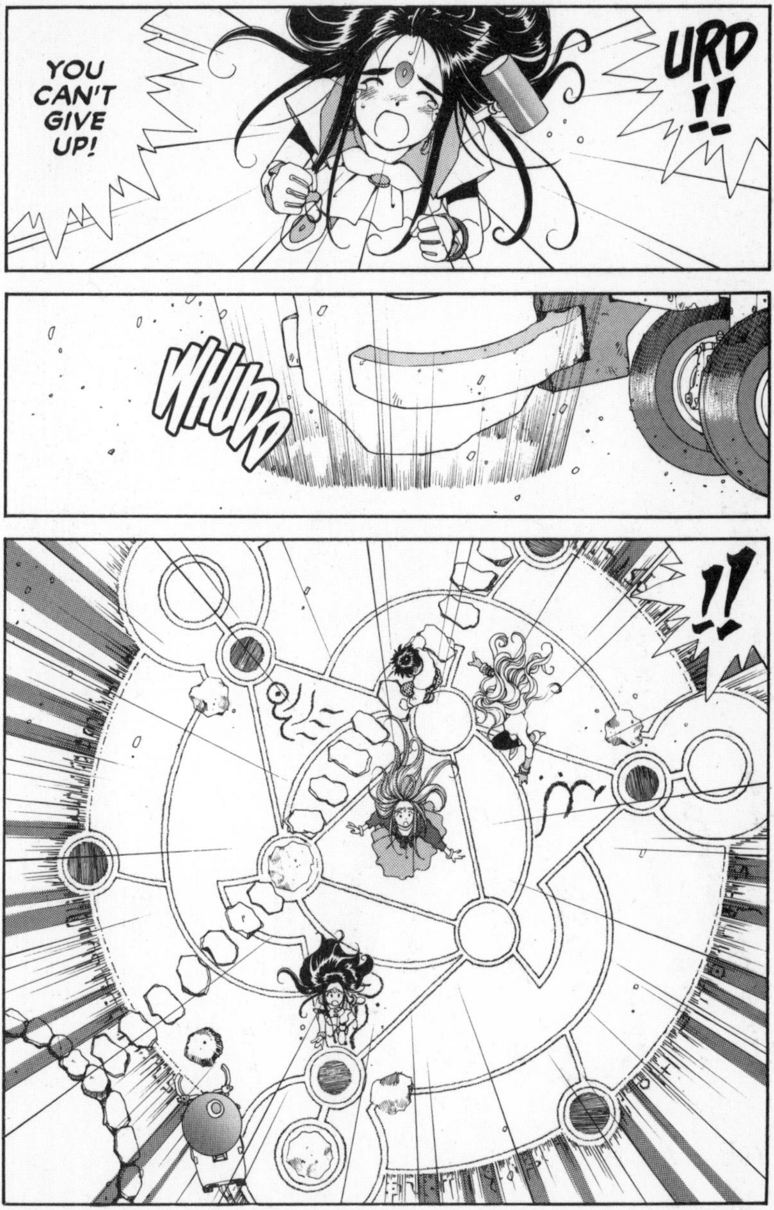
URD!!
YOU CAN'T GIVE UP!
WHUDD
!!

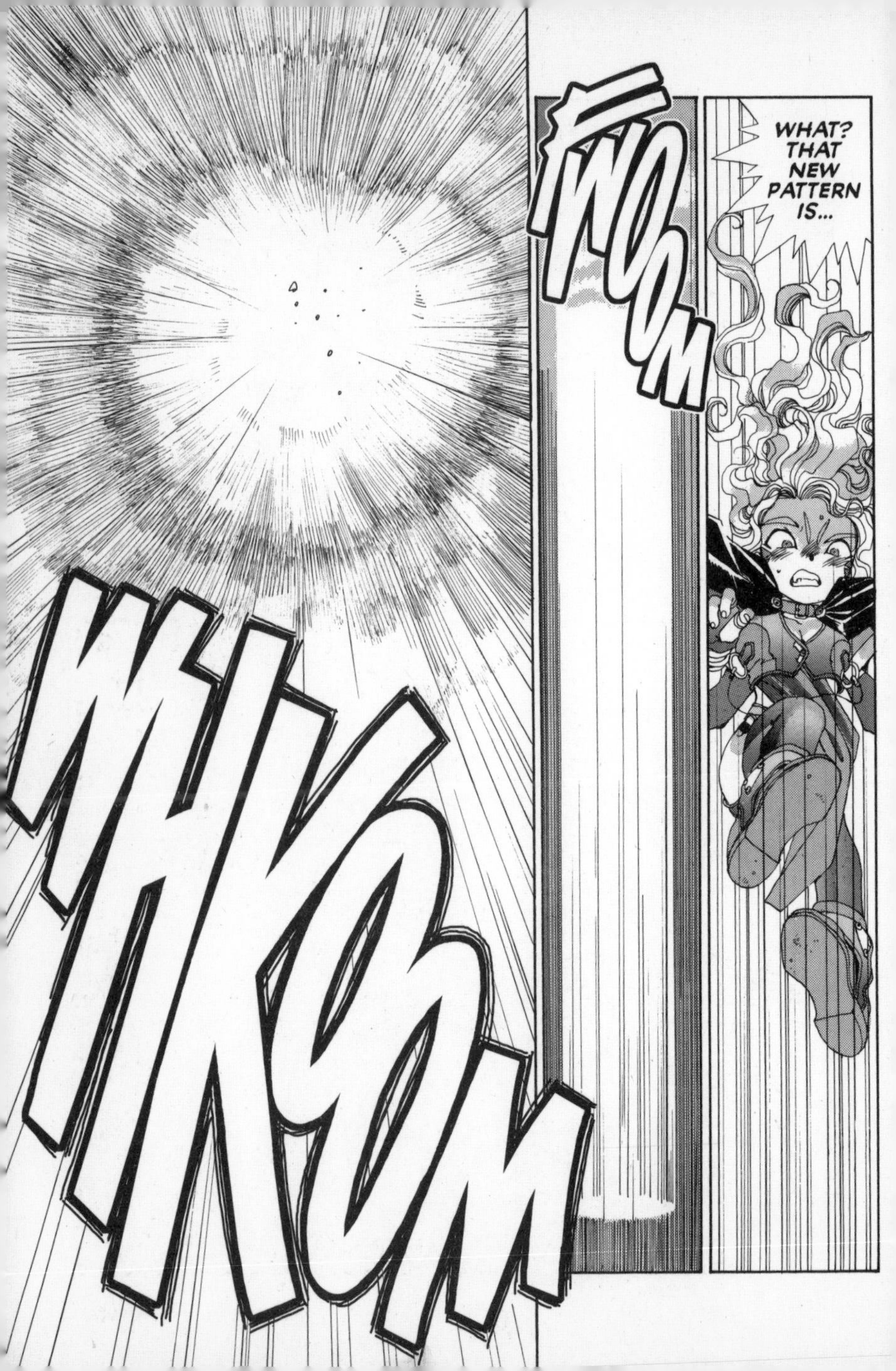
WHAT? THAT NEW PATTERN IS...
FWOOM
WHOOM

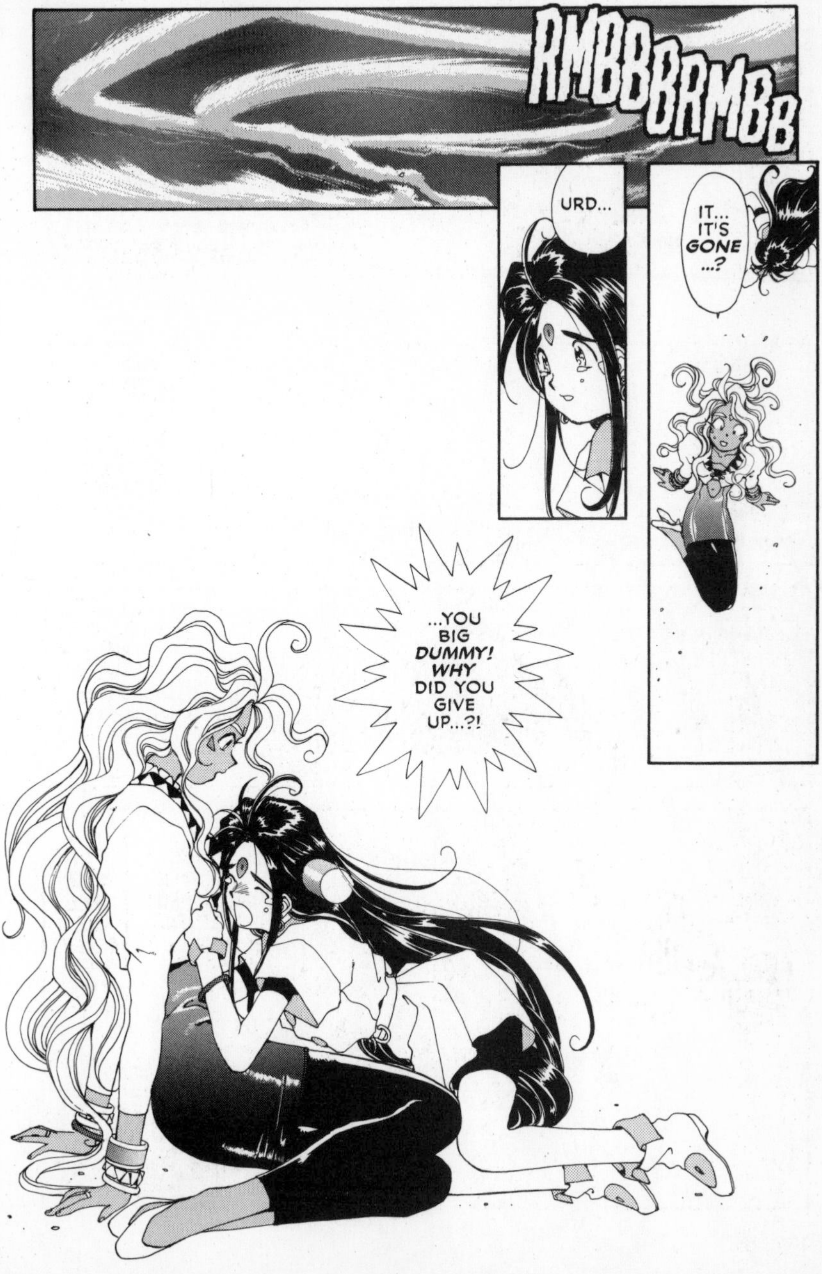
RMBBBRMBB
IT... IT'S GONE ...?
URD...
...YOU BIG DUMMY! WHY DID YOU GIVE UP...?!

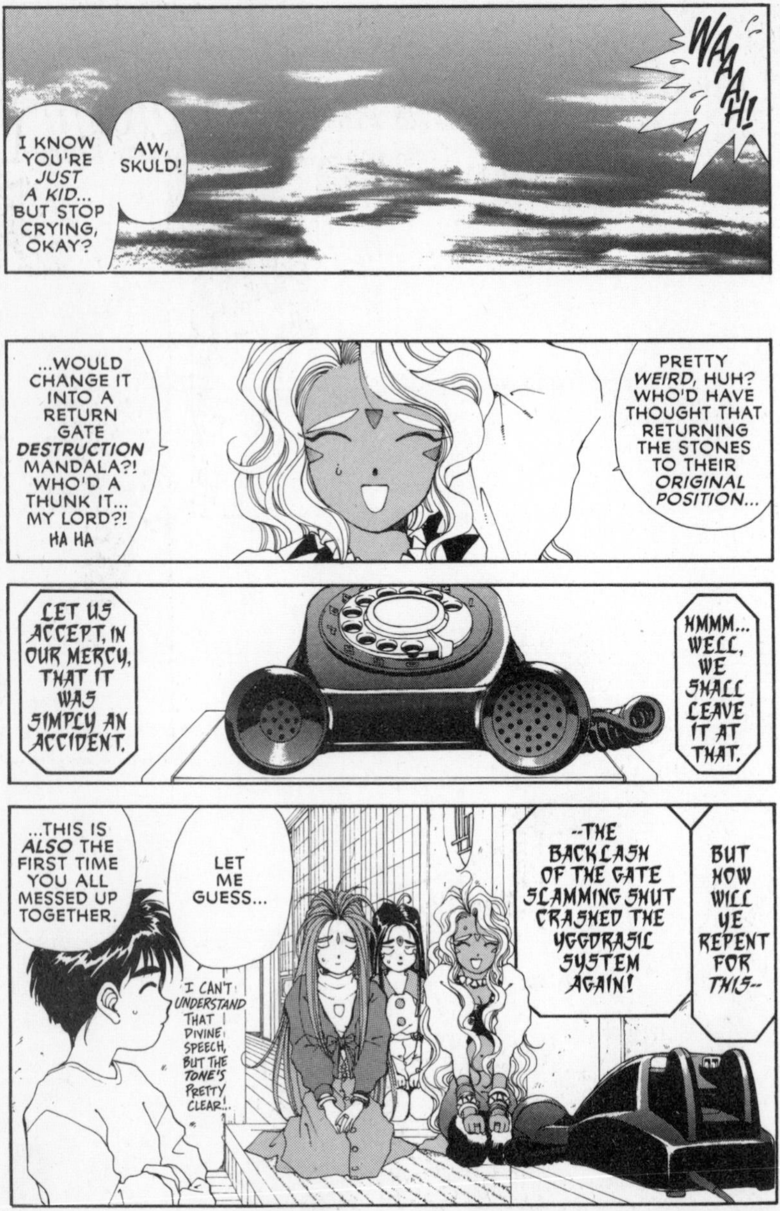
WAAAH!
AW, SKULD!
I KNOW YOU'RE *JUST* A KID... BUT STOP CRYING, OKAY?
PRETTY *WEIRD*, HUH? WHO'D HAVE THOUGHT THAT RETURNING THE STONES TO THEIR *ORIGINAL* POSITION...
...WOULD CHANGE IT INTO A RETURN GATE ***DESTRUCTION*** MANDALA?! WHO'D A THUNK IT... MY LORD?!
HA HA
HMMM... WELL, WE SHALL LEAVE IT AT THAT.
LET US ACCEPT, IN OUR MERCY, THAT IT WAS SIMPLY AN ACCIDENT.
BUT HOW WILL YE REPENT FOR *THIS*--
--THE BACKLASH OF THE GATE SLAMMING SHUT CRASHED THE YGGDRASIL SYSTEM AGAIN!
LET ME GUESS...
...THIS IS ***ALSO*** THE FIRST TIME YOU ALL MESSED UP TOGETHER.
I CAN'T *UNDERSTAND* THAT DIVINE SPEECH, BUT THE *TONE'S* PRETTY CLEAR!

THE ADVENTURES OF MINI-URD

With the Miracle Ingredient: MINI-SKULD!

FORWARD TO THE FUTURE!

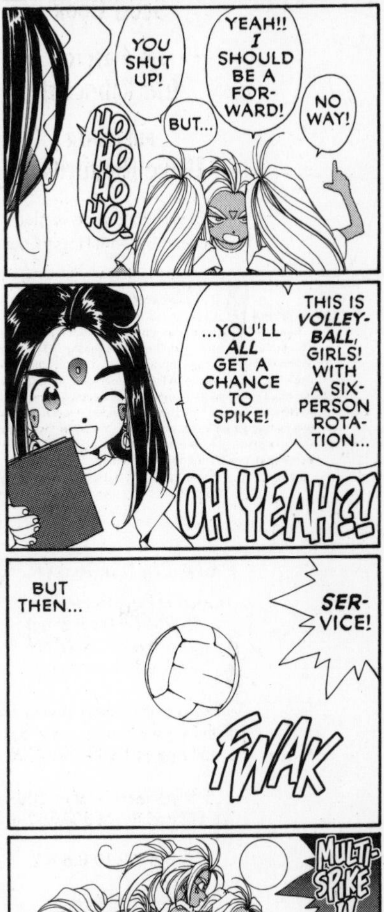
NO WAY!
YEAH!! *I* SHOULD BE A FOR-WARD!
YOU SHUT UP!
BUT...
HO HO HO HO HO!
THIS IS *VOLLEY-BALL*, GIRLS! WITH A SIX-PERSON ROTA-TION...
...YOU'LL *ALL* GET A CHANCE TO SPIKE!
OH YEAH?!
*SER-*VICE!
BUT THEN...
FWAK
MULTI-SPIKE!!
WILL YOU GUYS JUST *LISTEN* FOR ONCE?!

BLOOMERS OF DOOM

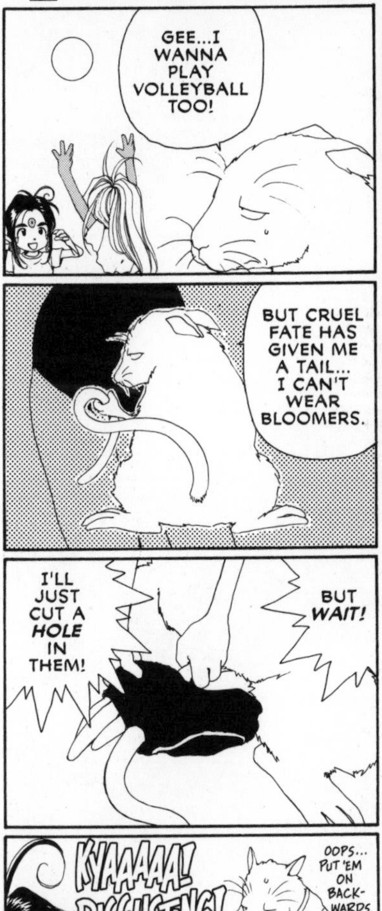
GEE...I WANNA PLAY VOLLEYBALL TOO!
BUT CRUEL FATE HAS GIVEN ME A TAIL... I CAN'T WEAR BLOOMERS.
BUT *WAIT!*
I'LL JUST CUT A *HOLE* IN THEM!
OOPS... PUT 'EM ON BACK-WARDS.
KYAAAAA! DISGUSTING!

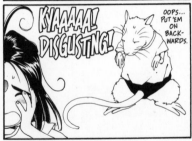

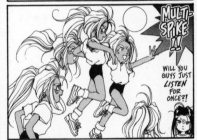

EDITOR
Carl Gustav Horn

DESIGNER
Scott Cook

ART DIRECTOR
Lia Ribacchi

PUBLISHER
Mike Richardson

English-language version
produced by Dark Horse Comics

Published by Dark Horse Manga

a division of Dark Horse Comics, Inc.
10956 SE Main Street
Milwaukie, OR 97222
www.darkhorse.com

To find a comics shop in your area,
call the Comic Shop Locator Service
toll-free at 1-888-266-4226

First edition: October 2007
ISBN: 978-1-59307-850-8

1 3 5 7 9 10 8 6 4 2

Printed in Canada

letters to the
ENCHANTRESS

10956 SE Main Street, Milwaukie, Oregon 97222
omg@darkhorse.com • www.darkhorse.com

NOTE: Full addresses and e-mail addresses will not be printed, unless you ask! All fan artwork, letters, and e-mails submitted become the property of Dark Horse Comics.

Dear Enchantress,

Thanks for looking at these pictures I sent! I just wanted to tell you all that I'm really looking forward to *Oh My Goddess!* Vol. 27. I thought I'd send in some fan mail for the first time since I really like the series. I saw some of the other fan mail printed in the book and I was kind of hoping mine would turn up in one too.

But of course you people would probably already have chosen right? (Ha Ha!) Anyway, I just hope you like them. I spent a long time working on these! Oh yeah, and please write me back if you have the chance!

Your Devoted Fan,
Anna M. B.
of Kansas

Oh and by the way . . . I'm twelve years old. ^_^ (Soon to be thirteen in December).

Anna (cool name—a classic), thank you very much for writing in with your fan art! I hope it's all right that it appears here in Vol. 7 rather than waiting for Vol. 28—as you may know, *Oh My Goddess!* goes on a new-old-new-old schedule where we release a "new" volume (never before printed in English—e.g., Vols. 26, 27, 28, etc.), then two months later an "old" volume (i.e., Vols. 5, 6, 7, etc.—*OMG!* stories previously released in a flopped, Western-style format as used to be standard), then a "new," etc. So rather than waiting the four months between Vols. 27 and 28, I thought it'd be OK to run your stuff here in-between, i.e., Vol. 7 ^_^

Vol. 27, of course, interrupts our regular "Letters to the Enchantress" to feature a preview of the upcoming novel *Oh My Goddess!—First End*, written by the long-time Japanese *seiyuu* (voice actor) for Urd in the *OMG!* anime, Yumi Tohma! Officially authorized by Kosuke Fujishima (and illustrated by the *Oh My Goddess!* character designer, Hidenori Matsubara), *First End* involves the domestic routine of Keiichi and the Goddesses in his life being upset when a sudden plague of the rabbit-like "bugs" infect Yggdrasil, the heavenly computer.

Nothing Skuld, perhaps with the help of Urd and Peorth, can't handle, you say? Not this time, as *Oh My Goddess!—First End* rapidly escalates within its first few chapters into a shocking drama that shakes the story we love to its core! Prepare to take another look at both the personal and universal meaning of Keiichi and Belldandy's relationship—and just how the two are alike. If you're an *OMG!* fan, you won't want to miss the *Oh My Goddess!—First End* novel, out in stores from Dark Horse this November!

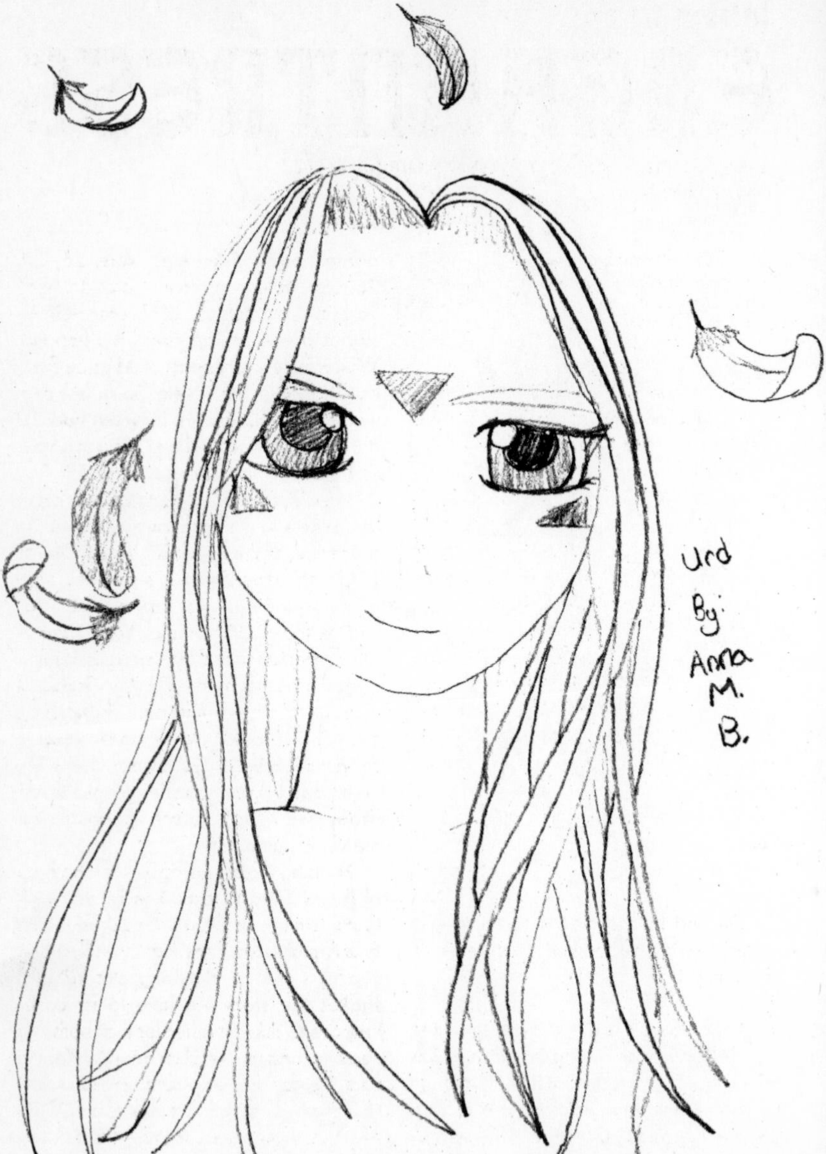
Urd
By:
Anna
M.
B.

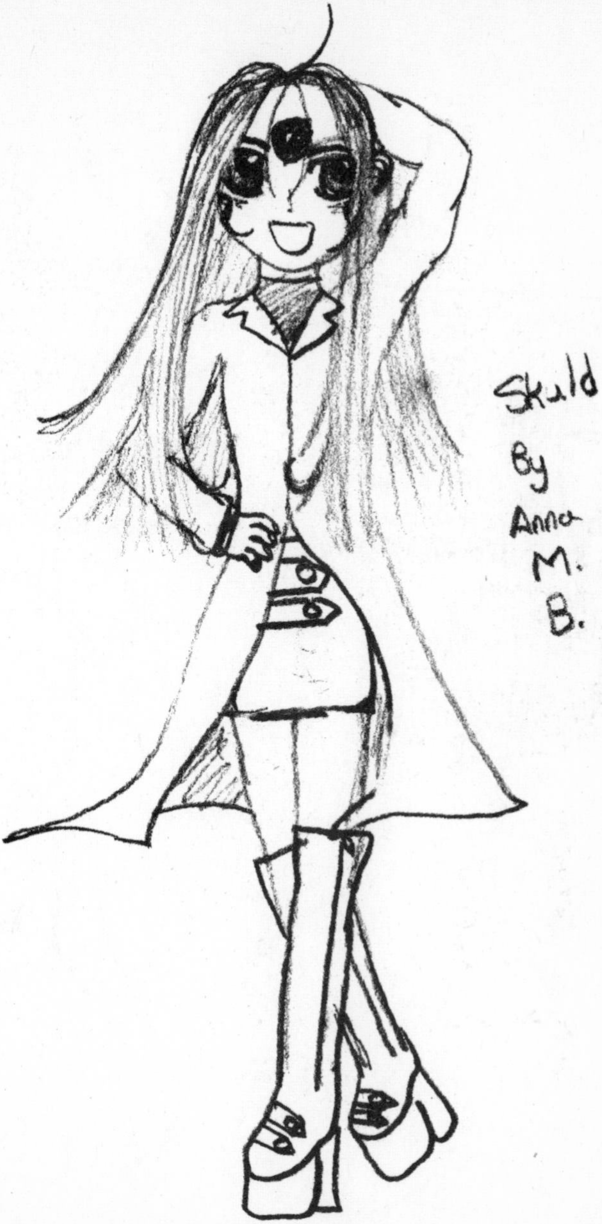
Skuld
By
Anna
M.
B.

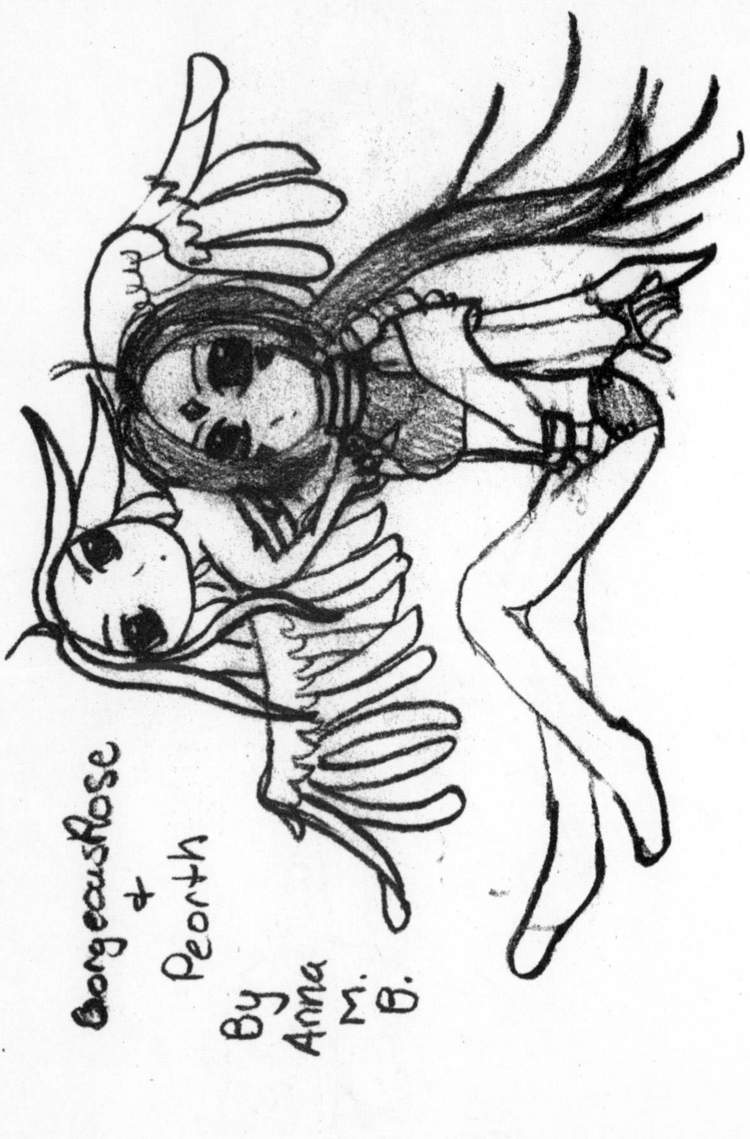
GorgeousRose
+
Peorth
By
Anna
M.
B.

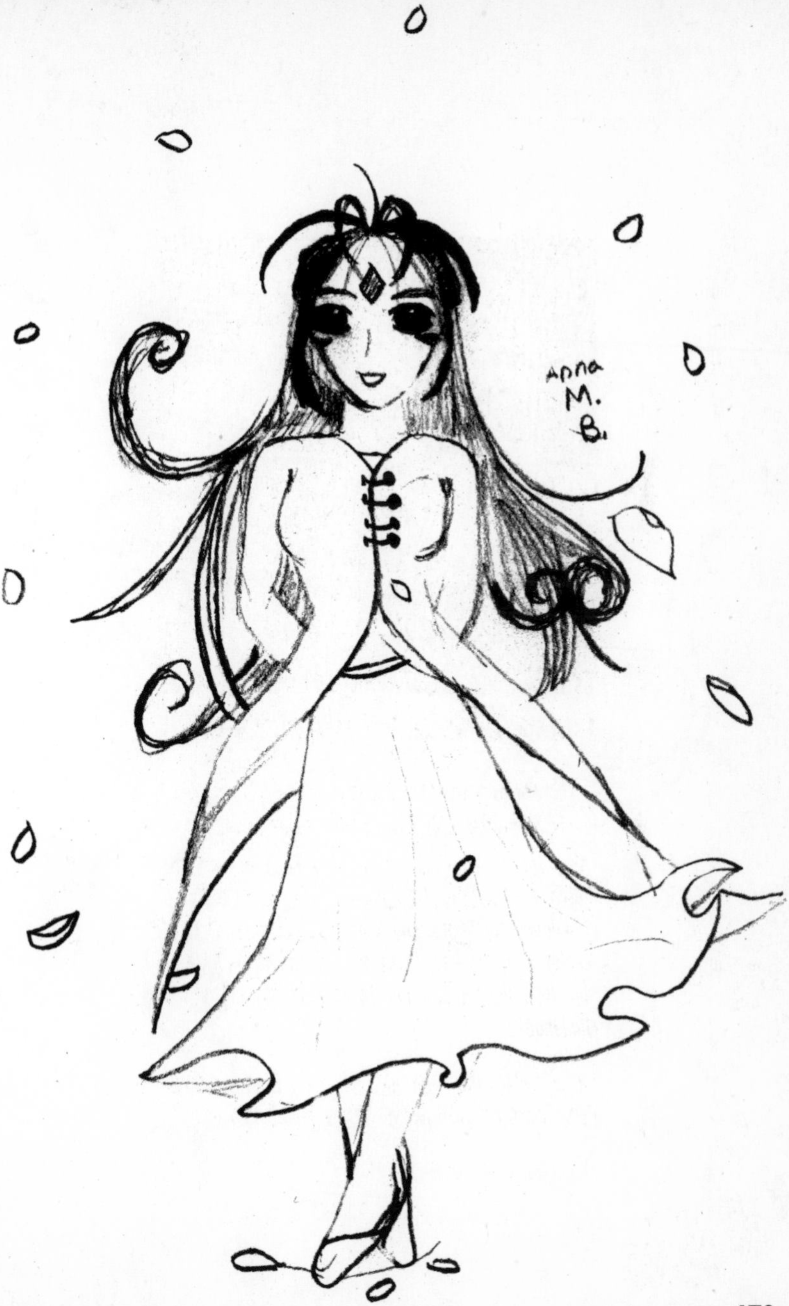
Anna
M.
B.

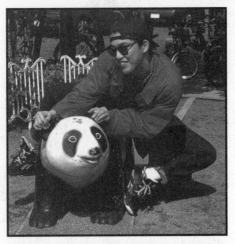

Creator Kosuke Fujishima in 1992!

His message to fans in the original Japanese *Oh My Goddess!* Vol. 7:

"Yes, yes y'all—check it out, my new machine: the Panda Bamboo 250!! Employing the latest in design, it completely annihilates any need for older models! We're pushin' it to the limit here! No one can touch this! Me and this thing are one and the same!! Anyone up for a challenge?!

"P.S.: Besides this, I am also riding my Elephant AAARR-RUNNNGHHH!* 600 and the Dance Rabbit 125 daily."

*The sound of an elephant's trumpet ^_^ —ed.

Kosuke Fujishima's Oh My Goddess!

Dark Horse is proud to re-present *Oh My Goddess!*
in the much-requested, affordable, Japanese-reading,
right-to-left format, complete with color sections,
informative bonus notes, and your letters!

 $10.95 each!

AVAILABLE AT YOUR LOCAL COMICS
SHOP OR BOOKSTORE
*To find a comics shop in your area, call
1-888-266-4226

For more information or to order direct:
•On the web: darkhorse.com
•E-mail: mailorder@darkhorse.com
•Phone: 1-800-862-0052 Mon.–Fri. 9 A.M.
to 5 P.M. Pacific Time.

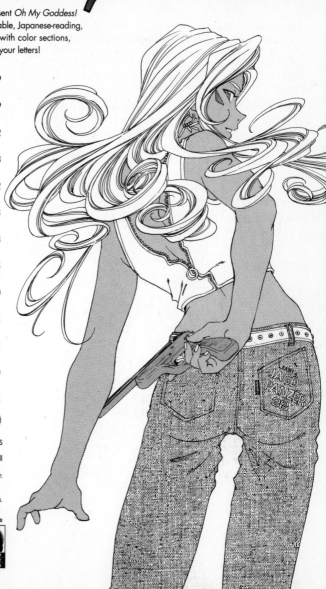

Kosuke Fujishima's

Oh My Goddess!

Can't wait on the Goddesses? Change directions!

Just gotten into the new unflopped editions of *Oh My Goddess!*, and found you can't wait to see what happens next? Have no fear! The first **20 volumes** of *Oh My Goddess!* are available **right now** in Western-style editions! Released between 1994 and 2005, our *OMG!* Western-style volumes feature premium paper, and pages 40% larger than those of the unflopped editions! If you've already got some of the unflopped volumes and want to know which Western-style ones to get to catch up, check out darkhorse.com's "Manga Zone" for a complete breakdown of how the editions compare!

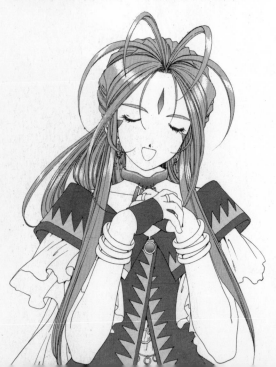

AVAILABLE AT YOUR LOCAL COMICS SHOP OR BOOKSTORE
*To find a comics shop in your area, call 1-888-266-4226
For more information or to order direct:
•On the web: darkhorse.com
•E-mail: mailorder@darkhorse.com
•Phone: 1-800-862-0052 Mon.-Fri. 9 A.M. to 5 P.M. Pacific Time.

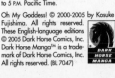

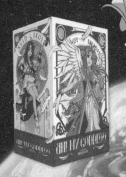
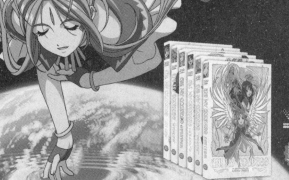